Dvořák to Duke Ellington

Dvořák to Duke Ellington

A Conductor Explores America's Music and Its African American Roots

MAURICE PERESS

OXFORD
UNIVERSITY PRESS

2004

OXFORD
UNIVERSITY PRESS

Oxford   New York
Auckland   Bangkok   Buenos Aires   Cape Town   Chennai
Dar es Salaam   Delhi   Hong Kong   Istanbul   Karachi   Kolkata
Kuala Lumpur   Madrid   Melbourne   Mexico City   Mumbai   Nairobi
São Paulo   Shanghai   Taipei   Tokyo   Toronto

Published by Oxford University Press, Inc.
198 Madison Avenue, New York, New York 10016

www.oup.com

Oxford is a registered trademark of Oxford University Press

Chapter 17 appeared in different form in *Black Music Research Journal* 13, no. 2 (Fall 1993).

Quotes from "Simple Song," "Agnus Dei," and "Fraction" from *Mass: A Theatre Piece for Singers, Players, and Dancers*, by Leonard Bernstein, texts by Leonard Bernstein and Stephen Schwartz, are used by permission of Leonard Bernstein Music Publishing Company LLC, Publisher.

Quotes from Langston Hughes, "Cross," from *The Weary Blues*, are used by permission of Alfred A. Knopf, New York, N.Y.

Library of Congress Cataloging-in-Publication Data
Peress, Maurice.
Dvořák to Duke Ellington : a conductor explores American music and its
African American roots / by Maurice Peress.
p. cm.
Includes bibliographical references and index.
ISBN 0-19-509822-6
1. Music—United States—African American influences.   2. Peress, Maurice.
I. Title.
ML200.P47 2004
780'.973—dc21   2003002793

9 8 7 6 5 4 3 2 1

Printed in the United States of America
on acid-free paper

To Lorca, Paul, and Anika

Acknowledgments

I wrote this book for the musically curious with catholic tastes. There has been no conscious plan to my research. I am a performer, a conductor, who found his way through some less traveled paths of American music history and now I feel the need to put it all in some coherent order. I view black and African American as culture, not simply as skin color.

I wish to thank those teachers who first unlocked for me the mysteries of music—before language and without end—Gerald "Jerry" Cnudde, Herschel "Harry" Freistadt, Philip James, and Martin Bernstein.

Thanks also to my Czech friends who unselfishly shared their knowledge and passion for Antonin Dvořák: author Josef Skvorecky and music scholars Dr. Jarmil Burghauser and especially Dr. Jitka Slavikova, who literally walked me through Dvořák's Bohemian homes and haunts and provided me with precious copies of holograph letters and manuscripts from his time in America.

Thanks to several wise and knowledgeable American music scholars and fellow musicians: my lifelong musical brothers, John Lewis and Howard Brofsky; and Dick Hyman, Mark Tucker, Ellie Hisama, Wayne Shirley, Dean Root, and, in particular, Reid Badger, who read my manuscript in its earliest and middling incarnations and urged me ever on.

I also wish to thank Sheldon Meyer of Oxford University Press, who offered me a contract based upon a two-page treatment; and associate editor Maureen Buja, who believed in my book even though it needed much more work and who eventually led me to the book's "without whom"—my marvelous, insightful editor, Manuela Kruger, who supplied that order and more.

I had expert editorial assistance as well from my gifted and generous daughter, Lorca Miriam Peress, who between her acting, teaching, and directing assignments arranged for clearances and vetted the manuscript through its sundry computer program upgrades. And finally, deepest thanks to my dear wife, Ellen Waldron Peress, my ever patient "ear" for new often raw text, read aloud for the first time, and my forever soulmate.

Contents

Art appeals to that part of our being . . . which is not

dependent upon wisdom; to that in us which is a gift and not

an acquisition . . . to the latent feeling of fellowship with all

creation [which] binds together . . . the dead to the living

and the living to the unborn.

—Joseph Conrad

Introduction

For some time now I have wanted to write a book about American music — what I learned from my work as a conductor, some of the composers with whom I shared the exquisite pain and pleasure of a world premiere (Leonard Bernstein's *Mass*, Duke Ellington's *Queenie Pie*, Morton Feldman's *Rothko Chapel*, David Amram's *Autobiography for Strings*), and what I discovered as I searched and sifted, preparing for my re-creations of historic concerts at which George Gershwin's *Rhapsody in Blue*, Ellington's *Black, Brown and Beige*, James Reese Europe's Clef Club orchestra, and George Antheil's *Ballet Mécanique* were given new life.

Some might consider the range of American music I have been concerned and involved with as unusually broad. I simply followed my muse and am now pleased to find that I am not alone. Other artists are letting their roots show. Where once there was a cultural divide between those who are moved by Dvořák and those who dig Ellington, I now find that many more people take immense pleasure from both. These names are not selected at random. There is an unbroken line that connects the Czech master and the American composer and orchestra leader with one another.

The first music I knew was Dad's Arabic folksongs, which he sang to the accompaniment of his oud, and Mamma's Yiddisher liederle, sung in a voice of the sweetest purity. I didn't understand the words. But the experience of seeing my parents away from their endless store- and housekeeping chores, becoming transfixed as they reconnected with their youthful dreams in strange fading faraways, marked me forever. They introduced me to the universal power of music. I have spent my life in music feeding on this power and passing it on. The odd combination of my parents' background—my father was from the ancient Jewish community of Baghdad; my mother came from a small Polish mill town—opened me to the affect of all manner of music, as Ellington used to say, "beyond category." So it is no surprise that it was to be the music of America, the multi-ethnic nation that welcomed them, wherein I parked my soul.

I began my professional musical life as a freelance trumpeter and arranger. I played at Bach concerts and on Broadway. I wrote pop arrangements for a quintet of lovely young harpists, "The Angelaires." For my Chamber Brass Players I arranged Renaissance and baroque music that we intoned in the old German *Turmsonate* tradition from atop the tower of Stanford White's Judson Memorial Church during the Greenwich Village Outdoor Art Show. In the army I wrote dozens of arrangements for big band. Count Basie once read down one of my originals, "Mad's Pad." How I evolved from these fragmented beginnings into a symphony conductor who worked closely with giants of American music has never ceased to amaze me.

Leonard Bernstein made possible my American music adventures when in 1961 he welcomed me into the land of the symphony orchestra by appointing me an assistant conductor with the New York Philharmonic. I continued to work with "Lenny" over the next twenty years. The high point was conducting the world premiere of his *Mass* for the opening of the John F. Kennedy Center for the Performing Arts.

A university post gave me the freedom to pursue my later interest, reconstructing and presenting historical American music concerts from the first half of the twentieth century, trying to better understand the roots of our American music. I uncovered far more than I anticipated about the symbiotic relationships—Mother would have said "one hand washes the other"—between musicians, black and white, out of which was forged a new and fresh "African American" music. As I researched these concerts, many lines led me to Antonin Dvořák, who spent the better part of three years (1892–95) in America as the director of the National Conservatory of Music. Among his dozen or so composition students were two who would become the teachers of Ellington, Gershwin, and Aaron Copland. The Bohemian master's observations and his radical statement that "the future American school would be based upon the music of the Negro," and my conviction that Ellington is the fulfillment of Dvořák's prediction, inspired this book.

1

Antonin Dvořák Comes to America

In 100 years America will be the center of music for the world.
—ANTONIN DVOŘÁK, quoted by former pupil Camille W. Zeckwer

I have always wondered why Dvořák came to live and work in America.

It could have been for the money — $15,000 per year for two years, one-half advanced to a bank in Prague. Dvořák's annual income at the time was far less, but his family enjoyed a comfortable life in Bohemia. The hardships of his apprentice years, when he supported his composing with odd jobs as an organist, violist, and itinerant piano teacher, were well past. With commissions for new works rolling in and an active catalog of over ninety compositions, including seven operas, eight (depending how one counted) symphonies, and dozens of smaller works, Dvořák was far too busy to accept the composing chair offered him by the Prague Conservatory. The Dvořáks and their six healthy children, aged four to fourteen, lived in a sizable apartment in Prague. They also enjoyed their cherished country house, Vysoka, a converted farm cottage with an apple orchard and pigeon coops set in gentle hills on the estate of Mrs. Dvořák's brother-in-law, Count Václav (Kunic) Kaunitz. No. I don't think that money alone induced Dvořák to come.

It could have been wanderlust, the pleasures of travel. Unlike Johannes Brahms, Dvořák's close friend and mutual admirer, who, "haunted by visions of seasickness,"[1] wouldn't travel to England to receive an honorary doctorate from Cambridge University, or Piotr Ilyich Tchaikovsky, who came to America for twenty-five days and couldn't wait to escape ("Despite [my] success . . . I was racked with homesickness and with all my soul craved to come back home"),[2] Dvořák came to enjoy touring. Between the fall of 1884 and the spring of 1891 he crisscrossed the English channel nine times to direct concerts of his music in London, Birmingham, and other major cities — which explains his proficiency in English.[3] Dvořák agreed to spend two consecutive years in America and, after a summer break in Bohemia, returned for a third. The Atlantic was no English Channel. This was more like emigrating.

It could have been for love. Dvořák might have needed distance between himself and Countess Josefina (Kunicova) Kaunitzova, his first, unrequited, love. Like Mozart before him, Dvořák married the sister of the woman who had once captured his heart. And there is reason to believe those who say he never quite got over this passion. How else to explain Dvořák's last-minute revision of his Cello Concerto, the crowning glory of his American works, on the occasion of Josefina's death in 1895? Dvořák expanded the coda, working in a song of his she admired, "Leave Me Alone . . . You really cannot comprehend this ecstasy with which love has filled me" (opus 82). The song had provided the theme for the second movement, but this time Dvořák adds a new countermelody for the solo cello, which one perceptive Dvořák scholar has identified as another of Josefina's favorites (from the final duet of Tchaikovsky's *Eugene Onegin*), conjuring up another emotionally significant text:[4] "Happiness was so easy to reach, it was so close."

Finally, it could have been politics. Dvořák's strongly held humanist convictions made America particularly attractive. Its welcome call, "Give me your tired, your poor, / Your huddled masses yearning to breathe free,"[5] had already beckoned tens of thousands of his Czech-speaking countrymen to emigrate to the United States. Dvořák and his folk-inspired music were closely identified with the national struggle to free Bohemia and Moravia from the domination, cultural as well as political, of the Austro-Hungarian Empire, a role he inherited from the father of "Czechish" music, Bedřich Smetana. Indeed, it was Dvořák's nationalist credentials that attracted Jeanette Thurber, founder of the National Conservatory of Music of America, to hire him as their new director, for at the top of her agenda was the establishment of an American school of composers.

Dvořák's influence on American music and musicians is evidenced by his work at the conservatory, by the widespread news coverage his novel ideas attracted, and by the distinguished and ongoing teacher-student legacy he initiated. Correspondingly, the impact of the New World on Dvořák was enormous. He produced a flurry of "American" works, among them four that remain his best known and loved: the Symphony in E Minor (*From the New World*), the *Humoresques*, the "American" String Quartet in A, and the Cello Concerto.[6]

Be it money, wanderlust, love, or politics; whatever the combination of causes that drew Dvořák to American shores, one of the most significant cultural exchanges in American history was about to begin when Dvořák, his wife, Anna, and their two oldest children boarded the SS *Saale* in Bremen on September 17, 1892, and, after nine stormy days, debarked onto a pier in Hoboken, New Jersey.

2

America and Negro Music

In the Negro melodies of America I discover all that is needed
for a great and noble school of music. They are Pathétic,
tender, passionate, melancholy, solemn, religious, bold, merry,
gay or what you will. It is music that suits itself to any mood or
purpose. There is nothing in the whole range of composition
that cannot be supplied with themes from this source. The
American musician understands these tunes and they move
sentiment in him.
—ANTONIN DVOŘÁK, *New York Herald*, May 21, 1893

Dvořák's famous announcement is often foreshortened, omitting perhaps his
most important appraisal, "The American musician understands these tunes
and they move sentiment in him"—an acute observation that only a few years
later would find a parallel in "the weird and intoxicating effect" on listeners
of the Scott Joplin rags, a desired effect noted by the composer himself.[1]

Narratives about the infectious peculiarities of African-rooted music
appear throughout American history. Even the earliest settlers of the New
World fell under its spell, a point brought home to me almost a half century
ago by my old German-born musicology professor, Kurt Sachs.

We were studying the origins of the dances found in seventeenth-
century European classical suites, among them the allemande, courante, and
gigue. Sachs, who took great satisfaction in upending assumptions, surprised
us with his discoveries that the courtly dances known as the sarabande and
the chaconne could be traced back to Africa via sixteenth-century dances of
New Spain and the Caribbean. According to Sachs, the "lewd, lascivious"
Creole/African *zarabanda*, a dance so beguiling it was outlawed by the
church, metamorphosed over time into the slow, stately sarabande. But "even
more than the sarabanda," the African-derived *chacona*, also known as the
chacona mulata, was sensuous and wild, the "most passionate and unbridled
of all dances."[2]

Sachs's deductions were stored in my youthful jazzer's memory bank.

Now that I am trying to tie things together, searching for ever-larger themes and continuities, I wonder if the ecstatic *zarabanda*, the Negro melodies that caught Dvořák's attention, and Joplin's "weird and intoxicating" rags share some extraordinary "affect"—to borrow a useful term from baroque theorists—that spans time and distance. Are the main themes of America's black music history—the slave gatherings, camp meetings, minstrelsy, and jubilees—connected by some common thread?

For a time, I found myself entrapped in historical quicksand, drawn ever deeper into questions about America's black music history before Dvořák came on the scene. And from what I have learned, and from everything I know as a performer, the answer to my question is yes.

Place Congo in old New Orleans (present-day Beauregard Square) was known for its Sunday afternoon slave gatherings "when not less than two or three thousand people would congregate to see the dusky dancers," who represented different African tribes: "Kraels, Minahs, Congos and Mandringas, Gangas, Hiboas and Fulas."[3]

America's first internationally celebrated musician, Louis Moreau Gottschalk, is said to have witnessed these dances as a boy, and it was his "Bamboula, danse de negres" (1846) that established his early reputation as a brilliant pianist and composer. Ellington's dramatic narration *A Drum Is a Woman* contains a "Place Congo" section.

Even earlier slave gatherings were commonly held throughout New England. In New York's Washington Square, after the Revolutionary War, when it was known as Potter's Field, "the Blacks [danced] joyful above, while the sleeping dead reposed below. In that field could be seen at once more than one thousand of both sexes, divided into numerous little squads, dancing and singing, each in their own tongue."[4]

In "camp meetings," during the religious revival movement of the late eighteenth and early nineteenth centuries, Negro congregants "instantly formed a superb choir." They created their own versions of hymns and Old Testament stories, "singing tune after tune—scarce one of which were in our hymn books." They could even be heard doing the Ring Shout in their tents, slapping their thighs and shuffling in rhythm.[5] For many of their white co-religionists, these Africanized Christian expressions were too darn hot. Yet there were those who found the music irresistible.

A remarkable article about spirituals and shouts sung by black Civil War soldiers appeared in the *Atlantic Monthly* in June 1867. It was written by a white army officer, Colonel Thomas Wentworth Higginson, a Unitarian minister, member of the Secret Six (a group of Bostonians who provided moral and financial support for John Brown's raid on Harper's Ferry), and Harvard gentleman. Higginson describes the music he encountered when he led the Thirty-first South Carolina volunteers, the first regiment of freed slaves to be mustered into national service in the Civil War.[6] Recalling that Sir Walter Scott had collected Scottish ballads "from the lips of ancient crones,"[7] Higginson found himself

> brought into the midst of a kindred world of unwritten songs. I had for many years heard of—"Negro Spirituals,"—I could now gather on their own soil these strange plants, which I had before seen as in museums alone. Often in the starlit evening, entering the camp—[I] have silently approached some glimmering fire, round which the dusky figures moved in the rhythmical barbaric dance the Negroes call a "shout," chanting, often harshly, but always in the most perfect time, some monotonous refrain. Writing down in the darkness, as best I could,—perhaps with my hand in the safe covert of my pocket, —the words of the song, I have afterwards carried it to my tent, like some captured bird or insect, and then after examination, put it by.[8]

Higginson's article included nineteen song texts, alas, not the music.

Minstrelsy, the ersatz Negro entertainment that swept across the nation well before the Civil War, crossed my path in the early 1960s when, as a young music director in Corpus Christi, Texas, I arrived at the symphony office one afternoon to find a minstrel troupe rehearsing in "my" auditorium! The show was a mostly amateur affair sponsored by the local Lions Club. Added to the blackface characters, insulting race jokes, and corny banjo tunes were equally offensive parodies of Jewish figures. Dressed in long black gabardine coats, with paste-on hook noses and side locks, they shrugged and whined as the rest of the cork-blacked cast whooped and hollered and rattled their tambourines. I was mortified.[9]

Over time I have come to understand that we cannot expunge our passage through minstrelsy, the dominant American entertainment vehicle of the nineteenth century. Black social historians such as Mel Watkins have begun to dig beneath the stereotypes, the cross-dressing, and the ludicrous "cork" masks, dissecting the humor, the social satire, and the banjo-fiddle-and-bones music, the better to understand our American past.[10]

For all of its contorted cartooning, minstrelsy played an enormous part in the process that brought America to embrace the music of African Americans as its own. Furthermore, its impact on black music and musicians was profound, for black entertainers would ultimately reclaim their birthright.

Several "authentic" all-black minstrel troupes advertising themselves as "the real thing" arose in the last quarter of the nineteenth century. They elevated the form, twisting the parody back on its African American roots, meanwhile finding in minstrelsy a vehicle for displaying their skills as composers, violinists, bandsmen, actors, singers, and dancers, the whole now carried to the highest professional standards.[11] For the finished, classically trained black musician, such as the violin teacher of David Mannes, John Thomas Douglas (1847–1886), black minstrels were the only game in town. And, irony of ironies, the cork-black mask became so intrinsic to the form that African American performers wore it on stage as well. In his poem "Black, Brown and Beige," Ellington celebrates the end of black minstrelsy.

> Yes, Harlem!
> Land of valiant youth,
> You've wiped the makeup from your face,
> And shed your borrowed spangles.
> You've donned the uniform of truth.[12]

Besides Corpus Christi, I have come across vestiges of the black minstrel past in unexpected places: in a photo of James Reese Europe's Clef Club, in the poem of Ellington's quoted above, and in an interview with Eubie Blake.

In the late 1970s I did an on-camera interview with Eubie Blake in his comfortably furnished brownstone home in Bedford-Stuyvesant, Brooklyn. It was for a television show I dreamed up for my orchestra, the Kansas City Philharmonic, about the influence of ragtime on symphonic music.[13] We called the show "Twelfth Street Rag," after the familiar song that took its name from what was once Kansas City's tenderloin strip. Well past ninety at the time, Eubie Blake was alert, charming, and as always, smartly dressed. After the interview ended and we were packing up, Eubie called me over. He had a final thought. "Remember," he said, looking me full in the face, that long piano tickler extended, "I never wore cork!"

It took me some time to realize the significance of what seemed a gratuitous remark. We were, after all, talking about ragtime.[14] Perhaps reminiscing brought Blake back to the old-time artists he worked with, including several who came out of minstrelsy in the late 1890s and moved smoothly into the ragtime era via the new all-black Broadway musicals, which, more often than not, retained minstrel "cakewalks" and "walk arounds." Many continued to wear cork. The most celebrated of these transitional figures was Bert Williams, who appeared in blackface as late as 1919, when he was a star of the Ziegfeld Follies.

The high point of Eubie Blake's career came when he and his song-writing partner, Noble Sissle, helped launch the second wave of all-black Broadway musicals with their electrifying *Shuffle Along* (1921), which featured the jazz-age hit "I'm Just Wild about Harry." It was this generation, the generation of the "New Negro" and the Harlem Renaissance, not that of cork-wearing artists such as Bert Williams, that Eubie Blake wanted to be identified with.

If ever there was a Moses of African American music, one who single-handedly led black musicians and their music into the land of respect, professionalism, and pride, it was James Reese Europe. Europe formed a cooperative brotherhood of Negro musicians, setting fee standards where there had been chaos and hurtful competition. His Clef Club Orchestra was the most celebrated large-scale Negro ensemble of its time. Jim Europe reads like a man who would cut a wide swath between himself and the degradations of minstrelsy.

The most familiar image of Europe shows him standing with great dignity, the central figure in a marvelous panoramic photograph taken on the occasion of his Clef Club's Monster Melange and Dancefest, held on May 11, 1911, in the Manhattan Casino. I have gone over this photo with a magnifying glass: it is for me a primary source. Europe is surrounded on the ballroom floor by a huge string orchestra of almost sixty players. In addition to the usual violins, cellos, and basses there are thirty-five strumming instruments—guitars, harp guitars, banjos, and mandolins. There are also ten pianists, a single trap drummer, and one flute. They are all in formal attire.[15]

Behind this impressive array, on the raised orchestra stage of the ballroom, sits yet another band, which includes the usual woodwinds and brasses.[16] They are fronted by a thirteen-man minstrel line in white trousers and black coats; six hold banjos, others hold tambourines, and several are in blackface. Among the "tambos" was Henry S. Creamer, composer of "After You've Gone" and "Way Down Yonder in New Orleans." The Interlocutor is Henry Troy, a lyricist and book writer who wrote "Gin House Blues" to music by Fletcher Henderson. William Tyers, among the most learned of Europe's musical colleagues, directs the minstrel band.[17] Jim Europe was not about to cut off the generation of musicians who carried the torch from minstrelsy. He simply brought them along.

A highbrow counterpart to black minstrelsy, Negro vocal ensembles known as Jubilees were established long before Dvořák arrived. The most celebrated of these was the Fisk Jubilee Singers, formed in 1871. Elegant in dress and manner, this group of nine singers and a pianist, all former slaves, presented their slave songs and spirituals in churches and on concert stages up and down the East Coast.[18] How apt is the epithet "Jubilee," taken from the Hebrew word for the ram's horn of celebration and the symbolic number

FIGURE 2.1

James Reese Europe and his Clef Club Orchestra on the occasion of a "Monster Melange and Dancefest" held in the Manhattan Casino, May 11, 1911. Note the blackface minstrel band on the stage in the rear. Courtesy of Maryland Historical Society.

fifty. On the Jubilee—the Sabbath of Sabbaths, forty-nine plus one—the Old Testament mandates that slaves be freed and that fields lie fallow.[19]

The Fisk Jubilee Singers made an enormous impression at the second World Peace Jubilee, a mammoth assemblage held in Boston in June 1872. Others performing included the Johann Strauss orchestra, the Grenadier Guards from England, and the French Garde Républicaine. Among the American musicians were two Negro violinists, Henry F. Williams and F. E. Lewis.[20] A twenty-five-foot bass drum was built for the occasion. With massed choristers, the total number of performers came to over 20,000.[21]

The World Peace Jubilees were the creation of the celebrated Irish-born bandmaster Patrick S. Gilmore, the composer of the Civil War hit "When Johnny Comes Marching Home." A contemporary description of the Fisk Jubilee Singers' appearance at the second World Peace Jubilee gives us some idea of the maddening mix of racism and adulation that African American musicians encountered:

> The immense audience of 40,000 people was gathered from all parts of the land; and the color prejudice that had followed the [Jubilee] Singers everywhere reappeared here in the shower of brutal hisses that greeted their first appearance. But the air of that radical New England city is not kindly to colorphobia, and a deluge of applause drowned the insult. And a day or two after, the Singers had a proud revenge.
>
> Mrs. Julia Ward Howe's stirring lyric, "The Battle-hymn of the Republic," was on the program, to be sung to the air of "John Brown" [the "unofficial theme song of black soldiers" who fought for the Union]. But for some unexplained reason the key was given to the orchestra in E-flat [making the high note a G at the top of the staff] and the first verses . . . taken by some colored singers of Boston . . . were a painful failure. The Jubilee Singers were to come in with the verse beginning, "He hath sounded forth the trumpet that shall never call retreat." . . . Fired by the remembrance of their reception on the previous day, and feeling that to some extent the reputation of their color was at stake, they sang as if inspired. Mr. White's masterly drill had made easy to them the high notes which others had failed. Every word of that first line rang through the great Coliseum as if sounded out of a trumpet. The great audience were carried away on a whirl-wind of delight. . . . One old man was conspicuous, holding his violon-cello above his head with one hand, and whacking out upon it his applause with the bow held in the other. When the grand old chorus, "Glory, glory, hallelujah," followed, with a swelling volume of music

FIGURE 2.2
Detail from illustration of Gilmore's second "World Peace Jubilee,"
Boston, June 1872. Drawn for *Harper's Weekly* by Thomas Worth

from the great orchestra, the thunder of the bands, and the roar of the artillery, the scene was indescribable. . . . The Coliseum rang with cheers and shouts of, "The Jubilees! The Jubilees forever!"

It was worth more than a Congressional enactment in bringing that audience to the true ground on the question of "civil rights."[22]

The success of the Fisk Jubilee Singers at the World Peace Jubilee immediately led to an invitation to appear before President Grant at the White House. During the next two decades, with changes in personnel, the Fisk Jubilee's music and artistry would become known to concertgoers throughout the United States and Europe. The name the "Jubilees" was appropriated by other Negro singing ensembles. At times more than one "official"—and several unofficial—ensembles were on tour at the same time. The Jubilees' final six-year-long world tour, which began in 1884, included appearances in the Holy Land and Asia.

Thanks to ensembles like the Fisk Jubilee Singers, the idea of an independent African American art music, drawn from slave gatherings, camp meetings, and Civil War bivouacs, became a reality. And thanks to minstrelsy, America's popular music was indelibly marked "African American" and well positioned to grow on its own. Nevertheless, it would take the honest enthusiasms of a world-class Czech composer to thrust "Negro" music into the center of the serious—read "European"—music establishment.

3

Dvořák's Symphony
From the New World

Dvořák arrived in the United States on September 28, 1892, as the country was feverishly putting the finishing touches on the four hundredth anniversary celebration of Columbus's landing in the New World. There was a national taking of stock. What had transpired over the last four centuries? What had we become? Where were we heading?

In apposition to the small role Christopher Columbus was assigned for the relatively tame 1792 celebrations, the master navigator was held forth as an iconic figure for the United States and its growing sense of empowerment. Any misgivings intellectuals might have had about the catastrophe Columbus had brought upon Native Americans and enslaved Africans—he introduced the practice of slavery in the New World—were swept aside in the euphoria. (The more recent 1992 celebration, sobered by revisionist debates, stands in stark contrast to what Dvořák encountered.)

Starting on Monday, October 10, 1892, New York City's island of Manhattan, draped in bunting and glowing with electric light signs, played host to a revelry that continued unabated for three days and nights. The borough was flooded with visitors. The Hudson and East Rivers teemed with naval flotillas and private boats that sailed out to greet them. Nightly fireworks exploded from atop tall buildings and gushed out in fiery "Niagras" from the flanks of the Brooklyn Bridge. Temporary arches, designed by Stanford White, were erected across Fifth Avenue. And the seventy-six-foot-high Columbus

Monument, the largest stone of which weighed thirty-six tons, was ceremoniously raised by proud Italian workmen in the center of the newly named Columbus Circle, where it still stands.[1]

From his temporary quarters just off Union Square, the staging area and principal hub for the all-day parades, Dvořák wrote to his friend Karal Baštař, noting the exact hour as well as the date:

> New York Clarendon Hotel,
> early morning at 7 hours 18 $^{14}/_{10}$ 92[2]

> Just imagine row after row [of marchers], an incredible procession of people working both in the fields of industry and the crafts, and huge numbers of gymnasts—among them members of the Czech Sokol—and crowds of people from the arts and also many nationalities and colors. And all of this went on uninterruptedly, from dawn until 2:00 in the morning. . . . Thousands upon thousands of people, and an everchanging sight! And you should hear all the kinds of music! . . . Well, America seems to have demonstrated all it is and all it is capable of! I haven't got enough words to describe it all.[3]

The original plan of having Dvořák direct a new cantata setting of Rodman Drake's "American Flag" at the Metropolitan Opera House on Columbus Day, October 12, was foiled on two accounts: the text "did not get to Dvořák in time to be completed," and the Metropolitan Opera House suffered a fire that forced the cancellation of the entire 1892–93 season. Dvořák's Columbus Day concert, his official introduction to the New York public, was moved forward to October 21, and to Carnegie Hall.[4]

In place of the cantata, Dvořák conducted the world premiere of his *Columbian Te Deum*, directing the Metropolitan [Opera] Orchestra, soprano Clementine DeVera-Sapio, bass Emil Fischer, and a chorus of three hundred.[5] The concert was preceded by a twenty-minute oration, "Two New Worlds: The New World of Columbus and the New World of Music," which was projected from the stage in those pre-microphone days by Colonel Thomas Wentworth Higginson, by then a venerable Americanist. Higginson's address could well have planted the idea for the title of Dvořák's most celebrated American work, the Symphony no. 9 (*From the New World*), which was completed within the next seven months. The speech was quoted in part in the next morning's *New York Herald*.

> The triumphs of our land in music . . . lie in the future. . . . If we were all made of unmixed English blood, we might have long to wait for them. . . . We are not all of English blood. We stand in one of the great German cities of the world and the other great musical race of

Europe is making our very byways Italian. . . . Let us hope that our guest tonight [Dvořák] . . . may consent to transplantation and may help add the new world of music to the continent which Columbus found.[6]

Higginson's theme underscored the sanguine expectations of Jeanette Thurber, whose gallant efforts on behalf of American music and musicians were remarkable for her time. In 1886, using her social position and wealth, she established the American Opera Company, dedicated to opera sung in English, and a sister institution, the National Conservatory, for the training of American-born singers here at home. The opera company made several tours under the baton of Theodore Thomas, the leading American conductor at that time, before its funding started to dry up. She then turned her full energies toward the Conservatory, which began training instrumentalists and composers as well as singers. Modeled after the Conservatoire de Paris, where she herself had studied, the National Conservatory of Music of America was, according to the Carnegie Hall program for Dvořák's belated Columbus Day concert, "founded for the benefit of Musical Talent in the United States . . . conferring its benefits free upon all applicants [regardless of color or gender] sufficiently gifted . . . and unable to pay." To assuage her backers, the program goes on to explain that the tuition was "loaned" to the budding artists with the understanding that they would pay it back once their careers were established.[7]

I wonder if Colonel Higginson spent time with Dvořák after the concert, perhaps talking about the spirituals and ring shouts he so eloquently lauded in the *Atlantic Monthly*? The choice of Higginson as the keynote speaker at the concert cannot be a simple case of serendipity. There appears to have been a plan afoot. Whether divine or woman-made, it would come to play itself out most dramatically.[8]

Higginson was not the only African American musical resource set before Dvořák. A young baritone, Harry T. Burleigh, was assigned to be his student assistant at the conservatory. Dvořák saw in Burleigh a reflection of himself as a student and befriended the youth: "If in my own career I have achieved a measure of success and reward it is to some extent due to the fact that I was the son of poor parents and was reared in an atmosphere of struggle and endeavor."[9]

When Burleigh first arrived in New York, he joined the men and boys' choir at the St. Philip's Free African Church, the second oldest African Methodist Episcopal Church in the country; it traces its origin to 1809, "when attendance at Trinity's Sunday afternoon African service had become so large, and the African-American parishioners so dissatisfied with having to worship separately, that they reached a decision to set up their own congregation."[10]

St. Philip's was then located in the tenderloin district at 161 West Twenty-fifth Street, less than a mile from Dvořák's house on East Seventeenth Street. Burleigh became part of the large African American community that had established itself around St. Philip's, many of them in apartment houses built and managed by the church.

There were at least two other musicians from St. Philip's enrolled at the National Conservatory: Edward B. Kinney, the church's organist and choirmaster, who was a member of Dvořák's composition class; and Charles Bolin, who studied piano and perhaps organ as well. This explains why the St. Philip's men and boys' choir performed under Dvořák (and Kinney) at a historic concert held in Madison Square Garden in 1894 that featured the conservatory's African American students. Eighteen years later the St. Philip's men and boys' choir participated in another historic concert, James Reese Europe's Clef Club Concert at Carnegie Hall, this time under the direction of their new organist and choirmaster Charles *Bohlen*—Bolin had taken a Germanic spelling for his name.[11] Burleigh, Bolin, and perhaps Kinney[12] were among the first of what, under Dvořák's prodding, would soon become well over 150 African Americans among the 600-plus students enrolled at the conservatory.

Dvořák led the Conservatory orchestra, which met twice a week. Burleigh served as the orchestra's librarian and copyist and filled in on double bass and timpani. I can attest that the conductor's lot is a lonely one. The orchestra librarian is among the few orchestral musicians we get to talk with off the podium, and the one we depend upon for a myriad of editorial details and drudge jobs.

Dvořák and Burleigh apparently worked well together. During his second year at the conservatory, Dvořák wrote to his family back in Prague that his son Otakar, age nine, "sat on Burleigh's lap during the Orchestra's rehearsals and played the tympani."[13] Victor Herbert, a lifelong friend of Burleigh's,[14] described the Dvořák-Burleigh relationship in a letter sent in 1922 to Carl Engel, chief of the Music Division of the Library of Congress: "Dr. Dvořák was most kind and unaffected and took great interest in his pupils, one of which, Harry Burleigh, had the privilege of giving the Dr. some of the thematic material for his Symphony. . . . I have seen this denied—but it is true."[15]

Burleigh learned many of the old plantation songs from the singing of his blind maternal grandfather, Hamilton Waters, who in 1832 bought his freedom from slavery on a Maryland plantation. Waters became the town crier and lamplighter for Erie, Pennsylvania, and as a young boy Burleigh helped guide him along his route. The family was Episcopalian, and young Harry sang in the St. Pauls men and boys' choir. Burleigh also "remembered his Mother's singing after chores and how he and his [step]father and grandfather all harmonized while helping her."[16]

At various times in his long life—he died in 1949 at age eighty-one—Burleigh described his student days with Dvořák. Taken together, his writings provide insight into Dvořák's ongoing Negro music education while he was composing what would become the symphony *From the New World*.

> Dvořák used to get tired during the day and I would sing to him after supper. . . . I gave him what I knew of Negro songs—no one called them spirituals then—and he wrote some of my tunes (my people's music) into the New World Symphony.[17]

Dvořák began working on various "American" themes in mid-December 1892, filling eleven pages of a sketchbook.

> Part of this old "spiritual" ["Swing Low, Sweet Chariot"] will be found in the second theme of the first movement . . . given out by the flute. Dvořák saturated himself with the spirit of these old tunes and then invented his own themes. There is a subsidiary theme in G minor in the first movement with a flatted seventh [a characteristic passed on to jazz, known as a "blue note"] and I feel sure the composer caught this peculiarity of most of the slave songs from some that I sang to him; for he used to stop me and ask if that was the way the slaves sang.[18]

In January 1893 Dvořák began a continuous sketch for the symphony:

> When Dvořák heard me sing "Go Down Moses," he said, "Burleigh, that is as great as a Beethoven theme."[19]

This, for Dvořák, was the ultimate compliment. He made his students compose dozens of themes before accepting one as appropriate for "development." He would then have them wrap the theme around the skeleton of an existing Beethoven sonata, imitating, measure by measure, the modulations and key relationships.[20]

Dvořák began working on the full score in mid-February 1893.

> Dvořák of course used Swing Low, Sweet Chariot, note for note. . . . It was not an accident. He did it quite consciously. . . . He tried to combine Negro and Indian themes. The Largo movement he wrote after he had read the famine scene in Longfellow's Hiawatha. It had a great effect on him and he wanted to interpret it musically. [That Burleigh's grandmother was part Indian may help to explain why

Dvořák often equated or confused Indian with African American music.][21]

Burleigh's influence was profound. Within one week, May 21–28, 1893, a spate of articles about Dvořák's views on Negro music and the completion of his new symphony appeared in the *New York Herald* and, by means of the newspaper's new "exclusive" Atlantic cable, its sister paper, the English-language *Paris Herald*.

The oft-quoted *New York Herald* interview that begins, "In the Negro melodies of America I discover all that is needed for a great and noble school of music,"[22] came out on Sunday, May 21. It traveled under the Atlantic at the speed of light and made the front page of the *Paris Herald* the following morning. *Paris Herald* stringers were quickly dispatched to Vienna and Berlin to interview famous musicians about Dvořák's curious theory. So strong was the notion of German musical authority that French musicians of note, such as Camille Saint-Saëns, conveniently nearby in Paris, were not consulted.

Among those interviewed were Joseph Joachim, a distinguished violinist and pedagogue, who may have already been exposed to American Negro music through his student, Will Marion Cook; Anton Rubinstein, the pianist, composer, and founder of the Saint Petersburg Conservatory; and Anton Bruckner, the Viennese composer and organist. Their reactions to Dvořák's theory appeared on the front page of the *Paris Herald* on three consecutive days, Friday through Sunday, May 26–28, and, thanks to cable, in the *New York Herald* in a single condensed article on Sunday, May 28. What would normally take several days by steamship was being accomplished in hours. But there was more.

Elsewhere in the May 28 edition of the *New York Herald*, Dvořák exploded the time bomb that had been ticking all week:

ANTONIN DVOŘÁK ON NEGRO MELODIES
The Bohemian Composer Employs Their Theme And Sentiments In A New Symphony
Dr. Dvořák's explicit announcement that his newly completed symphony reflects the Negro melodies, upon which . . . the coming American school must be based . . . will be a surprise to the world.[23]

The editorial page also took notice of Dvořák's Negro melody idea, describing it as a "welcome utterance."[24]

With two bold strokes Dvořák empowered American musicians of all stripes by setting a "great and noble" example, meanwhile apprising the general public about something that in my view they already suspected but were perhaps afraid to acknowledge.

Dvořák's notions about the future of America's music, now broadcast on both sides of the Atlantic, created no small amount of controversy, catching the American music establishment off guard. The *Indianapolis Freeman*, a black weekly, would recall a decade later that Dvořák's prediction "fell upon the ears of the American white people like a heavy clap of thunder."[25] Among the naysayers were the American composers Edward MacDowell and John Knowles Paine. MacDowell was particularly bitter: "We have here in America been offered a pattern for an American national music costume by the Bohemian Dvořák . . . though what Negro melodies have to do with Americanism in art still remains a mystery."[26]

On the other hand, Dvořák's ideas provided just the imprimatur that was needed by composers like Arthur Farwell, who were especially interested in Indian music. When Farwell established his own composer-governed Wa Wan Press in 1902, his declared intention was to "launch a progressive movement for American music, including a definite acceptance of Dvořák's challenge to go after our own folk music."[27]

Black musicians were ecstatic. The *Freeman* article recalls Dvořák's statements as "a triumph for the sons and daughters of slavery and a victory for Negro race achievements," referring to him as "Pan [father] Antonin Dvořák, our greatest friend from far across the sea."[28] According to William Warfield, the distinguished bass-baritone and former president of the National Association of Negro Musicians, this bond with Dvořák "lives on in black music circles."

I was curious about the interviews with "Eminent Musicians from Berlin and Vienna" about Dvořák's "Negro Melody Idea" that had been summarized in the *New York Herald*, and I found an opportunity to visit the morgue of the *Paris Herald* to read them in their original unabridged form. The comments of Joachim, Rubinstein, and an American composer, Arthur Bird, as reported by an unnamed Berlin correspondent, seemed thoughtful and respectfully curious, and in the case of Bird most insightful:

> JOSEF JOACHIM: . . . It may be a very good idea to try and merge the American Negro melodies into an ideal form, and that these melodies would then give the tint to the National American Music.
>
> ANTON RUBINSTEIN: . . . If there is a great literature of these Negro melodies, Dr. Dvořák's idea is possible. . . . Ah, so they are going to allow Negros free musical education. That is very interesting. . . . They may develop a new melody. . . . It is refreshing of course. . . . In twenty five years or fifty years we shall perhaps see whether the Negros can develop their musical talent and found a new musical style.

ARTHUR BIRD: . . . I wonder whether the Negro melodies . . . simple, sad, musical, [would] lose from being instrumented.[29]

The comments from Vienna, under the heading "A Cold Water Douche," were far less hospitable to Dvořák's thesis:

"German musical literature," Professor Anton Bruckner declared, "contained no written text emanating from the Negro race, and however sweet the Negro melodies might be, they could never form the groundwork of the future music of America."

Evidently Bruckner never heard of Beethoven's African Polish friend, the composer and virtuoso violinist George Polgreen Bridgetower. Beethoven composed a violin sonata for Bridgetower titled "Il mulattica," which he later rededicated to Rudolphe Kreutzer, whose name it carries still.

The final comments, which were not included in the *New York Herald*'s summary article, were attributed to Hans Richter, conductor of the first performances of the *Ring* at Bayreuth. His post as "the celebrated leader of [Vienna's] Imperial Opera Orchestra and Philharmonic Concerts" would be taken over by Gustav Mahler three years later. It is the unnamed Viennese reporter's voice we hear as much as the maestro's:[30]

[Richter] is very enthusiastic concerning America and believes greatly in its future music, but he could not realize that this could emanate from the Negro race, nor would he admit that persons playing by ear [more racist assumptions] could be taught music properly, or had ever given evidence of talent in this respect. He spoke of the gypsy race of Hungary, every man, woman and child of which plays by ear, but said that it was quite an exceptional thing for a gypsy to play from written music.[31]

These conflicting sets of interviews from Berlin and Vienna are a case study of reportorial spin in action. I have learned not to take newspaper critics too seriously ever since Peter Pretsfelder, a clever press agent, chastised me when I complained about a long semi-favorable revue: "Don't read your reviews," he said. "Measure them!"

It was a busy eight days at the two *Heralds*, and the articles could not have happened spontaneously. Thanks to the miracle of the paper's new commercial cable, "tongues . . . were wagging" over "Doctor Dvořák's Bold Declaration" on both sides of the Atlantic. I have no doubt that some yet-to-be-identified éminence grise at the *New York Herald* designed this clever international publicity campaign.[32] By now it is obvious that Jeanette Thurber, her friends and supporters, and the *New York Herald*, which had been staunchly pro-abolition, shared strong—and in my view noble, if naive—ideas about racial equality. Dvořák's enthusiasms were a tonic.

On Wednesday of this stormy week, Dvořák completed the scoring of his *New World* Symphony, and in keeping with his normal practice, he carefully signed and dated it: "*Fine,* Praised be to God! May 24, 1893, at nine in the morning." In an unusual gesture, Dvořák returned to the score later that day to add a euphoric note: "Family arrives at Southhampton! (telegram 1:33)."

One could view this "famous entry" as some quaint exuberance.[33] I see it as both a revelation and a symbolic dedication—the blessing of his loved ones—vesting them with the New World energy and sense of future he had written about only seven months earlier: "I haven't got enough words to describe it all."[34] Dvořák's impressions of America were now captured for all time in his symphony, a symphony that "reflects the music of the Negro."

Artists are sensitive heralds of change; they are the first to recognize a new spirit in the world around them. I believe that Dvořák was aware of something I have long felt. Black Americans, more often than not, dominate American language, fashion, dance, and music—what we see, the way we move, and what we hear—a truth revealed to Dvořák over one hundred years ago.

Within a week, Dvořák and his reunited family would leave by train for Spillville, Iowa, a quiet little Czech-speaking farm village, where they were to spend their summer. It was Joseph J. Kovařik, an American of Czech ancestry, who told Dvořák about Spillville. Kovařik, who had transferred his violin studies from the Prague Conservatory to the National Conservatory at Dvořák's urging, earned his keep as the maestro's American secretary and amanuensis. They made a large and lively group as they boarded the train at the Grand Central Depot on Forty-first Street and Park Avenue: the Dvořáks, their six children, and an aunt (not Josefina), plus Kovařik and a cook. En route they sampled the thrills of The World's Columbian Exposition of 1893, Chicago World's Fair.

4

The Chicago World's Columbian Exposition of 1893

The Chicago World's Fair of 1893 celebrated America, its industry, and its people. It was among the first events of its kind to honor the achievements of women. Almost overnight, the fair and Chicago became a gathering place for the nation's gifted and talented from every scientific and artistic discipline.

Little remains of the original fair. Surreal silvertint photographs offer proof that a magnificent White City, a combination of Venice's Piazza San Marco and the Roman Forum, arose for one glorious summer only to disappear like Atlantis. But the fair's countless exhibitions and day-to-day events were meticulously recorded in thick official state and institutional volumes. These contain long lists of participants, a kind of who's who at the fair. The blatant exception was black America.

In my search for evidence of African American music at the fair I found, behind the official neglect of Negro achievements, a complex and broad-ranged black presence. There were the elite Negroes who worked and gathered around the Haitian Pavilion. They conspired to produce "Colored People's Day," an "honor day" event mixing race politics and high art that constituted their brief moment in the sun. There was an African tribe direct from the Gold Coast via Paris, the so-called primitive, yet highly sophisti-cated denizens of the "Dahomey Village," disdained, however, by most of the Haitian Pavilion crowd. Finally, there was the ever-looming large musical underbelly of the fair—the piano "professors" (soon to become ragtimers),

FIGURE 4.1
Chicago World's Fair 1893. View across the Court of Honor, east to west.
Photograph by C. D. Arnold courtesy of the Chicago Historical Society.

the "hootchy kootchies," the sideshows, and the surrounding pleasure
houses. Most significant to my story is the role played by the fair in hasten-
ing the emergence of ragtime, a "rhythm" that would shape popular music,
and in turn no small amount of classical music, over the next three decades.

Nine years after the fair closed, an ironic postscript to all three of these
black presences arrived in the form of a "Negro Musical Comedy" that made
quite a stir on Broadway and enjoyed an even greater success in London.
Created by many of the elite artists who were at the fair, it was titled *In Dahomey* and boasts a masterful score by Will Marion Cook, chock full of ragtime.

The Dvořák family detrained in Chicago on June 4, 1893, to spend a day at the fair. They would visit again on their way back to New York at the end of the summer. Dvořák himself returned from Spillville in early August for an extended ten-day stay.[1] His first four days were spent in preparation for a gala concert he conducted on "Bohemian Day," August 12, another "honor day" event. The rest of the time was for taking in the sights. A contemporary diary reports that

> Dvořák spent part of each day sightseeing and visiting. At night he went to the Austrian restaurant, "On the Midway," where he took his meals and enjoyed imported Pilsner beer. The Tavern [Old Vienna] also boasted a touring [strolling] brass band. The band members got quite excited when Dvořák first came into the restaurant . . . and began to play Austrian and Slovenian dances. Dvořák soon discovered that the musicians were largely Czech and got absorbed in conversation with them.[2]

It is more than likely that Dvořák also heard Edison's early phonograph and saw a demonstration of projected images, harbingers of the immense changes that the performing arts would undergo in the approaching century. The composer was besieged by visitors. Among them was Theodore Thomas, conductor of the Chicago Symphony and overall music director of the fair, who arranged to have a string quartet come to Dvořák's hotel, the Lakota, to read through the "American" Quartet, just completed in Spillville.

Harry T. Burleigh was also in Chicago, rehearsing music for "Colored People's Day." At the Dvořák Archives in Prague I came upon a letter from Burleigh that Dvořák had saved from the summer of 1893.[3] Written with pen and ink in longhand on three sheets of Hotel Lakota stationary and apparently left there for Dvořák the day after his "Bohemian Day" concert, Burleigh introduces his friend Will Marion Cook, director of the "Colored People's Day" concert, to Dvořák:

August 13, 1892[3]

Dear Doctor,

I want to introduce to your consideration Mr. Will M. Cook, a [here he begins to write "vi" for violinist, then writes over it "fo"] former pupil of the great Joachim. [Cook wished to be known as a composer, not a violinist, and Joachim, his biggest credit, was also a composer.] Mr. Cook has marked ability in the line of composition and desires very greatly to meet you and speak with you about his work. He has composed an opera ["Uncle Tom's Cabin"], the principal role of which I will sing.

You remember I sang Mr. Kinney's two songs at your last concert at the Conservatory last May. [This line is very curious if we think of Burleigh as Dvořák's intimate. I believe that by mentioning Kinney, Burleigh wanted to establish Cook by association as another gifted Negro composer. We know that Cook would not abide a racial description.]

I am going away from Chicago to-day but will leave this note for you, and Mr. Cook will call and see you. [Victor Herbert arranged to have Burleigh work in Saratoga's Grand Union Hotel that summer as a wine steward and occasional singer with the orchestra. Burleigh would be returning to Chicago in less than two weeks for the "Colored People's Day" concert.]

I sincerely trust you will listen to his work and give him your opinion.

Hoping you will be blessed with continued good health and success and that I will see you in the Conservatory next September I have the privilege to remain

> Yours very truly,
> Harry T. Burleigh

Dvořák was leaving for Spillville on August 18, so Cook had but five days in which to arrange a meeting with the busy Maestro. The ever-enterprising Cook succeeded in getting through. I suspect he impressed Dvořák with his command of German. His music for "Uncle Tom's Cabin" must have made a good impression as well, for Cook joined Dvořák's composition class the following month. Cook was on a roll, but he had another audition to pass: convincing his old mentor Frederick Douglass to speak at "Colored People's Day."

That "Colored People's Day" had been placed late on the calendar (August 24), toward the waning days of the fair, and only after much prodding of the fair directors, was but one of many slights that inclined Douglass, director of the fair's Haitian Pavilion, toward boycotting the whole proceeding. The Haitian Pavilion, the unofficial headquarters for "Colored People's Day," was the one place at the fair where African Americans like James Weldon Johnson, on a summer break from his job as a country schoolteacher in Henry County, Georgia, might have taken some pride and felt at home.[4] Johnson, who was working as a carpenter and "chairboy," met the poet Paul Laurence Dunbar at the Haitian Pavilion. Dunbar, then twenty-one, was serving as a clerk for Douglass, the proud, battle-weary abolitionist fighter. And it was at the Haitian Pavilion that Will Marion Cook sat down to reason with Douglass, an old family friend, who had once helped fund his violin studies in Europe.

Cook prevailed. When the announcement for "Colored People's Day" appeared in the *Daily Columbian*, the official newspaper of the fair,[5] Douglass was the lead attraction:

> At 2:30 in Festival Hall the Honorable Frederick Douglass will deliver an oration "Race Problem in America." Mme. S. Jones, the famous "Black Patti," Mr. Sidney Woodward of Boston, Mr. Harry Burleigh of the National Conservatory of Music of America, will sing selections from the famous opera "Uncle Tom's Cabin" written by Mr. Will M. Cook. Miss Hallie Q. Brown, the distinguished elocutionist will recite stirring and patriotic selections. The famous Jubilee Singers will render their quaint and plaintive plantation melodies. Mr. Joseph Douglass, the gifted violinist [grandson of Frederick Douglass and a teacher of James Reese Europe] will play several selections.

In a review of the concert that appeared two days later[6] no mention was made of the Jubilee Singers. But two other National Conservatory musicians besides Burleigh and Cook were listed on the program: a last-minute replacement for Sissieretta Jones with the extraordinary appellation Desiree Plato (Mme. Jones canceled because her "advance" didn't arrive in time); and Maurice Arnold Strathotte, Dvořák's favorite student, who was the accompanist for the entire program. The report announced that there were 3,000 in attendance, among them "2,000 blacks . . . professors, teachers, Bishops, [and] musicians." Douglass spoke for nearly an hour, taking the opportunity to lash out at the directors of the fair and at a nation that had turned its back on Reconstruction:

> The management of the fair slapped the face of the colored race, [which suffered] unchristian, unconstitutional treatment. . . . We Negros love our country. We fought for it. We ask only that we be treated as well as those that fought against it. . . . Judge us not by comparison with Caucasian civilization, but with the depths from which we came.[7]

Picking up the theme set by Douglass, Paul Dunbar read an original "Ode to the Colored American":

> And their deeds shall find a record
> In the registry of Fame.
> For their blood has cleansed completely
> Every blot of Slavery's shame.
> So all honor and all glory
> to those noble sons of Ham—

The World's Columbian Exposition

The gallant colored soldiers
Who fought for Uncle Sam![8]

On May 4, directly under the *Daily Columbian* masthead, a line drawing appeared with a caption announcing "The Arrival of the Dahomans" [*sic*].

Sixty-seven subjects of King Behanzin, ruler of Dahomey [set up camp] on the Midway Plaisance. [They came] from cities and bush regions along the slave coast of the Gulf of Guinea, West Africa. [They were shivering] from the cold raw air [as they] groaned along under heavy trunks. There were two children and twenty women in the party, among the latter [were] seven of the bravest "warriors" . . . Amazons hideous with battle scars and with the lines of cruelty and determination on their faces. [The Dahomans] have been en route for two months. . . . Through an interpreter they said the climate . . . was much better than that of Paris where they were on exhibition for a week. The camp is in mourning for one of the band who died in New York. [They] brought along toenails and part of his wool and will carry them back to Africa. Their cheeks were branded at childhood with their family names. Some were unbranded. A few spoke French and wore a Godo or T cloth.[9]

The Midway Plaisance, emblazoned by George Washington Gale Ferris's gigantic wheel, which rose well over two hundred feet above the ground,[10] was part carnival, part restaurant row, and a place where exotic entertainments were staged—a place to get away from the heady formal pavilions dedicated to man's good works.

The Dahomeyans were assigned a camping ground at the farthest outskirts of the Midway, according to a sinister hierarchy of human development as conceived by the "Head of the Department of Ethnology for the Chicago World's Fair," Frederick Ward Putnam. Putnam was a professor of anthropology at Harvard University and a proponent of social Darwinism. In 1993 I came upon the culmination of Putnam's madness at a fair centenary exhibit mounted at the Chicago Museum of Science and Industry. Among the artifacts on display were a pair of nude, life-sized figures, male and female, composites of students attending Harvard and Radcliffe in the 1890s, which were held up at the fair as "the most advanced examples of human development"!

In fact, Putnam's "order of human development" plan was compromised by practical realities, for Dvořák's favorite beer stop, "Old Vienna," was placed amid other outcast groups: the Bedouin Encampment, Sitting Bull's Camp, the Chinese Village, the Indian Bazaar, and Cairo Street—famous for its "hootchy kootchies" and their *danse du ventre.*

ARRIVAL OF THE DAHOMANS.

FIGURE 4.2
"The Arrival of the Dahomans." Drawn by Huit
for the *Daily Columbian*, May 4, 1893.

The presence of the Dahomey Village was taken as an affront by the
Haitian Pavilion intelligentsia, but Henry Krehbiel, music critic of the *New
York Tribune*, a great admirer of Dvořák and among the earliest serious students of Indian and African American music, was fascinated by what he saw
and heard there:

> I listened repeatedly during several days to the singing of a Dahomen
> minstrel who was certainly the gentlest and least assertive person in
> the village, if not in the entire fair. All day long he sat beside his little
> hut, a spear thrust in the ground by his side, and sang little descending
> melodies in a faint high voice. . . . To his gentle singing he strummed
> . . . upon a tiny harp. . . . His right hand . . . played over and over again
> a descending passage of dotted [quarter and eighth notes] in thirds; with
> his left hand he syncopated ingeniously on the highest of two strings.
>
> A more striking demonstration of the musical capacity of the Da-
> homans was made in the war-dances which they performed several
> times every forenoon and afternoon. These dances were accompanied
> by choral song and the rhythmical and harmonious beating of drums
> and bells. . . . Berlioz in his supremest effort with his army of drum-
> mers produced nothing to compare in artistic interest with the harmo-
> nious drumming of these savages. [Krehbiel was probably referring to
> Berlioz's Requiem, which employs ten drummers playing twelve ket-

tledrums that span the entire chromatic scale.] [We] attempted to
make a score . . . but were thwarted by the players who, evidently di-
vining our purpose when we took out our notebooks, mischievously
changed their manner of playing as soon as we touched pencil to
paper.[11]

Judging by Krehbiel's account, I find it hard to believe that Cook and
Dunbar could resist being drawn to the Dahomeyans as well. But we do
know that vaudeville stars Bert Williams and George Walker—their future *In
Dahomey* collaborators—"with an added coat of black," filled in as extras at
the 1894 San Francisco World's Fair when some members of the Chicago
Dahomey troupe were late in arriving. The outcome of this experience was
described by Mary White Ovington, sociologist and cofounder of the National Association for the Advancement of Colored People (NAACP):

> They became in turn spectators and studied the true African. This
> contact with the dancing and singing of the primitive people of their
> own race had an important effect upon their art. Their lyrics recalled
> African songs, their dancing took on African movements, especially
> Walker's. Anyone who saw Walker in "Abyssinia," the most African
> and the most artistic of their plays, must have recognized the savage
> beauty of his dancing when he was masquerading as an African king.[12]

It is no coincidence that Dahomey was the back-to-Africa state of choice
for the 1902 runaway hit *In Dahomey*—music by Will Marion Cook, lyrics by
Paul Dunbar, libretto by Jessye A. Shipp, and starring Williams and Walker.[13]
The Broadway show, which reopened in London at the Shaftesbury Theatre
on May 1903 for a highly successful run of seven months, does indeed have
a scene with Williams and Walker and the cast in full jungle regalia, an
atavistic spoof not uncommon in shows by African American authors and
musicians, including Duke Ellington's *Queenie Pie*.

The unifying element of *In Dahomey* is ragtime. Its rhythmic gestures
not only infuse the show's strutting banjo tunes, such as "Emancipation
Day," a Negro high holiday that Ellington also interprets in *Black, Brown and
Beige*; ragtime also hides just below the surface of the most charming and
gentle of Cook's ballads, "Brownskin Baby Mine":

> She ain't no violet,
> She ain't no red, red rose
> An tho' the lily of de valley's sweet
> She's sweeter yet I knows.
> She ain't no tulip rare
> Nor mornin' glory fine;

But 'mongst de flowers fair kaint none compare
With brownskin baby mine.[14]

The emergence of ragtime, immediately following and as an outcome of the fair, has often been suggested but never explored. Enough hard and circumstantial evidence placing ragtime at or around the fair has surfaced to warrant a closer look.

> The wheels clicked merrily and the brothel doors stood ajar. Concert saloons blossomed out with extravagant shows. . . . Beer flowed, champagne corks popped, the "professors" [an honorific for barroom piano players] and Negro bands played gay tunes, and the girls worked double shifts. . . . Chicago . . . the wickedest wide-open town in the nation.[15]

We know that among the hundreds of entertainers who flocked to the fair were several important ragtime players and composers. Scott Joplin was there, as were Ernest Hogan and Jessye Pickett. Pickett was playing his "Dream Rag" in one of Baltimore's innumerable brothels when thirteen-year-old Eubie Blake "learned it off of him" by watching his fingers through the window. Pickett later told Blake, "I learned it ['The Dream Rag'] at the Fair."[16] Ragtime historian Rudi Blesh suggests that the piano "professor" known as Jack the Bear was the real author of "The Dream [Rag]," which would place him at the fair as well.[17] We can only imagine the myriad musical interchanges that took place among ragtime players at the fair and the vastness of what was stored in their memory banks. We do know that within a few years of the fair's closing, ragtime sheet music sales caught on "like wildfire."[18]

A handful of obscure articles about ragtime at the fair were published, mostly in Negro newspapers. In a 1915 interview in the *Chicago Defender*, Will Marion Cook, by that time an established composer and conductor and a respected authority on "Negro music," places ragtime directly at the fair:

> About 1888 marked the starting and quick growth of the so-called "ragtime." [Cook would have been eighteen at the time and still studying in Europe]. As far back as 1875, Negros in questionable resorts along the Mississippi had commenced to evolve this musical figure [a reference to ragtime's predecessor, the cakewalk], but at the World's Fair in Chicago, "ragtime" got a running start and swept the Americas, next Europe, and today the craze has not diminished.[19]

The distinguished researcher Lawrence Gushee has turned up an even earlier Cook interview from 1898, when he was still an unknown composer

The World's Columbian Exposition

struggling in New York. Cook was responding to the proposition that Negro music—as exemplified by such ephemeral "clap-trap compositions as . . . 'The New Bully,' 'A Hot Time in the Old Town,' and 'All Coons Look Alike to Me'"—was degenerate when compared with "soul stirring slave melodies." Cook responded:

> One special characteristic of these songs is the much advertised "rag" accompaniment. . . . This kind of movement, which was unknown until about fifteen years ago, grew out of the visits of Negro sailors to Asiatic ports, and particularly those of Turkey, when the odd rhythms of the *danse du ventre* [literally, belly dance] soon forced itself upon them; and trying to reproduce this they have worked out the "rag."
>
> During the World's Columbian Exposition at Chicago, the "Midway Plaisance" was well filled with places of amusement where the peculiar music of the "muscle dance" was continually heard, and it is worthy of note that after that time the popularity of the "rag" grew with astonishing rapidity and became general among Negro pianists.[20]

Cook's evasive answer was atypical; he rarely missed an opportunity to strike back at the musical snobbery that plagued him throughout his career. More significantly, the interview came at the very time he had found a new friend in Ernest Hogan, the composer of the offending "All Coons Look Alike to Me." Published in 1896, Hogan's song contained the first musical usage of the word "rag" in print;[21] the sheet music offered an optional piano arrangement, a "Choice chorus, with Negro 'Rag' Accompaniment," suggesting that ragtime began as a rhythmic imposition, dare we say improvisation, on an already composed piece. This was exactly the way Eubie Blake demonstrated ragtime for our television show in 1979, playing Chopin's "Funeral March" straight, "as they were going to the cemetery," and then *ragged*—with rag accompaniment—"when they headed home." Eubie ended the music with a flourish, clinching the argument. "That's Ragtime!" and he beamed.

Ernest Hogan had his own ideas about the birth of ragtime, which he connected to his controversial song "All Coons Look Alike to Me." In *100 Years of the Negro in Show Business*, Tom Fletcher reconstructs several conversations that he had with Hogan. Their last meeting took place in a nursing home in 1908, toward the end of Hogan's life:

> Hogan was out in Chicago . . . seeking a little "sport" [the chronology strongly suggests this happened during the fair or soon after]. . . . The piano player seemed very blue. "He must of had something on his mind," said Hogan, "because he was plunking and talking to himself. . . . Each night found me in that same house asking him to play and

sing that song. . . . There was no protection for songs in those days, so when I left Chicago the song left with me."

Laughing, [Hogan] asked me to hand him [his] concertina which he played exceptionally well. He started playing "All Coons Look Alike to Me" and while he played he talked. "Son," he said, "this song has caused a lot of trouble in and out of show business, but it was also good for show business because at the time money was short in all walks of life. With the publication of that song, a new musical rhythm was given to the people. Its popularity grew and it sold like wildfire. . . . That one song opened the way for a lot of colored and white songwriters. Finding the rhythm so great, they stuck to it . . . and now you get hit songs without the word 'coon.' Ragtime was the rhythm played in back rooms and cafes and other such places. The ragtime players were the boys who played just by ear their own creations of music which would have been lost to the world if I had not put it on paper."[22]

Cook and Hogan (via Fletcher) do more than simply confirm the notion that ragtime, without which there would not be an American music, took root in the fair's catalytic proving ground. Instead of the anonymous, noble-savage image traditionally imposed on African American musics—for want of a paper trail, that accompanying documentation that art and cultural historians have come to expect—we find here composers who, through the application of accurate notation, attention to form, harmonic refinement, and adroit piano voicings, crafted the improvisations of the piano "professors" into a coherent whole and delivered a music that seems inevitable.

Dvořák headed back to Spillville via the Chicago, Milwaukee, and St. Louis Line, crossing the "sweeping currents" of the Mississippi River at Prairie du Chien. He detrained a short time afterward at Calmar, just across the northeast border of Iowa; from there he traveled the last few miles to Spillville on a horse cart.[23] In the summer of 1993, accompanied by a few Czech friends,[24] I made a Dvořák anniversary pilgrimage to Chicago and (via Iowa City) to Spillville, where we attended the Dvořák in Spillville Centennial Celebration. Driving through endless miles of corn-fruited plains, we crossed the Mississippi at Rock Island. And the river obliged us with a rare breaching of its banks, flooding the surrounding towns and fields.

The tiny farm village of Spillville seemed caught in a time warp. The squarish brick house where the Dvořák family spent their summer, known these days as the Bílý Clock House, was intact. The upper floor, where the family slept, is now a modest museum. In a glass case Indian artifacts mingle with a stub of a pipe used by Dvořák. Lying nearby is a fading Dvořák letter.

The Bili Clock House reminded me of another homespun shrine I visited in Czechoslovakia, the little upstairs study in Vysoka, which remains as Dvořák left it when he died in 1904. The walls are covered with awards, among them laurel wreaths and large presentation ribbons lettered with the date and venue of long-ago concerts. In a place of honor, framed in glass, hangs a diploma of honorary membership presented to Dvořák by the New York Philharmonic Society. At the back of Dvořák's desk, along with other reference books, is a copy of the harmony text used by the National Conservatory, evidently sent in advance of his trip to familiarize him with their program. Dvořák's handwritten notations indicate he gave it a thorough review. There is also a guide to New York (c. 1880) with photos of the harbor teeming with sailing ships. Scattered along the windowsills and wainscoting are photos of students with grateful greetings. Three photos stood out among all the others: Chief Big Moon; his wife, Large Head; and John Crow.

Dvořák's son Otakar wrote a memoir in 1961 about his boyhood trip to America. Although sixty-eight years had passed, he had never forgotten the Indians he met in Spillville. He described them as "medicine men" belonging to a tribe of thirty or so Iroquois who lived in tents "south of town, across the creek. . . . My father was interested . . . in their songs and instruments. . . . Father received photos from the Indians. These photos were among my father's prize possessions."[25]

The high point of the Spillville Dvořák Centennial Celebration was a grand parade led by a high school marching band huffing out a Sousafied "Goin' Home," from the *New World* Symphony. The band was followed by a horse cart carrying Otakar's son, Antonin Dvořák III. Beside him were his son and grandson, Antonin IV and Antonin V, who had traveled from Czechoslovakia for the occasion. Dressed in a nineteenth-century hat and coat and with a full beard, Antonin Dvořák III looked every centimeter like "the old man" to all of us pilgrims.

The Maple Leaf Limited train still winds its way alongside the broad sweeps of the Hudson estuary. It traces the bittersweet route of Dvořák and his family on the last leg of their end-of-summer journey of 1893. The leaves were beginning to turn, a reminder that the family were about to separate once again. Otakar and little Antonin would remain with their parents on East Seventeenth Street. The others would return to Prague.

When Dvořák detrained into the smoke and soot of the Grand Central Depot,[26] he was carrying the completed scores of his *New World* Symphony and his new "American" String Quartet. They would both be premiered at Carnegie Hall during the 1893–94 season, the most triumphant of the composer's life.

5

The National Conservatory
of Music of America

The National Conservatory of Music of America was represented in full force at the brilliant Carnegie Hall premiere of Dvořák's Symphony no. 9 (*From the New World*) on December 16, 1893. Dvořák, his wife, and their two sons Antonin and Otakar sat in a box of honor with Maurice Arnold (Strathotte), the student composer for whom Dvořák had the highest hopes.[1] Jeanette Thurber and her husband, Frances B. Thurber, sat proudly in an equally prominent box nearby. Victor Herbert led the cello section of the New York Philharmonic on the stage below. Scattered in the balconies were other students: Harry T. Burleigh, who had copied some of the orchestra parts now resting on the stands of the players; and a fifteen-year-old cornetist, Edwin Franko Goldman (the future composer and director of his own "Goldman" band), who had already played some of the music from the symphony when he tested the trumpet passages for Dvořák as he was orchestrating to see if they sat well on the instrument.

I wonder how many students were present at the first rehearsal of the slow movement, when the conductor, Anton Seidl, sent for the orchestra's tuba player. The tuba player thought he had the week off, for Dvořák did not call for a tuba in the score. But a last-minute decision was made—by either Seidl or Dvořák—to reinforce the bass trombone part with a tuba, further underpinning the mysterious chorale that opens the Largo movement and sets a somber mood for the hauntingly beautiful English horn solo, the "Goin' Home" tune. And at thousands of performances ever since, a lone tuba player sounds the seven notes at the beginning and end of the slow movement and then remains trapped onstage for the rest of the symphony with nothing to do.

The English horn solo made a lasting impression on Maurice Arnold (Strathotte) and two of his fellow composition students, Harvey Worthington Loomis and William Arms Fisher. Dvořák had described the slow movement as "a study or sketch for a longer work, either a cantata or an opera . . . based on Longfellow's 'Hiawatha.'"[2] But how do we explain that thirty or so years later, just when the copyright was running out, Loomis, Arnold, and Fisher—independently of one another—fitted the English horn tune from the Largo of the symphony with a Negro spiritual text and had it published? Arnold came up with "Mother Mine" (New York: H. Flammer, 1927); Loomis used "Massa Dear" (Boston: C. C. Birchard, 1923); but it was Fisher's adaptation using his own text, "Goin' Home" (Boston: Oliver Ditson, 1922), that eventually established itself as a popular Negro spiritual. This has to be more than coincidence. I think that Dvořák told members of his composition class that the English horn solo was conceived as a wordless Negro spiritual—for Hiawatha!

What was the outcome of Dvořák's prediction about a new school of American music? How did his students at the National Conservatory fare, three in particular: Rubin Goldmark, grandson of a Hebrew cantor and nephew of the celebrated Viennese composer Karl Goldmark; Maurice Arnold (Strathotte), Dvořák's "favorite"; and proud, feisty Will Marion Cook, a man ahead of his time?[3]

Rubin Goldmark (1872–1936) became best known as a teacher. Starting in 1924, he headed the composition department at the Institute of Musical Art and its successor, the Juilliard School, holding the post until his death. Goldmark also founded the Bohemian Musical Society. In the winter of 1917, a Brooklyn-born teenager, Aaron Copland, began studying privately with him, a relationship that lasted until Copland left for Paris four years later and began work with his new teacher, Nadia Boulanger. George Gershwin, forever in pursuit of a conservatory equivalency diploma, came to Goldmark for a short period in 1923.[4]

While Goldmark was still studying with Dvořák he composed a Piano Trio, op. 1, which he dedicated to his teacher. The trio was premiered at the conservatory on May 8, 1893, a few weeks before Dvořák left for Spillville, with Victor Herbert offering his "kind assistance" as cellist. The Piano Trio is said to be the piece that moved Dvořák to declare, "Now there are two Goldmarks."

The Piano Trio, op. 1, contains no overt Americanisms, no cakewalk licks, no Indian tunes or spirituals. It sounds Viennese.[5] Goldmark's more mature, unblushingly American symphonic work *The Call of the Plain* (1925), which I dusted off for a Dvořák American Legacy concert at the Prague Spring Festival in 1992,[6] pales in comparison with the fresh ragtime- and blues-inspired works that his star pupils, Copland and Gershwin, were writing around the same time.

In the winter of 1993 I talked with the conductor, composer, and publisher Arthur Cohn, who had studied with Rubin Goldmark in the early 1930s. Cohn retained a vivid memory of his teacher, in particular the hundreds of themes he wrote, and the months "lost," before Goldmark finally allowed him to begin composing in earnest. I pointed out that similar "endless revisions of the theme" had been reported by several students of Goldmark's own teacher, Dvořák.[7] To my surprise Cohn did not recall Goldmark ever making known his work with Dvořák. Dvořák's star has risen and sunk beneath the horizon several times during the twentieth century. The same is true for his fellow romantic composers, Tchaikovsky and Brahms, but I'll wager that if Goldmark were alive today he would have his Dvořák apprenticeship engraved on his calling card.

Nor did Cohn recall Goldmark mentioning Aaron Copland, whereas "he rarely missed an opportunity to bring up Gershwin." Gershwin had already composed the *Rhapsody in Blue, An American in Paris,* and the [Piano] Concerto in F, and was the darling of Broadway by the time Cohn was studying with Goldmark. Copland's big pieces—*El salón Mexico* (1936), *Billy the Kid* (1938), and, above all, *Appalachian Spring* (1944)—were yet to come.

Goldmark was particularly proud, said Cohn, that he "helped Gershwin with his *Lullaby* for string quartet." Edward Jablonski, a longtime friend of Ira Gershwin and the biographer of George, dismisses the import of the Goldmark-Gershwin relationship: "It can hardly be claimed that Gershwin 'studied' with Goldmark. . . . They met perhaps three times." In my view, three meetings between a master teacher and an advanced musician who happens to be a genius can be deeply influential.

Gershwin did not live long enough to issue reflections on his early years. As is often the case, various spokespersons have arisen to fill the gap. And it saddens me that the only statements about Goldmark by Gershwin biographers are dismissive or poke fun at a man Jablonski himself describes as "fine and respected . . . a most sought after teacher of piano and theory then in New York."[8] Had he lived, Gershwin might have contributed his own encomium alongside that of Copland, who wrote a moving tribute to his teacher in 1956 on the occasion of the twentieth anniversary of Goldmark's death:

He was one of the outstanding musicians and composers of his period. American musicians . . . tend to forget that only half a century ago so-called classical music was thought of as an exotic growth in the American landscape. Because of that, the men of Rubin Goldmark's time had their work cut out for them: they had first to acclimatize the art of music in a bleak native environment. . . . In a very real sense these men were the pioneers, we owe them a debt, if for no other reason that they helped make possible our present day musical flowering.[9]

Edwin Franko Goldman, the young trumpeter in Dvořák's conservatory orchestra, recalled Maurice Arnold in a memoir: "My instructor in harmony at the conservatory was Maurice Arnold, who in those days was known as Maurice A. Strathotte. Dvořák was very fond of him, and considered him his most promising pupil." [10]

Maurice Arnold was born in St. Louis, Missouri, in 1865. His first lessons came from his mother, a piano teacher. In 1883 Arnold left the Cincinnati College of Music to study composition in Europe. He was eighteen at the time and already a fine pianist and violinist. Arnold rejected the first teacher he found, Heinrich Urban, in Berlin, "[because] he discouraged me when I attempted to imbue a suite with a Negro Plantation spirit."[11] Arnold had independently arrived at the idea of incorporating African American music into his compositions a decade before he began his studies at the conservatory. This was around the same time that the Boston-based composer George Whitefield Chadwick was composing a Scherzo (1884) for his Second Symphony that made "American references."[12] Arnold's particular interest was duly noted by Dvořák: "Among my pupils . . . I have discovered strong talents. There is one young man upon whom I am building strong expectations. His compositions are based upon Negro melodies, and I have encouraged him in this direction."[13]

On January 23, 1894, still flushed with the enthusiastic reception given his new symphony, Dvořák directed the National Conservatory Chorus and Orchestra in a benefit concert at Madison Square Garden for the New York Herald's Free Clothing Fund. This concert has received little attention in the Dvořák canon. Upon examination we see that this was not some quiet school recital for parents and friends, but rather a significant Thurber-Dvořák "event"—the conservatory on parade. Especial attention was given to the achievements of its African American students, in particular Maurice Arnold, whose work was being held up as an example of the new American school to come.

Dvořák was the drawing card. The Herald review reported that "long before the hour fixed for the opening, the [Madison Square Garden] hall

MME. JONES, THE "BLACK PATTI."

FIGURE 5.1
Sissieretta Jones wearing
medals awarded on her
concert tours. Unsigned
drawing for the *New York
Herald,* January 24, 1894.

was filled with an immense throng of people. . . . There was hardly standing room,"[14] and that the large and distinguished audience included Maestro and Mrs. Anton Seidl. The review also noted that "each soloist, with one exception, belonged to the colored race."[15]

Sissieretta Jones—the same "Black Patti" who did not show up at the fair for Cook's "Uncle Tom's Cabin"—was the featured guest star of the evening.[16] For the grand finale she joined with "baritone soloist" Harry Thacker Burleigh, an all-Negro choir, and the orchestra in a performance of Stephen Foster's "Old Folks at Home," arranged for the occasion by Dvořák, who conducted. Jones's portrait appeared in the *Herald,* rendered by a staff artist in those pre-photoengraving days. It shows her formally posed, her ample bosom replete with medals and awards. There is a smaller portrait of Burleigh.

Dvořák bestowed a high honor upon two of his students—one (possibly both) African American—when he invited them to the podium and turned over his baton. Edward B. Kinney, organist and choirmaster of St. Philip's A.M.E. Church, directed the orchestra and the 130-voice all-black choir, among them the boy sopranos and altos from St. Philip's, in the "Inflammatus" from Gioachino Rossini's Stabat Mater, with Sissieretta Jones as soloist.

The Conservatory of Music of America

Maurice Arnold led the orchestra in his brand-new composition, *American Plantation Dances*.

Dvořák referred to this work in an earlier *Herald* interview:

> "When I first came here last year I was impressed with this idea—to study and build upon plantation melodies—and it has developed into a settled conviction. These beautiful and varied themes are the product of the soil." And saying so Dvořák sat down at his piano and ran his fingers lightly over the keys. It was his favorite pupil's adaptation of a southern melody.[17]

I was delighted to find a copy of Arnold's *American Plantation Dances* safely tucked away in the stacks of the New York Public Library Music Division.[18] It was published in the form of a condensed autograph score—most probably in Arnold's own hand—and instrumented for a standard European symphonic ensemble, with one exception. The fourth movement calls for "blocks of sandpaper," which were used by kit or trap drummers in the dance bands and theater orchestras of the early 1900s. The sandpaper blocks underline a triplet rhythm in the woodwinds, a rhythm that soon accelerates into a rollicking cakewalk. This must be the first usage of sandpaper blocks in a classically scored work, but also the first pop-music effect.[19]

There were no orchestral parts to be found, but by following Arnold's carefully notated indications I recreated a full score and a set of parts of the *American Plantation Dances*, which I performed with my student orchestra at Queens College and with the Karlovarski Symphony at the Prague Spring Festival in 1992. The second movement, a lilting skipping dance for solo clarinet, is striking because it reminds everyone of the celebrated Humoresque no. 7, the **dah-dadah-dadah-dadah** one that introduced so many of us to Dvořák. They share the same gavotte rhythm, phrase lengths, and plagal cadences. The clarinet tune must be the one that Dvořák tinkled out for the reporters. There is really no other candidate. It predates the Humoresque no. 7 by a year and probably was its inspiration. Arnold's choice of solo instrument, in the light of Goldman's memoir, conjures up a lovely image:

> Dvořák was greatly interested in the Negroes, and especially their music. In the students' orchestra there were a number of them. I recollect a first violinist named Craig, a clarinetist named Bailey and in particular Harry T. Burleigh. . . . Often when the first clarinet had a solo passage, Dvořák would go over to Bailey and put his arms around him and cry *Bravo!*

I picture a happy Papa Dvořák at the Free Clothing Fund concert, bursting with pride as Arnold conducted his *American Plantation Dances* and Bailey tootled forth, his theory made manifest for all to behold.

Arnold's final movement builds into a full-blown cakewalk, swung out by the oboe and accompanied by busy figures in the strings. And according to the *Herald* review, the performance was a toe-tapper: "There is such a gay swing about the last movement that nearly every boy in the choir marked time with his head. And I am pretty sure that under cover of that friendly gallery front, they were all patting 'juba.'"[20]

I wish I could report that Arnold's more mature music fulfilled the promise of his *American Plantation Dances*. I studied all fifteen of Arnold's published chamber works listed in the catalog of the British Library. Among them are a few provocative pieces that date from before or during Arnold's time with Dvořák: a "Valse elegante" for two pianos, eight hands, and "Dance de la Midway Plaisance, 'souvenir of the famous Persian Danse du Ventre,'" recalling his visit to the Chicago World's Fair when he was the accompanist for "Colored People's Day."

Maurice Arnold Strathotte's prominent participation in a black pride program sets one to thinking that he must have been African American. John Clapham makes a passing reference to "the black student Maurice Arnold" in his book *Dvořák*,[21] yet he is not described as a Negro by two contemporary chroniclers who were careful to so designate: Edwin Franko Goldman and the *New York Herald* reporter who reviewed the Free Clothing Fund concert.

There can be no doubt that Arnold lived as a white person at the end of his life. His last address, 120 East Eighty-ninth Street, was in the heart of Yorkville, then Manhattan's German district.[22] I am reminded of a Langston Hughes poem, "Cross," the genesis of *The Barrier*, an opera composed by Jan Meyerowitz that made a lasting impression on me when I saw it as a young college student and that I had the pleasure of conducting in 1961:

My old man died in a fine big house.
My ma died in a shack.
I wonder where I'm gonna die,
Being neither white nor black?[23]

Does Arnold's lifelong ambivalence about his name or his "modesty" have to do with his double identity? The bulk of his later work, while well crafted, is undistinguished. Perhaps one could find more interesting music among his larger, unpublished works, but Arnold's manuscript scores, like those of so many other American composers of the period, including Cook and Europe, have disappeared.[24]

Dvořák and the well-meaning folks at the *Herald* and the conservatory rightly believed that the *American Plantation Dances* pointed in the direction of a new school, but there were miles yet to go. The *American Plantation Dances*, despite its inspired moments, clings safely to tradition. Except for

The Conservatory of Music of America

throwing in a lick on sandpaper blocks, Arnold was in the unenviable position of trying to paint an African American landscape using a European palette, thus canceling out many of the unique qualities in Negro music that first attracted Dvořák and, as he astutely observed, "moved sentiment in" American musicians.

Over the next three decades, a new kind of American orchestra would evolve, with its own unique sound. Its instrumentation would allow a style of inflected playing that mirrors the language and song of the people from which it flows.

How were the *American Plantation Dances*, which Dvořák had touted so mightily, perceived by other African American students at the conservatory—in particular, Will Marion Cook? Cook might have been one of several Negro violinists in the conservatory orchestra at the Free Clothing Fund Concert.[25] I say "might have been," because Cook left the conservatory sometime during the 1893–94 season. According to an oft-quoted memoir that he wrote a half century later:

> I was barred . . . from the classes at the National Conservatory . . . because I wouldn't play my fiddle in the orchestra under Dvořák. I couldn't play; my fingers had grown too stiff. Dvořák didn't like me anyway; Harry T. Burleigh was his pet. Only John White, the harmony and counterpoint teacher, thought I had talent, and insisted that I attend his classes.[26]

The "fingers had grown stiff" remark resonates with another story about Cook's abandoning the violin in anger after a critic offered qualified praise by referring to his race. One source is Tom Fletcher, who knew Cook as early as 1908, when he (Fletcher) was managing the path-breaking Memphis Students ensemble, "the first modern jazz band," led by Cook.[27] The tale is further dramatized by Duke Ellington, who devotes a chapter to Cook in his autobiography, *Music Is My Mistress*.

> When he [Cook] first returned to New York and did a concert at Carnegie Hall, he had a brilliant critique the next day in the newspaper . . . "the world's greatest Negro violinist."
> Dad Cook took his violin and went to see the reviewer at the newspaper office . . . and smashed it across the reviewer's desk. "I am not the world's greatest Negro violinist," he exclaimed. "I am the greatest violinist in the world!" He turned and walked away from his splintered instrument, and he never picked up a violin again in his life.[28]

Cook did pick up the fiddle again when he joined James Reese Europe's historic Clef Club Concert at Carnegie Hall in 1912. But what I find hardest to believe is Cook's story that he was fed up because Burleigh "was Dvořák's pet." Dvořák's real pet—the fellow to beat—was Maurice Arnold. Not only does Cook's memoir gratefully recall how Burleigh staked him to a bed and meals when he was traveling up from Washington, trying to break into Broadway; in an interview he gave during the London run of *In Dahomey*, Cook touted Burleigh, transforming aspiration into fact: "Soon you will have the opportunity of seeing a negro composer of serious music in London. I refer to Mr. Harry T. Burleigh whose chamber music and symphonies are well known."[29]

If Cook was heading toward a parting of the ways with Dvořák and the National Conservatory, the Free Clothing Fund concert would have forced the issue. Violinists were ubiquitous in those days. Nevertheless, the directors of the conservatory would have wanted every violinist of color on parade at that symbolic event. And I doubt that Dvořák, who remarked upon the lack of wind instrumentalists at the conservatory, would have noticed Cook's absence among a dozen or more violinists. Nor would he have "barred him from classes," which has the ring of an official dictum. No, I think that Cook saw himself as a golden boy. He was enrolled in the Oberlin Conservatory at age twelve. With the financial assistance of Frederick Douglass, he was then sent to Berlin, where he joined the violin class of Joseph Joachim, friend of Mendelssohn, Schumann, and Brahms. Cook, who had excerpts of his opera performed at the Chicago World's Columbian Exposition, could not bear the idea of literally playing "second fiddle" behind Sissieretta Jones at a special concert that Dvořák presented to show off his African American pupils, and certainly not for a composer-conductor who wrote Negro-inspired music as tame as Maurice Arnold's.

I believe that Cook's stubborn refusal to "play my fiddle in the orchestra under Dvořák," before or after the Free Clothing Fund event, was a convenient way to deal with his envy. I also wonder if Cook came to the realization that for all Dvořák's enthusiasms about African American music, the European models he imposed upon his students were not where Cook was heading as a composer. Beethoven's formulations were of no interest to him. He was already working out his own African American idiom—the "Uncle Tom's Cabin" arias, following the play, were no doubt sung in dialect[30]—and he had plans. Within the year Cook and Paul Laurence Dunbar would sign a contract with the music publishers W. Witmark and Sons for *Clorindy: The Origin of the Cakewalk*, a novel musical theater piece that Cook had conceived, though it had yet to be committed to paper.[31]

The basic difference between Arnold's and Cook's Negro-inspired music was vividly brought home to me when I recorded their works in a single session with the Prague Radio Orchestra on September 24, 1998. The orchestra read through Arnold's *American Plantation Dances* as if it were an old (European) friend. The only challenge was getting two cakewalk tunes to fly. Arnold assigned them both to the oboe, known far more for its lyric singing than for beckoning us onto the dance floor. On the other hand, the tunes in Cook's overture from *In Dahomey*, which require the underlying, steadily prodding pulse of ragtime, took some time to settle in.

For the grand finale of the Free Clothing Fund concert, Dvořák made his own setting of Stephen Foster's "Old Folks at Home," which he described as "a very beautiful American folk song . . . that he [Foster] *happened to write down* [author's italics]. American music is music that lives in the hearts of the people, and therefore this air has every right to be regarded as purely national."[32] These days Dvořák would be liable for such a statement about a work under copyright. In fact he was simply echoing the sentiments of a great majority of African Americans. W. E. B. Du Bois himself thought that "The Old Folks at Home" was justifiably part of black heritage.[33]

The Dvořák archive in Prague holds the sheet music from which Dvořák made his soli, chorus, and orchestra version of "The Old Folks at Home," five pages sliced out of a collection of minstrel songs "old and new" published by the Oliver Ditson Company; with an arranger's credit, "As Sung by E. P. Christy" (Christy being the very successful minstrel troupe leader who paid Foster for the right to claim the song as his own).[34] Dvořák's orchestration follows the printed music in almost every detail. He assigns the verses to Burleigh and Madame Jones and adds a few touches: a rising arpeggiated figure that leads into the choir's entrance and his own fine four-part choral harmonization of the refrain, "All the world is dark and dreary." Only as an afterthought does Dvořák affix his name, squeezing it between the title and Stephen Foster's name: "Arranged for Soli, Chorus, and Orchestra by Antonin Dvořák."[35]

The *Herald*'s reviewer reported that just before Dvořák began the finale, Mr. Friedlander, a violinist, stepped out of the ranks and presented Dvořák with a gold-fitted baton of ebony

> as a token of loving esteem to their distinguished director. Dr. Dvořák was too much overcome by his feelings to reply. He thanked the orchestra by gestures that were more eloquent of his appreciation of their kindness than any words could have been, and then taking up the beautiful present he commenced to conduct. Appropriately enough, seeing that Dr. Dvořák is the apostle of national music, the first number he directed with his baton was his own arrangement of

America's most popular folksong, "The Old Folks at Home," which he scored specially for this concert.[36]

At the end of the concert, Dvořák, who fastidiously dated and saved every scrap of paper carrying his sketches as well as his finished scores, gave the "Old Folks at Home" manuscript to Burleigh as a gift, thereby returning the work that "lives in the hearts of the people" to the man who embodied Negro music for him.[37] Goldman recalled the concert fifty years later: "a Negro chorus participated in 'Swanee River,' and Dvořák beamed with joy."[38]

The Free Clothing Fund concert reads as an intensely poignant yet joyous event, one of those rare concerts when the performers and the audience are magically joined. Above all, Dvořák comes off as an unusually warm and nurturing human being. A mensch. It is no wonder that after the composer's death in 1904, Sylvester Russell, a leading black journalist with a national following, was moved to close his obituary: "If it were possible the Afro-American musicians alone could flood his grave with tears."[39]

Yet, many in the audience at the Madison Square Garden Music Hall were aware that Jeanette Thurber's unique conservatory, as dramatized by the concert before them, was but a tiny oasis in a vast desert of bigotry. The promise of Reconstruction was long broken. The incidence of lynchings—practically the only mentions of African Americans I came across as I thumbed through hundreds of pages of the *Daily Columbian*—was at its height. And coursing its way between the lynchings and the love-ins was a small but stubborn third stream of thought: a rejection by members of the black intellectual elite, the "talented tenth," led by W. E. B. Du Bois, of the Europeanization, the whitening, of Negro art.

6

Paul Laurence Dunbar, *Clorindy,* and "The Talented Tenth"

Some prominent black intellectuals with ideas of their own "for the development of Negro genius"[1] were at odds with the efforts of Dvořák and the conservatory, and their supporters in the press, on behalf of Negro music. In Washington, D.C., on December 8, 1896, John Wesley Crummell, a distinguished African American minister, brought together a high school Latin teacher, two fellow clergymen, and a young poet to explore the idea of forming a black learned society, an African Institute. The poet, Paul Laurence Dunbar, had already distinguished himself by introducing Negro dialect into his poetry, consecrating as authentic folk art that which had been parodied in minstrelsy. The five men agreed on a statement of purpose:

> To promote the historical and literary works of Negro authors. To gather in its archive valuable data, historical or literary works of Negro authors. To aid, by publications, the vindication of the race from vicious assaults, in all the lines of learning and truth. To publish an annual collection of original articles. To raise the standard of intellectual endeavor among American Negros.[2]

They considered inviting distinguished black women to join, but the question was left unresolved. For their second meeting Crummell chose the symbolic day of March 5, the anniversary of the Boston Massacre, the day that Crispus Attucks, the first African American hero, was killed. William Edward Burghardt Du Bois, a twenty-eight-year-old classics teacher from

Wilberforce University with a doctorate in anthropology, joined the group, now expanded to nineteen. At the suggestion of Dunbar, described by Crummell as "the shining star . . . a model of the younger men of genius on whom the future of their people depended," it was agreed their name be changed from the African Institute to the American Negro Academy. They were no longer outsiders looking back; they were now full and equal citizens looking ahead.[3]

At Crummell's invitation, Du Bois submitted a paper that he read to the assembly, "The Conservation of the Races."

> For the development of Negro genius, of Negro literature and art, of Negro spirit, only Negros bound and welded together, Negros inspired by one vast ideal, can work out in its fullness the great message we have for humanity . . . if the Negro is ever to be a factor in the world's history—if among the gaily-colored banners that deck the broad ramparts of civilization is to hang one uncompromisingly black, then it must be placed there by black hands, fashioned by black heads and hallowed by the travail of two hundred million black hearts beating in one glad song of jubilee.[4]

Further into the paper, Du Bois narrows his sights and offers a musical reference:

> We are the people whose subtle sense of song has given America its only American music, its only American fairytales, its only touch of pathos and humor amid its mad money-getting plutocracy.

Dunbar's poetry had been discussed as "a demonstration of how necessary it was for educated blacks to turn to their own race and history in order to discern the truth within," and Du Bois's paper seemed to be urging just such an approach.[5] Nevertheless, once the enthusiastic applause subsided, several members rose to question Du Bois's views, and an all-too-familiar separatist-versus-assimilationist debate ensued.[6] Before adjourning, the members drew up a wish list of forty-nine leading black intellectuals they would invite (all males).

Despite the academy's professed interest in "Negro literature and arts," it wasn't until 1903 that a musician was invited to join, and then only as a "corresponding member."[7] This honor was bestowed upon Samuel Coleridge-Taylor, an African English composer who called ragtime "the worst sort of rot." The academicians apparently liked their music bland, at least on the record. Cook wrote about such high-minded blacks—among them his own mother, an Oberlin graduate in the class of 1865—who "loved the Dunbar lyrics but weren't ready for Negro songs."

Only a few months before the academy meetings began, Dunbar met with Cook in New York City. Cook had been on a "long siege of persuasion" to get Dunbar reinterested in *Clorindy*.[8] One such skirmish must have taken place in September 1896, when fate brought Cook, Dunbar, Williams and Walker, Victor Herbert, and the Casino Theater—where *Clorindy* would eventually make history—together.

According to Dunbar's journal, this was the same month he gave a recitation under Edison's new "focusable [electric] lamps" at the Lyceum Theater on Twenty-third Street and Fourth Avenue.[9] Dunbar also traveled out to Far Rockaway to visit William Dean Howells, the dean of American letters (a meeting that led to a glowing review in *Harper's Weekly*).[10] And he hung out with Cook, Burleigh, and James Weldon Johnson, his friends from the Chicago World's Fair days, who introduced him around New York's show business crowd. Among those he met were Johnson's brother, the composer J. Rosamond Johnson.[11] Wouldn't these young African American artists be curious about the appearance, for the first time on Broadway, of black entertainers, Williams and Walker, in a white show with music written by Burleigh's friend Victor Herbert? Herbert's *The Gold Bug* was opening on September 21 at the Casino Theater. The show needed a lift, so at the last minute the producers turned to the popular vaudeville team, breaking the color line, but to no avail. The show lasted three days. But Cook evidently saw it. In a letter to author Alain Locke written in 1936, Cook recalls that *The Gold Bug* was "a most dismal flop . . . W and W an overnight riot."[12] This dovetails neatly with Cook's memoir about going up to New York from Washington, D.C., for meetings with Williams and Walker about his newest ideas for *Clorindy*.[13]

Whether or not Burleigh, Dunbar, and the Johnson brothers caught *The Gold Bug* with Cook, they constituted a core group of black writers, musicians, and vaudeville stars who together would create the new all-black musicals that Americanized Broadway, moving the Great White Way from the waltz to ragtime. *Clorindy: The Origin of the Cakewalk* was the first to break through.

Dunbar and Cook finally came together to work on *Clorindy* in Washington, D.C., sometime in the winter of 1897–98.[14] Four years had passed since the Chicago World's Fair, a time when Dunbar and Cook, two fatherless men in their twenties, came under the influence of a living legend, Frederick Douglass. When Douglass died in 1895 at age seventy-seven, Dunbar wrote: "He was no soft tongued apologist . . . / To sin and crime he gave their proper hue / And hurled at evil what was evil's due." They were now a far more mature and focused pair. Each had since encountered—and survived—new, enormously powerful mentors. Cook's disillusionment with the well-meaning Dvořák did not seem to crush his spirit. It might even have helped clarify his goals. Dunbar was probably relieved to set aside the Ciceronian notions of Crummell and the American Negro Academy.

We have both men's versions of their *Clorindy* collaboration. Working from letters and personal interviews, Paul Dunbar's biographer assembled the Dunbar version in 1907:[15]

> Will Marion Cook and his brother John were in Washington and came over [to see Dunbar] asking, "How about finishing *Clorindy?*" Paul agreed. It was just what he needed—comic relief after his hardships in England and the seriousness of his first novel [*The Uncalled*].
>
> The three gathered at John's house, around the big piano. John [a future Clef Clubber] thumped out the rhythm with musician's magic as Will hummed the tune. Paul walked back and forth, composing out loud. Sometimes a rhyme wouldn't come, or a balky phrase refused to fit the meter.
>
> "Here," Will said. "Have another beer." Refreshed, Paul began dictating again. Will scribbled down the words beneath the notes and jumped up to do an impromptu dance. A cakewalk. *Clorindy*'s subtitle was *The Origin of the Cakewalk*. Will read off the names of their [six] songs. . . . "We've got a hit show," Will said, slapping Paul enthusiastically on the back. "Wait till it gets to New York. You'll see."

One of the songs, "Who Dat Say Chicken in Dis Crowd?," became the hit of the show:

> Who dat say chicken in dis crowd?
> Speak de word agin' and speak it loud
> Blame de lan' let white folk rule it,
> I'se lookin' fuh a pullet
> Who dat say chicken in dis crowd?

Cook set the word "chicken" with an upward leap of a third on a catchy, short-long, ragtime rhythm—also known as the doo-dah lick and the Scotch snap—the "hook," in current songwriter jargon, that made "Who Dat Say Chicken in Dis Crowd?" first on everyone's humming list as they left the theater. But underneath the clever dialect and spanky rhythms lies social commentary. Dunbar juxtaposes power—"de lan' let white folk rule it"—with a simple search for sustenance.

Cook's version of their collaboration dates from a memoir written in 1944, the last year of his life.[16] Cook recalls how Williams and Walker liked his idea for a show about the origin of the cakewalk and that it was around the same time he was "barred from classes at the National Conservatory." Cook

FIGURE 6.1
Sheet music cover, "Who Dat Say Chicken in Dis Crowd," 1898

moved back to Washington but he didn't give up: "After a long siege of persuasion I finally got Paul Laurence Dunbar to consent to write the *Clorindy*
libretto (which was never used) [*sic*] and a few of the lyrics."

On one hand, Cook's fifty-year-old memory was accurate, the "siege"
lasted from the signing of the contract in 1895 to their actual collaboration in
the winter of 1897–98; but there is reason to question the minimal role Cook
assigns to Dunbar. According to Mercer Cook, Abbie Mitchell, his mother-
to-be, "auditioned for Paul Laurence Dunbar and Harry T. Burleigh for a
role in *Clorindy* . . . before she ever met my father." If this is true, Dunbar
must have stayed in touch with *Clorindy* well beyond the all-night session
they both describe.[17] Will Marion Cook continues:

Paul Laurence Dunbar and *Clorindy*

[We were] fortified by two dozen bottles of beer, a quart of whiskey . . .
a porterhouse steak cut up . . . with onions and red peppers, which we
ate raw. Without a piano or anything but the kitchen table, we
finished all the songs, all the libretto and all but a few bars of the ensembles by four o'clock the next morning.

According to both narratives, Cook and Dunbar wrote the book and
songs for *Clorindy* in one inspired and beery night. As for the rest of their
conflicting Rashomons—a paradigm of every theatrical "if it weren't for me"
collaboration story I have ever known—somewhere between them lies the
truth. Nevertheless, the product of their efforts, reworked and cakewalked-up
by the theater-smart Ernest Hogan, would produce a triumph. Cook's description of the opening night, July 5, 1898, is exultant:

My chorus sang like Russians, dancing meanwhile like Negroes,
and cakewalking like angels, black angels! When the last note was
sounded, the audience stood and cheered for ten minutes. . . . Negroes
were at last on Broadway, and there to stay. . . .Gone was the uff-dah of
the minstrel! Gone the Massa Linkum stuff! We were artists and we
were going a long, long way.[18]

Cook may have compressed time in his *Clorindy* memoir and forgotten
about his brother John's role at the piano, but incidents that stuck in his mind
have the ring of truth. By now it is clear that Cook danced to his own drummer. Proud, defiant, and worldly, he felt entitled. Ultimately, it was Cook's
chutzpah that turned the corner for *Clorindy*.

Cook learned that Ed Rice, producer of *Rice's Summer Nights* for the
Casino Roof Garden, at Thirty-ninth and Broadway, was holding weekly auditions for new acts. Cook showed up uninvited with his already-rehearsed
chorus and his own orchestrations to offer excerpts from *Clorindy*. His professionalism must have impressed John Braham, the English conductor of
the Casino orchestra—he had conducted the American premiere of Gilbert
and Sullivan's *H.M.S. Pinafore*—since Braham turned the baton over to
Cook for the audition.[19] In his memoir, Cook remembers that Braham stood
up to an irate Ed Rice when he walked in late to the auditions and began
shouting, "No nigger can conduct my orchestra on Broadway!"[20] Nonethe-
less, Cook and Dunbar's show crossed the color line on merit, and the
Clorindy company, with Cook at the helm, was officially invited to appear.

Clorindy was scheduled to start late, after eleven o'clock in the evening,
in the hope of attracting regular theatergoers up to the Casino Roof Garden,
"where the patrons could dine and watch lighter entertainments" after their
show downstairs let out. Cook reports that the plan worked: "When we

finished the opening chorus, the house was packed to suffocation. The big audience heard those heavenly Negro voices and took to the elevators."

Clorindy: The Origin of the Cakewalk, despite its being only about an hour in length and its under-the-stars venue, was the first all-Negro musical-comedy piece with an original score—written, composed, directed, conducted, choreographed, and orchestrated—by African Americans on Broadway. James Weldon Johnson, a firsthand chronicler of black art and artists from the 1890s through World War II, describes Cook as "the first competent composer to take what was then known as rag-time and work it out in a musicianly way. His choruses and finales in *Clorindy*, complete novelties as they were, sung by a lusty chorus, were simply breath-taking. Broadway had something entirely new."[21]

Neither the stuffed shirts at the American Negro Academy nor the believers in Dvořák's prophecy at the National Conservatory could have envisioned the direction that African American music was taking. Dunbar and Cook would soon be joined by other gifted Negro musicians and playwrights. Among the more prominent were Bob Cole; the Johnson brothers, James Rosamund and James Weldon; and James Reese Europe. "Nothing would stop us," said Cook, "and nothing did for a decade."

7

James Reese Europe

In 1912 David Mannes established his reputation as a music educator by or-
ganizing the Music Settlement [School] for Colored People. Mannes's path
crossed with that of James Reese Europe and his Clef Club Orchestra, and
history was made when Mannes invited them to appear at Carnegie Hall in
a benefit concert for the school.

My own path crossed with that of David Mannes in 1949. I was sitting
in the first trumpet chair in the Mannes School of Music Orchestra at one
of our regular Saturday morning rehearsals, held in the charming if small
concert hall built behind the adjoining pair of elegant East Side town
houses that made up the school. Maestro Carl Bamberger[1] stopped the rehearsal and introduced the founder of our school to us. Mannes was then an
elderly man in his nineties, at least six feet tall, bone thin, and distinguished
looking, with a good head of pure white hair. He stood very straight and had
a wonderful smile. He talked to us briefly (about what I cannot remember),
stroked something out on a fiddle, and left us to our work. It was unimagin-
able that anyone at the Mannes School that I knew then—most of the faculty were Viennese transplants who communicated in German with one
another—had any connection with African American music, no less its
namesake. Nowhere in today's chronology of the Mannes College [neé
School] of Music is its predecessor, the Music Settlement School for Colored People, acknowledged.

In his autobiography, *Music Is My Faith*, Mannes tells the story of how he met his teacher, John Thomas Douglas, "the man who helped shape my life":

> One morning when I was practicing in the basement of our house [215 West Twenty-fifth Street, in the Tenderloin district, up the block from St. Philip's A.M.E. Church], the doorbell jangled in our areaway. Mother opened the door to a rather fine-looking Negro, well-dressed, short and stout, wearing a moustache and a goatee a la Napoleon III.[2]

In response to his mother's broken (Yiddish-inflected?) English, Douglas "proceeded to speak in good and fluent German" and introduced himself as a violin teacher, saying that it was apparent that her son, little David, badly needed one.

As a young violinist, John Douglas played for two upscale black-owned musical entertainment companies: the Hyer Sisters, who toured "refined operatic and dramatic plays on black history,"[3] and the "All-Negro" Georgia Minstrels, one of the most famous companies of its kind, which featured such stars as Sam Lucas and James Bland, the composer of "Oh, Dem Golden Slippers." During this period Douglas copyrighted his own opera, *Virginia's Ball* (1868), possibly the first opera written in the United States by an African American. Around 1877 Douglas was apparently sponsored by wealthy Philadelphians—Mannes believed they were employers of Douglas's mother —to study in Dresden and Paris. It was shortly after Douglas's return to the United States that David Mannes, then a boy of thirteen, became his pupil. Mannes's memory of Douglas remained vivid even sixty years later:

> He composed much music, of which piles of manuscript in his home were ample evidence. He occasionally played at entertainments given by people of his race, but outside of his friends few knew of his existence. He tried to enter a symphony orchestra in this country, but those doors were closed to a colored man. Being of a modest and retiring nature he was not able to insist on being heard. Douglas was like a fish out of water, ahead of his time by thirty or forty years.[4] He grew despondent and later on began to drink. . . . I recall so vividly my playing Mazas, Pleyel and Viotti duets with him, for two violins, violin and viola, and cello and violin. In this way I learnt to read at sight and to play with better rhythmic values. I believe I was his only pupil, but there never was a question of payment. . . . In order to augment his meager income he learnt to play the guitar and played it remarkably. I remember his performance of his own arrangement of the "Tannhauser March." . . . I was always aware of his artistic and intellectual

superiority, and envied him his musical erudition; an envy which awakened the desire in me for further knowledge. Now do you realize how much John Douglas meant to me?

So began David Mannes's "cherished plan of founding the Music Settlement [School] for Colored People in memory of my old friend and teacher."

The Third Street Settlement School, the first of several New York City music school settlements "planted in poorer neighborhoods, especially among the foreign population," opened in 1894.[5] In 1910 Mannes, by then the dashing concertmaster and assistant conductor of the New York Symphony, became the Third Street Settlement's director and immediately set out to establish a new Settlement School in Harlem, which he opened in 1912. Mannes was its driving force, and he put himself in charge of engaging African Americans to the faculty.[6] This led to his friendship with James Reese Europe. It was Europe who suggested that the Clef Club orchestra play at a benefit for the new Music Settlement School for Colored People in its first year of operation.

Through his brother-in-law, Walter Damrosch, musical director of the New York Symphony and a darling of New York society, Mannes had access to patrons, the press, and Carnegie Hall, where he often conducted the New York Symphony's concerts for children. Jim Europe saw this as an opportunity to present Negro music, in all its depth and range, in the mecca of concert artists, and to support the new school, which was already providing employment for some of his musicians. Mannes and his board used their connections to publicize the concert, embracing a few concepts from Dvořák and Du Bois: "New York's first formal concert exclusively of Negro music. Of all the races the Negro alone has developed an actual school of American music . . . national, original, and real. . . . And this concert will be from beginning to end a concert of Negro music by Negro musicians."[7]

The first Clef Club concert was a great success.[8] It led to more Carnegie Hall concerts on behalf of the school by Europe and his "Negro Symphony Orchestra."[9] Their third and last appearance was praised by the *New York Times*: "an interesting concert. . . . These composers are beginning to form an art of their own."[10] But a week or so later, *Musical America* began urging that Europe's orchestra "give its attention during the coming year to a movement or two of a Haydn Symphony."[11]

Critics writing for monthly or weekly magazines such as *Musical America* get to read a handful of instant newspaper reviews and have time to gossip with other reviewers before writing their own. *Musical America* was offering not just another review, but a consensus. Perhaps Jim Europe was forewarned about this slight. Something ticked him off. Three days after the

Carnegie Hall concert there appeared a bold and painfully frank interview with Europe in the *New York Post* titled "The Negro's Place in Music." Much of it reads to me as a tongue-in-cheek send-up, reeking with sarcasm.

Europe called upon racial stereotypes to explain his lack of oboes and horns. "Our people are not naturally painstaking" was his reason for why he would have to import a black oboist from Africa, where "Sudanese boys begin receiving rigorous training in the British Regimental Bands at the age of twelve." He also noted that the mouth of the Negro is so shaped that it is "exceedingly difficult to make him more than a passable player of the French horn." Only in South Africa, where "prolonged training has corrected this handicap," would he be able to find black French hornists—unsaid was the fact that without oboes and horns "a movement or two of a Haydn Symphony" was out of the question. Later in the article Europe offers his own manifesto:

> We have developed a kind of symphony music that, no matter what else you think, is different and distinctive, and that lends itself to the playing of the peculiar compositions of our race. . . . My success had come . . . from a realization of the advantages of sticking to the music of my own people.

Europe's strongest opinions were saved for the African English composer Samuel Coleridge-Taylor, who could be said to follow a European tradition that traces back to Haydn:

> Coleridge-Taylor lived too much among white men: he absorbed the spirit and feeling and technique of white men to such an extent that his race sympathy was partially destroyed. His work is not real Negro work. It partakes of the finish and feeling of the white man. To write real Negro music, a Negro must live with the Negros. He must think and feel as they do.[12]

By the time of the fourth annual Carnegie Hall concert on April 12, 1915—which Europe and his renamed Tempo Club begged out of at the last minute—the dichotomy between the white-controlled board of the school and its director, J. Rosamond Johnson, was growing. Ignoring the call for a bit of Haydn, Johnson presented mostly African American music, albeit strictly in classical Negro forms, such as spirituals. The concert also included the tenor Roland Hayes in one of his earliest New York appearances. The white members of the board were soon gone, and the school, suffering from a financial crunch, closed six months later.

Mannes's only public response was, "Our school came into life at least twenty years too soon." He did not give up supporting African American music and musicians. In the final chapter of his book, titled "Credo," Mannes declares his sympathetic "devotion to the college for colored people, Fisk University of Nashville, of which I have been elected a trustee." And so ended the debt David Mannes owed John Thomas Douglas.

Savants at the Music Settlement School, the National Conservatory, the American Negro Academy, and *Musical America* tried, in different ways, to squeeze the Negro music genie into a schnapps bottle. But African American music had a destiny of its own. Just before his death in 1919, Europe wrote:

> I have come back from France more firmly convinced than ever that Negros should write Negro music. We have our own racial feeling and if we try to copy whites we will make bad copies. . . . We won France by playing music which was ours [i.e., the new rage called jazz] and not a pale imitation of others, and if we are to develop in America we must develop along our own lines.[13]

Europe was touching on an issue—using European models or developing along "our own lines"—that affected white as well as Negro composers. American whites had been living and growing up with and intrigued by Negro music for the better part of two centuries, and many of them were composing music that, rather than being a "pale imitation," was indistinguishable from that of African American composers. What Jim Europe was courageously and insightfully arguing for, the preservation of "racial feeling," lies less in the printed notes, as almost all of the Clef Club repertoire demonstrates, than in the *way* the music is performed—incisive rhythm, a wider tonal palette, nonpitch sounds, African and in turn Caribbean survivals in language and dialect, priority given to the dance, blurring of the lines between audience and performer, and between performer and composer—a holistic "performance practice" aesthetic, inseparable from the mere notation of the music, that has eluded scholars of African American music throughout the twentieth century.

I wonder how different the direction of American music would have been if Europe hadn't died so young. He had the ear of the public and the respect of his fellow musicians, and his mission was clearly defined. His sudden loss, which made the front page of most major newspapers, was no less traumatic to his time than Martin Luther King Jr.'s was to my generation. Not until Ellington emerged from the Cotton Club in the early 1930s and "took to the road"[14] both here and abroad would there be an African American musical leader to take his place.

The double helix of African American music was drawing tight, producing the generation of Gershwin, Ellington, and Copland, the American school that Dvořák anticipated. Born within a year of one another, these composers' formative years were marked by a proliferation of ragtime—all three were brilliant ragtime pianists—and early jazz bands. Theirs was also a moment of equilibrium in the history of American music, when our musical language was commonly held by white and black alike, when jazz and classical didn't seem so far apart.

The critic Gilbert Seldes was struck by this in 1924 when he wrote his *Seven Lively Arts*, which equated vernacular American artists with European masters: George Herriman's Krazy Kat with Picasso (it is a little-known fact that the satirical cartoonist was a mulatto Creole from New Orleans), Whiteman's jazz with the music of Stravinsky, and Jim Europe's conducting with that of Karl Muck, former music director of the Boston Symphony.[15]

"Jazz burst upon a startled world at the touch of a hundred or more orchestra leaders in 1915," said Paul Whiteman.[16] By 1915 Ellington had already composed his first piece, "Soda Fountain Rag." By 1915, Copland had tried his hand at composing, a song, "Lola," and a "Waltz [which] makes sense," and came to "the daring decision to spend my life as a musician";[17] and by 1915, George Gershwin had composed his "Ragging the Traumerai." Already prophesied in its title was the highbrow-lowbrow duality that would haunt him throughout his life.

8

George Gershwin and African American Music

Gershwin's supreme artistic achievement, *Porgy and Bess*, "an American Folk Opera," is perhaps the best-known American music-theater piece of the twentieth century. It is a rare night that *Porgy and Bess* is not onstage somewhere in the world, be it a full-blown production at La Scala or a bus-and-truck affair in the Czech Republic. Its songs enjoy a life of their own, inspiring hundreds of arrangements. The metamorphic Miles Davis–Gil Evans gloss on *Porgy and Bess*, recorded in 1958, is regularly performed live at concerts of jazz classics.

Speaking of jazz classics, Gershwin's "I Got Rhythm" is second only to the twelve-bar blues as the jazz musician's jamming and composing harmonic scheme of choice. Charlie Parker's "Anthropology," Sonny Rollins's "Oleo," and Ellington's "Cottontail" are arguably the most familiar of well over 150 jazz compositions built upon "Rhythm" changes.

As I see it, and hear it, Gershwin's symbiotic connection with African American music goes beyond that of most white American musicians born at the turn of the century. I have imagined Hollywood scenarios that, it turns out, have a grain of truth: little George, the street ragamuffin on roller skates, sprawled outside the Manhattan Casino at 155th and 8th, listening to one of Jim Europe's bands; Gershwin, the Tin Pan Alley dandy spending endless hours at black and tan clubs, that "ear" of his sopping it up.

We must assume, if only from his legendary "party piano" prowess, that Gershwin was blessed with total musical recall and the ability to play at once what he imagined or retained in his inner ear. I know dozens of musicians with these gifts, but only a handful who possess the genius to create original art. Gershwin was already twelve when his parents bought an upright piano for his brother, Ira. But he had been doodling around on a friend's instrument, feeling his way through a slowly pedaled piano roll or two, and to the family's surprise, when the piano arrived, "George twirled the stool down to size . . . and began to play an accomplished version of a then popular song."[1] Two years later Gershwin dropped out of high school to become a Tin Pan Alley pianist and song plugger at Remick's, a music publisher that "issued more ragtime compositions than its next ten competitors combined."[2]

Gershwin had more-than-casual encounters with black music and musicians. He did study, for a typically short time, with the master ragtime pianist Luckey (Charles Luckeyeth) Roberts (1887–1968). In a 1962 interview with jazz historian Terkild Vinding, Roberts recalled:

> Bert Williams and Will Vodery [an African American musician who was Ziegfeld's principal orchestrator] were the ones that got me to teach Gershwin. . . . He didn't have a tune in his head [!]. He was selling orchestrations at Remick's and stood behind the counter. Will Vodery said: "Son, help him along. He's very ambitious." He couldn't play jazz, but he had two good hands for the classics. . . . George knew everything I played, cause I was teaching him.[3]

Eubie Blake spoke of Gershwin's ragtime piano skills: "James P. Johnson and Luckey Roberts told me of this ofay piano player at Remick's . . . good enough to learn some of those terribly difficult tricks that only a few of us could master."[4] Gershwin also picked up ideas from listening to the white ragtime virtuosos Les Copeland and Mike Bernard, and gave credit to their influence while describing their techniques in the introduction to *George Gershwin's Song Book*, a limited edition of "party piano" arrangements of his hit tunes.[5]

By the time Gershwin left Remick's in 1917, he was moving away from ragtime piano and becoming enamored of the Broadway songs of Jerome Kern and Irving Berlin. He was studying classical composition and piano, accompanying pop singers, recording player-piano rolls, and going to concerts. His musical education would never stop. Nor would ragtime and the blues ever leave his side.

Soon after his Remick period Gershwin tried his hand at a piece for string quartet, a bluesy affair he later recycled as an aria in an ambitious failure, *Blue Monday Blues*—an operatic episode "ala Afro-American [*sic*]" that played for one night as part of the *George White Scandals of 1922*.[6]

Buddy DeSylva's "letter opera" libretto for *Blue Monday Blues* weaves a tragic tale of a lovers' quarrel set in a Harlem bar. Gershwin and DeSylva seem to be trying to portray Negro pathos and passion, and especially Negro sexuality—fantasized and whispered about, if rarely seen onstage—but stock characters and low-life dialogue prevail. The word "nigger," expunged in later versions, is casually tossed about in some misguided effort to add authenticity.

The story: Joe and Violet (Vi) are lovers. Joe has just made a big score in a craps game. He is awaiting a return telegram from his mother "down South," whom he hasn't seen for a long while, telling him that he can visit her. Joe has kept his plans from Vi, who is very possessive and jealous. He sings, "I'm going to see my Mother, Mother mine," and goes offstage before Vi' enters. She is immediately "hit upon" by Little Walker, a manipulative hustler (he bears an amazing resemblance to the future Sportin' Life). Vi's response is instantaneous: "My Joe gave me this revolver just to use on guys like you." The telegram arrives. Little Walker, who knows about Joe's plan, wastes no time in telling Vi that "Joe's going South in the morning, that telegram is from another woman down there." "You lie!" she hisses. Seething with jealousy, Vi confronts her lover, demanding to see the telegram. Joe refuses. "I warned you never to cheat on me!" she shouts, and shoots him. The music throbs as Joe lies dying, and Vi rips open the telegram. In a monotone she reads aloud: "Your mother has been dead for two years, wire if you'll be coming." Vi wails, "Oh forgive me Joe, forgive me," and collapses. Joe says, "It's all right Honey," and with his dying breath he sings a reprise of "I'm going to see my Mother, Mother mine."

If this stereotypical libretto wasn't enough to sink *Blue Monday Blues*, the sometimes charming, often crude musical score and its pit orchestration—one of the few examples of Broadway scoring from the 1920s that has survived—did little to keep it afloat. Theater orchestrations were thought of as worthless ephemera, more often than not tossed out with the scenery once a show closed. Will Vodery's original orchestration for *Blue Monday Blues*, found among his papers in the Library of Congress,[7] turns out to be surprisingly bland and literal. Even with the Paul Whiteman band in the pit for the *Scandals of 1922*, Vodery was still scoring for an English music-hall orchestra from the time of Gilbert and Sullivan: woodwinds and brasses in pairs and a string ensemble with extra violas to provide rhythmic back beats. The one addition was a trap drummer. Vodery ignored the jazz band sounds—banjo, saxophones, rhythm tuba, and colorful jazz mutes for the brass—we associate with Whiteman and his principal arranger, Ferde Grofé. Of course it is possible that Whiteman's musicians, among the hottest players of the day, added some of their own jazz color and phrasing.

Blue Monday Blues does have some good songs and a flashy ballet built on a tune that would resurface two years later as "Fascinatin' Rhythm." Otherwise it is rife with naive opera clichés and corn; Gershwin inserts the "good evening, friends"—for my younger readers, the "how old are you"—tag on the closing chord, ending sourly on a flatted seventh. But the major cause of the show's failure was in its casting.

The Harlem characters in *Blue Monday Blues* were played by white singer-actors in blackface, a crucial mistake that Gershwin would not forget. Broadway audiences, who only a season earlier welcomed with open arms the all-black musical hit *Shuffle Along*, knew the real thing. The use of blackface, in this instance, cannot be explained away as a vestige of the old minstrelsy style that clung to Al Jolson and Eddie Cantor well into the 1930s. *Blue Monday Blues* was no doubt hobbled by its anomalous book and orchestrations, but it was fatally brought down by its adherence to the color line. One wonders if an African American cast was ever considered.[8] In perhaps the only reference I ever heard him make about race, Duke Ellington said that he believed his 1947 show *Beggar's Holiday*, with a book by John Latouche, did not succeed because people "were not ready for an integrated love affair on Broadway."[9]

Blue Monday Blues was an important step in Gershwin's career even if it only brought him together with Whiteman, for this would lead to their landmark collaboration on the *Rhapsody in Blue* two years later.[10] But *Blue Monday Blues* also indicates that Gershwin was drawn to black themes early on. By the time he turned to *Porgy and Bess* a decade later, he had come to a crucial aesthetic realization about his Negro-influenced music. Gershwin recognized that what he heard in his inner ear, the fulfillment of his muse, could only be realized through the voices of African American singers.[11]

In spite of all of the obvious shortcomings attached to characterizing a race, we still recognize that the "racial feeling" to which James Reese Europe referred thrives and continues to evolve in a large part of the African American community. Leontyne Price, the most distinguished Bess of all time, told a young African American singer in a master class that her rendition of "My Man's Gone Now" lacked the "cultural context that is captured in the music." Price then asked, "You don't mind my getting sisterly about it? . . . I can tell from the way you answered 'Yes, ma'am' that you know what I'm talking about." Then she described and demonstrated how the song's sighing refrains must be "like moaning in church."[12]

"Moaning in church" is exactly what Gershwin experienced in Hendersonville, North Carolina, when he visited with DuBose and Dorothy Heyward—authors respectively of the book and the play *Porgy* on which the opera is based—for another round of southern acculturation. Gershwin, the big-city man-about-town, had already spent the better part of the summer of

1934 steeping himself in the music and life of the venerable Gullah community on the Sea Islands off the coast of Charleston, South Carolina—the exact setting of the Heywards' *Porgy*. Heyward described the Hendersonville encounter:

> We were about to enter a dilapidated cabin that had been taken as a meeting house by a group of Negro Holy Rollers, [when] George caught my arm and held me. The sound that had arrested him was the one to which . . . through long familiarity, I attached no special importance. But now, listening with him, and noticing the excitement, I began to catch its extraordinary quality. It consisted of perhaps a dozen voices raised in loud rhythmic prayer. The odd thing about it was that while each had started a different tune, upon a different theme, [the whole] produced an effect almost terrifying in its primitive intensity. Inspired . . . George wrote six simultaneous prayers [for *Porgy and Bess*] producing a terrifying invocation to God in the face of the hurricane.[13]

The "simultaneous prayers" remind me of a *davenning minyan*, a Jewish prayer group, something Gershwin was familiar with. Each *davenner* (worshipper) picks up the mode or key center established by the cantor or prayer leader and takes off on his own, embellishing the text, emphasizing an important phrase or word with raised voice. On musical cues from the leader, the whole congregation comes together for special tunes that mark a particular passage or the end of a section. This is precisely how Gershwin scored the storm scene.

Gershwin was not the only Jewish composer of the period who felt compelled to write pieces about African Americans. Besides *Porgy and Bess* (1935), there is *The Emperor Jones* (1921), by Louis Gruenberg, and *Show Boat* (1927), by Jerome Kern and Edna Ferber. The phenomenon transcends simple parallels of simultaneous song prayer, or similarities between the poignant modes of Jewish cantorial improvisations and black music, both of which may share a common North African–Middle Eastern source. I see these African American–inspired pieces by Jewish composers and librettists as private metaphors of their own suppressed mix of angst and cultural pride, a change of ethnicity being a way of coming out from hiding.

I remember my own 1930s consciousness "not to be too Jewish." How often we were encouraged to sublimate, or even hide—yet never to give up— our Jewishness! Changing one's name, from Beilin to Berlin, Gershovitz to Gershwin, Kaplan to Copland, was quite common. Bernstein, in a biting imitation of his mentor, Serge Koussevitzky, told me how "Koosy" had cautioned him: "Vid da name Boynschtine, a chob you'll neveh hev." The Holocaust and the establishment of Israel forever abolished such sophistry. A younger Jewish generation would now write about themselves.

So we find the conductors Koussevitsky and Fritz Reiner programming the first performances of twenty-six-year-old Leonard Bernstein's *Jeremiah Symphony* in the winter of 1944; by this time the dreadful reality of the Nazi death camps had become common knowledge. In the third movement of his symphony, Bernstein sets a biblical text from Lamentations, to be sung in the original Hebrew, "the cry of Jeremiah as he mourns his beloved Jerusalem, ruined, pillaged and dishonored after his desperate effort to save it."[14]

Kurt Weill was perhaps the first composer to put his art at the service of his Jewish origins in the gigantic pageant *The Eternal Road*, produced in New York in 1936.[15] Arnold Schoenberg, Gershwin's friend and erstwhile teacher, signaled his return to the Jewish fold in 1939 most appropriately, with his orchestral declamation *Kol nidre*, which uses as its text a prayer that some scholars believe was introduced into the liturgy as a disavowal for Jews forced to convert during the Spanish Inquisition, thus opening the door for their return.

Had Gershwin lived on into the "it's OK to be Jewish" generation, his original plan—to write a work for the Metropolitan Opera based upon the Jewish mystical folk tale "The Dybbuk"—might have come to pass. Instead, his folk opera *Porgy and Bess* was performed for the first time at the Met in 1993.[16]

In the fall of 1967, while preparing for a stage production of *Porgy and Bess* in Corpus Christi, Texas, I visited with Alex Steinert, the assistant conductor and rehearsal pianist for the original 1935 production. Steinert, a Harvard man who had won a Prix de Rome in composition, seemed eager to share his memories of *Porgy*, clearly the pinnacle of his career. He showed me the score he conducted from: not a full orchestral score but a heavily marked piano-vocal score full of paper clips indicating cuts, the excisions made to tighten for Broadway parameters the longer, slower, operatic pace of Gershwin's original score.[17] Steinert reminisced about the cast—John Bubbles's way with the ladies, his own infatuation with a young dancer. He played for me recordings cut on huge eighteen-inch discs, the stylus needle moving from inside to out; these were air checks of the original *Porgy* cast singing excerpts from the show at a Gershwin memorial concert Steinert conducted. He showed me movies of the storm scene he took from the pit of the Alvin Theater. It was my introduction to a rich trove of *Porgy and Bess* legendry and memorabilia.

In 1992, I spoke with other musicians who played for the original *Porgy and Bess* production, tracking them down from the signatures they left on the orchestral parts they used in 1935–36. I was trying to put an end to the "orchestration question" that has followed George Gershwin beyond the grave.[18]

Because, in his original fall from grace, Gershwin did not orchestrate the jazz-band accompaniment for his *Rhapsody in Blue* in 1924,[19] the orchestrations of all his subsequent scores—*An American in Paris*, the Concerto in F, "*I Got Rhythm" Variations*, and *Porgy and Bess*—were looked upon with suspicion. Gershwin saw the "orchestration question" as a challenge to his legitimacy as a serious composer, and he had to defend himself from whispered as well as published imputations that the scoring of his music was done by others.

Virgil Thomson, who seemed unable to resist *outré* remarks whenever "the Gershwins" came up in our conversations, volunteered that Alexander Smallens—who conducted the premiere of Thomson's *Four Saints in Three Acts* just six months before he did the same for *Porgy*—had done "wholesale reorchestration" on *Porgy and Bess*, an imputation that conflicts with his outrageous crack "I do not like . . . gefilte fish orchestration,"[20] made in his review of the work in 1935. Milton Rettenberg, a childhood friend of the Gershwins and the first pianist to play the *Rhapsody in Blue* after George, told me more than once that at the opening-night party for *Porgy and Bess*, "Paul [Whiteman] said that George should have let Adolf [Deutsch] do the scoring."[21]

The original *Porgy and Bess* orchestral parts and score (a bound photo reproduction of Gershwin's manuscript) are housed with the papers of the Theater Guild, the producers of the show, at the Beinecke Rare Book and Manuscript Library at Yale University. The four-hundred-plus-page score is entirely in Gershwin's hand. The full score contains no changes in orchestration and, to my surprise, none of the major cuts. Like Steinert, Broadway conductors rarely bring cumbersome full scores into the pit. The full score at the Beinecke was a reference copy for checking suspicious notes in the parts or, as I discovered, for penciling out all but the necessary parts in the brass and strings to reduce the size, and the cost, of the orchestra when audiences started to dwindle and the show was about to go on the road.[22]

Sometimes reorchestrating can be done in the parts. But outside of a few "hits" penciled into the drummer's music to underscore stage action—and the cuts—I found no emendations in the parts. I did find, however, fascinating written comments left there by the players.

In Gershwin's time, orchestral parts were still copied out by hand. (Nowadays computer programs produce print-quality parts.) Only when a work was established would a publisher invest in the engraving and printing of multiple sets of scores and parts for sale and/or rental.[23] So all that existed in 1935 was the single hand-copied set of parts for *Porgy and Bess* now at Yale, the same set that traveled with the show from Boston to New York and that was used again on the road for East and West Coast tours. A core group of in-strumentalists—usually the first violinist, a lead trumpet, and the drummer—traveled with the show. The rest were hired locally. Many if not most of these players signed and dated their parts as a matter of pride, like leaving one's mark on a mountain summit or deep in a cave. Some added cryptic messages along the borders or on the occasional blank page, such as a warning to the next user about a difficult passage. One player kept a record of the show's run-ning time from night to night. In Boston, before the cuts were implemented, the show came down well past eleven. Another recorded the night that Gershwin died. One comment is in Chinese characters.

With the help of an old union directory, I was able to contact several of the "first-run" pit musicians who had signed their names. Without exception, they were eager to tell stories about their time with *Porgy*.

Henry Denecke, retired and living in Wisconsin, was the show's original drummer. Denecke first studied with and later joined his father, who played for Joseph Rumshinsky in the Yiddish theaters on Second Avenue. Denecke also played percussion for the world premiere of Edgard Varèse's *Ionisation* and Béla Bartók's *Music for Two Pianos and Percussion*, with the composer and his wife, Ditta Pasztory, at the pianos and Sol Goodman on timpani. "But *Porgy and Bess*," he said, was "the high spot in our lives."[24]

One *Porgy and Bess* recollection that stayed with Denecke was being in the check-in line at a hotel in Chicago when the clerk tried to turn away Ann Brown, the star of the show, whom Denecke knew from his Juilliard days. Be-ing a drummer, Denecke was also, by tradition, the librarian for the *Porgy and Bess* pit orchestra. He told me that at the end of the run, "George's per-sonal valet/driver, Paul Mueller, came to pick up the parts." Gershwin had no intention of allowing his work to be tossed away with the scenery. I located Mueller, who told me that while he was in on many of Gershwin's most per-sonal secrets, he had never heard about a ghost orchestrator.[25]

Many celebrated composers with a deadline to meet have asked for help in orchestrating. Bernstein publicly acknowledges several orchestrators in the printed score of *Mass*. But Gershwin had something to prove. He made a habit of scoring the overtures for many of his Broadway shows, keeping his hand in and demonstrating for himself, if not for others, that he was a com-plete composer.[26] Strictly Broadway composers such as Kern and Irving Berlin suffered no such doubts. They were not expected to orchestrate any more than to sew costumes.[27]

When the time came for scoring his Broadway-bound folk opera *Porgy and Bess* the whole orchestration affair so haunted him that he insisted on scoring it himself, a monumental task that no Broadway composer since the days of Victor Herbert would have considered undertaking. Even master or-

chestrators such as Bernstein, Morton Gould, Kurt Weill, and Ellington depended upon others to orchestrate their Broadway shows.[28] The composer's
place was in the house, watching and listening to the total work and making
himself available for refinements, eleventh-hour inspirations, and reworkings
of the music—not buried in a smoke-filled room with a gang of copyists
scratching out parts.

I find more than enough evidence in Gershwin's scores that his orchestrations were his own. On the one hand, there are some fine touches
in his earliest orchestrations that might not have survived the formal conservatory education he coveted: the solo role he assigns to a bluesy, derby-
muted jazz trumpet in the slow movement of the Concerto in F, and the
four taxi horns in his *American in Paris*, their random pitches (G, A-flat, A,
and B) brilliantly worked into the fabric of the work. But there are too many
examples of naive, meaningless, and even counterproductive scoring that
indicate an apprentice or a journeyman at work.[29] If Gershwin was getting
help, it wasn't very special.

Then there were the tryout sessions, private orchestral readings of his
orchestrations. There is a recording of Gershwin conducting a tryout of several of his *Porgy and Bess* orchestrations on July 19, 1935, months before rehearsals began with the real *Porgy* pit orchestra.[30] Any listener familiar with
the music is instantly aware of changes that Gershwin subsequently made.
This was not the first time he checked out his orchestrations. A decade earlier Gershwin had arranged for a private orchestral reading of his Concerto
in F, his first full-fledged symphonic orchestration, before sending it to Walter Damrosch and the New York Symphony.[31] These tryout sessions do not
jibe with apocryphal stories about a ghost scorer. They show Gershwin playing it safe, making sure his orchestrations "sounded" before putting them before the public.

Several of the principals from the forthcoming production sang in the
Porgy and Bess tryout session: Ann Brown, a recent graduate of Juilliard, sang
Bess; Todd Duncan, a member of the music faculty at Howard University,
sang Porgy; and Abbie Mitchell, who starred in *Clorindy* and *In Dahomey*,
sang Clara. This is the only recording we have of Abbie Mitchell singing
"Summertime." Born in Baltimore in the early 1880s of Jewish and African
American parentage, Mitchell must have been in her early fifties at the time.
She is in marvelous voice, sounds appropriately youthful, and convincingly
blends classical diction and dialect. Morton Gould was the orchestral pianist,
and we can hear him playing a bit of the opening "Jasbo Brown honkytonk
piano solo." The recorded tryout session offers a rare glimpse of Gershwin rehearsing from the podium. He comes off a thorough professional, seasoned,
efficient, and clear.

How could this take-charge guy with the Hell's Kitchen accent allow the "original cast" recording to be compromised three months later by the RCA Victor company? How did Gershwin rationalize the flouting of his dictum that only black voices sing *Porgy and Bess* when Brown, Duncan, and Mitchell were replaced by two white singers, Helen Jepson as Bess and Clara, and Lawrence Tibbett as Porgy?[32]

In the spring of 1968 I did a full dress production of *Porgy and Bess* with my orchestra in Corpus Christi, Texas. When I asked Reverend Harold Branch, the minister of St. John the Baptist Church in Corpus Christi and the only African American member of the city council, how he felt about our orchestra mounting *Porgy and Bess*, his first response was that his "manhood was not threatened." Then he countered, "It would be an opportunity for African American talent to show itself in our town."

Porgy and Bess presents dramatic and vocal challenges that only superb artists can meet, and it has led to operatic careers for many African Americans. Nevertheless, in the 1960s many black critics and artists dismissed *Porgy and Bess* as a white man's exploitation and plagiarism of black art. Others, like Reverend Branch, were conflicted. Ellington's angry assessment of the work—"Gershwin's lampblack Negroisms"—still stings.

I was not surprised by the controversy and emotion *Porgy and Bess* generated, but I was unprepared for its mysteries. The Corpus Christi production took place in spring of 1968. And I came away from that experience believing that *Porgy and Bess* belongs as much to the black singer-actors who bring it to life as it does to the Heywards and the Gershwins.

We were fortunate to engage William Warfield to sing Porgy. Robert Guillaume—now a television actor, then a classically trained lyric tenor whom I had met in Vienna—sang Sportin' Life. Our Bess was Martha Flowers.[33] Clara was sung by a young student from Texas Southern University in Houston, Faye Robinson, who went on to a fine career in opera. TSU also supplied our *Porgy* ensemble and choir, which was under the direction of Ruthabell Rawlins.[34]

I remember well my first rehearsal with the choir—how their singing took the music to a level I had never imagined in my mind's ear. There was far more music in the room than appeared on the page. It was richly layered with expressive details; like an oriental carpet or mosaic, step away and the details blend into a shimmering, lustrous whole.

During the rehearsals for *Porgy* and at the performance I was made aware of an arcane underlife that has attached itself to the work. Irving Barnes, who sang the role of Jake, the Fisherman, asked me if he could stop by TSU on his way to Corpus Christi and meet with the choir. He had been in several major productions of *Porgy and Bess* and had some pointers he would like to give them. I said, "Be my guest." I suspect it was what Barnes told them that inspired the choir to do something I shall never forget.

In the final scene Porgy tells the folks of Catfish Row that he is going to New York to find Bess. He begins to sing the closing song, "Oh Lawd, I'm on My Way," and the company answers, "I'm on My Way to a Heav'nly Lan'," a familiar sentiment for African Americans, a spiritual of faith and trust in God when faced with the impossible. In Corpus Christi the choir made it into a personal *Porgy and Bess* anthem.

On the final "Oh Lawd," the sopranos hold a B above the staff—not the most comfortable note—for five measures, meanwhile the rest of the cast sings "but you'll be there." The sopranos rejoin the others on the four final words, "to take my han'," again ending on high B. At this point the whole cast is supposed to cut off, leaving the orchestra to play out the last bluesy phrase as the curtains close. When the curtain in Corpus Christi's Del Mar Auditorium reopened for bows, the chorus was still holding the final chord with the sopranos on high B! The curtain closed and reopened. They were still holding the chord. I found myself crying. Later that night, as my family and I were leaving the cast party, the choir gathered around us and sang, "Oh Lawd, I'm on My Way."

9

Leonard Bernstein

Never look back upon roads not taken. The roads you did take,
they are the story of your life.
—VIRGIL THOMSON, on his ninetieth birthday

My curiosity about Dvořák and American music came to the surface rather
recently, but its seeds were planted in the 1960s. Had I not met Leonard
Bernstein, who jump-started my symphonic career, and Duke Ellington,
who reawakened my love for jazz, the first part of this book—my idiosyncratic take on African American music and musicians from the first half of
the twentieth century, with Dvořák as splendid guidon—could not have
come about.

When Bernstein was appointed music director of the New York Philharmonic in 1958, he instituted a novel assistant conductors' program, ostensibly to develop American talent. One of the first to be chosen was my upstairs neighbor and musical colleague at the Mannes School of Music, Stefan
Bauer Mengelberg, nephew of the famous Dutch conductor. What seemed
a world away suddenly came within reach, and I too applied.

In February 1961 a letter arrived from the Koussevitsky Foundation inviting me to meet Bernstein at a gathering to be held in his studio apartment
at the Osborne, Stanford White's massive brownstone-and-stained-glass
edifice that stands diagonally across the street from Carnegie Hall. In the in-
tervening years, an eruption of towering glass-sheathed buildings has formed
a canyon around Fifty-seventh and Seventh, and the Osborne's once proud
stance now seems tired and squattish. But I thought I was crossing the Rubi-
con when I entered the lobby on a Friday afternoon, March 10, 1961. I was
playing a pair of Young Audience concerts earlier that day with my brass

quintet, the Chamber Brass Players, thinking I would be less nervous than if I just waited about; besides, I needed the money. After the concerts, we five brass players crammed into a small sedan, with the tuba as a sixth passenger. By the time I struggled out of the car when it dropped me off for my meeting with Bernstein, my Irish tweed suit and hand-loomed wool tie were a rumpled mess. Under my arm, in the hip fashion of the day, I carried my green corduroy trumpet bag.

The Osborne was intimidating: a long canopy, liveried doormen, bird-cage elevators. "Yes, Mr. Bernstein is in Studio 2DD on the second floor," intoned the elevator man. He pivoted the hand lever across the crescent-shaped brass guide, and after a second's pause the ancient hydraulic car floated up in silence. I entered the studio to find five or six other men in their twenties seated about, not knowing whether to talk or study the ceiling. I was glad I had my horn with me. Its familiar tubes and twists under the corduroy kept my hands occupied.

Bernstein arrived, cigarette in hand. He explained that according to our résumés, all of us were qualified to be assistant conductors with the Philharmonic. Therefore he was following the lead of Harvard's Medical School: when faced with more deserving applicants than they had room for, the medical school faculty came up with the novel idea of holding cocktail parties, where they would meet and observe the candidates in a social setting to help them decide whom to accept.

To start things off, Bernstein asked each of us why he wanted to become a conductor. One frustrated fellow immediately questioned the entire proceeding, demanding that Bernstein sit at the piano so that he could demonstrate his conducting prowess. Another told of playing viola in several orchestras and said that he found most conductors to be charlatans (oops). "It was time that a player from the ranks, one with orchestral experience, be noticed," he said.

When my turn came, I told Bernstein the truth: that I had been curious and passionate about music ever since I was a little boy, and that my dad sang and played Arabic folksongs for me on his oud. That got him! I also explained that when I was a Boy Scout I used to fit two bugles together, making a kind of sliding trumpet, so I could get the "in-between notes," and that even though I was now playing the trumpet professionally, teaching theory, writing arrangements, and conducting whenever the opportunity arose, it was only when I was leading an orchestra that all of my musical interests came together and I became totally focused, without nervousness, and fully occupied with the music. When the gathering ended, I was the first to leave. In my heart I felt that I would be chosen.

Among the many part-time gigs I had at the time was teaching harmony, sight-singing, and theory one day a week at the Ninety-second Street YMHA. I worked with teenagers in the afternoon and adults in the evening. In between I would swim for an hour in the Y pool, which is where I was when a call came from my wife warning me that "a very haughty lady, Miss Helen Coates, called. She wants you to phone her at once; it's about the Philharmonic." I was still in my wet bathing suit when Miss Coates, who introduced herself as "Mr. Bernstein's personal secretary," told me that I had been chosen to be one of his assistants. She said that I would receive a confirmation in the mail, "But say nothing to anyone about this until the official announcement appears in the newspapers."

A month passed. Finally, the announcement appeared in the *New York Herald Tribune* on April 12, 1961. The heading read "3 Assistant Conductors Named by Philharmonic for 1961–62," and below were three postage-stamp-sized photos and the simple caption, "John Canarina and Maurice Peress, two New Yorkers, and Seiji Ozawa, of Japan."

Our Philharmonic year began in late September with a four-day tour to Philadelphia, Baltimore, Richmond, and Washington, D.C. Bernstein conducted Beethoven, Strauss, Ravel, and the glorious American soprano Eileen Farrell sang Wagner excerpts. The season ended in late May with an homage to Stravinsky on his eightieth birthday, coupled with the Piston Violin Concerto with soloist Joseph Fuchs, and the Brahms Second Symphony. Then came a week of acoustical testing of the new Philharmonic Hall. Our magnificent orchestra was humbled in the cold space and at the last minute the sound wizard Maestro Leopold Stokowski was called in. He mounted the podium and asked for the first two chords of the *Eroica* — "Trombones and tuba as well, E flat!" Whap, whap went the band. He stood listening and gave his prophetic assessment: "It will never do."

In between, there were thirty-three weeks of subscription concerts, including the notorious Glenn Gould–Bernstein brouhaha over the Brahms First Piano Concerto with public disclaimers by Bernstein — "I do not agree with Mr. Gould's interpretation . . . but I have agreed to conduct out of respect to him as an artist" — which set off a mini-scandal. There was my official debut with the orchestra, Eric Satie's tongue-in-cheek *Parade*, a Dada ballet score punctuated with ragtime, pistol shots, ratcheting roulette wheels, and a clattering typewriter with bell. "Just stand there and let it happen," said Lenny. You bet.

There were eleven guest conductors, sixty-three soloists, four weekly rehearsals, a dozen or so recordings, four televised Young People's Concerts, a special television broadcast of *Carmen*, formal balls, and a hysterical luncheon with a doddering dowager, Minnie Guggenheimer.[1]

I studied 134 major works in rehearsal and performance, score in hand.

Leonard Bernstein

When I left the Philharmonic I had enough repertoire to get me through several seasons in a regional orchestra. I also had what I call my "orchestral finishing school" diploma, earned by hanging around a world-class maestro, his band, and the formidable Miss Helen Coates. Miss Coates, who became "Nonnie Helen" to my children, taught stage deportment, how to bow and recognize the orchestra and soloists, and green room etiquette by commentary and example; she conveyed to us the social and political persona appropriate for a maestro.

Meanwhile, my musical world had been reconfigured. I signed on with Columbia Artists, the most powerful of classical music managements. Almost overnight, Columbia helped me get a two-year contract with the Corpus Christi Symphony, my first music directorship with a professional orchestra. In my first season I worked with Andrés Segovia, Mischa Elman, Benny Goodman, Julius Katchen, and Alexander Brailovsky. The New York Philharmonic retained me as an assistant conductor to cover their summer concerts. I was still on a roll two years later when I became the Joffrey Ballet's first live-music conductor. Said Bernstein, "I know—too fast, too slow."

The Joffrey Ballet made an appearance at the White House Festival of the Arts in the summer of 1965. It was there that I met Duke Ellington and heard *Black, Brown and Beige* for the first time, setting the stage for my gradual return to jazz and my double career.

10

Gershwin's *Rhapsody in Blue*

I sincerely believe in jazz. I think it expresses the spirit of
America and I feel sure it has a future—more of a future than
of past and present. I want to help that future pan out.
—PAUL WHITEMAN, in Paul Whiteman and
Margaret McBride, *Jazz*

One would be hard pressed to think of an American musical event that has
been written about more than Paul Whiteman's launching of George Gershwin's *Rhapsody in Blue*. Whiteman was among the brightest stars in popular
music in the 1920s. His bands crossed the Atlantic on ocean liners and played
for some of the same society parties up and down the East Coast where James
Reese Europe's bands once held sway.[1] He made hit records for Victor, and
his was about to become one of the first radio orchestras. A Denver-born,
corn-fed, cheery bear of a man, mild mannered and well spoken, Whiteman
won over the movie colony during his band's extended run at the Alexander
Hotel in Los Angeles. For five months in 1923 he delighted London audiences and charmed many British aristocrats with his natural manner as well
as his music. The following winter Whiteman's flagship orchestra was back
in New York, appearing nightly at the posh Palais Royal Restaurant, their
home port since 1920. Vincent Sardi Sr. was captain of the staff. Despite Pro-
hibition, high society came in droves to eat and to listen—and especially to
dance—to the music of the hottest dance band of the moment. Whether it
was the London audiences' warm reception of his music, the urgings of cultural intellectuals such as Gilbert Seldes, the news that the Vincent Lopez
band was planning to play at the Metropolitan Opera House, or his own
timely intuition, somewhere in the fall of 1923 Whiteman embraced the idea
of presenting his music in a formal concert setting.

In preparation for my sixtieth anniversary re-creation of the Aeolian Hall concert of 1924—"Same Day, Same Hour, Same Block"—I interviewed several Whiteman sidemen who played in the original concert. Violinist Kurt Dieterle painted a vivid picture of the band's ace trumpeter, Henry Busse (pronounced "bus-ee")—his raccoon coat, derby hat, and stylishly unbuckled galoshes, and his ever-present cigar.[2] I can easily imagine Busse walking the few blocks through the theater district from the Palais Royal on Forty-eighth and Broadway to Aeolian Hall between Forty-second and Forty-third Streets just west of Fifth Avenue; in cultural terms, however, the walk was a thousand-mile trek. For Busse was about to set up his horns on the same stage where Max Schlossberg, New York's leading classical trumpet teacher, played in Walter Damrosch's New York Symphony. This must have evoked a curious mixture of pride and trepidation, but there is no doubt he welcomed the challenge. Busse was famous, the recording star of "Whispering" and "Hot Lips," and rich, earning much more than the symphony boys. One wonders if he felt his behavior to be slightly sacrilegious. This was, after all, a first. No dance band had ever before appeared on that or any other American concert-hall stage—James Reese Europe's 1912 "just before jazz" Clef Club Concert had long been forgotten—and the whole of musical New York buzzed with excitement.

Aeolian Hall, one of New York's most prestigious concert facilities, took up the lower third of a nineteen-story building on the then-upscale business thoroughfare of West Forty-second Street. The building, which has since been radically reconfigured, also served as the Aeolian Piano Company's corporate headquarters and their primary New York showroom. Whiteman titled his concert "An Experiment in Modern Music." It was scheduled for Tuesday afternoon, February 12, 1924, at three o'clock.

Today such a program would be billed as "An Experiment in Jazz." But in 1924, jazz bands, black and white, encouraged by critics like Seldes, believed they had a place at the forefront of the newest trends in music. And why not? All of the master composers of Europe were borrowing from them: Stravinsky, Ravel, Milhaud, and Satie, to name a few. The event was described, in the Victorianisms of the time, as the concert that "made a lady out of jazz" and "made an honest woman out of jazz," and, because it took place on Lincoln's birthday, as the "emancipation proclamation of jazz."[3]

Whiteman's "experiment" was brilliantly planned and staged. Enlisted as patrons and patronesses were American culture mavens Gilbert Seldes and Carl Van Vechten; music critics and writers Deems Taylor, O. O. McIntyre, and Fannie Hurst; prominent musicians Walter Damrosch, Leopold Godowsky, Jascha Heifetz, Fritz Kreisler, Sergei Rachmaninoff, Moritz Rosenthal, and Leopold Stokowski; opera divas Amelita Galli-Curci, Alma Gluck, and Mary Garden; and financier Otto Kahn, the president of the Metropolitan

Opera. Whiteman invited them to the band's luncheon rehearsals at the Palais Royal. Together they raised and contributed money, wrote program notes, spoke glowingly from the stage, and packed the house with glitterati. It was the highlight of the 1923–24 concert season.

The follow-up was equally brilliant. The "experiment," with a few changes, was repeated at Carnegie Hall and Philadelphia's Music Academy. A spring tour was booked by the impresario F. C. Coppicus, who ran the Metropolitan Opera Musical Bureau. Whiteman and Gershwin rode with the band, now twenty-four strong (an extra saxophone was added), in a pair of specially outfitted railroad cars. Aboard were three Chickering grand pianos—two white ones for the band and an ebony concert grand for Gershwin—all carefully husbanded by Emil Neugebauer, the tuner and technician for the celebrated concert pianist Joseph Levine. Before the heyday of radio, touring and recording were how Whiteman brought his band to the attention of the public. And this was a whirlwind tour: twenty concerts in eighteen days in the major concert halls of such cities as Rochester, Pittsburgh, Indianapolis, Cleveland, Cincinnati, and St. Louis. In Ann Arbor, Michigan, Milton Rettenberg (another sideman I got to know and the source for much of the detail herein described), a recent graduate of Columbia Law School and boyhood friend of the Gershwins, took over as the *Rhapsody in Blue* piano soloist for the rest of the tour. Gershwin had to get back to New York to prepare for the new George White *Scandals* of 1924. Soon after Whiteman and his band returned to New York, they recorded (for Victor) the two big new pieces from his "experiment": the *Rhapsody in Blue*, with Gershwin as soloist, and Victor Herbert's *Suite of Serenades*. The Aeolian Hall concert was clearly the high point of Whiteman's career, one he tried in vain to repeat as he sought out "other Gershwins" and staged other "experiments." Inevitably, the slow theme of the *Rhapsody in Blue* became his musical signature, just as his bald, round, mustachioed caricature became his logo.

Gershwin's *Rhapsody* is indisputably the first American orchestral work shaped from blues and ragtime that crossed over to find a welcome place in the standard orchestral repertoire, albeit at first in a symphonized version. Dvořák's prediction was coming true, and dance-band leaders—Europe, Cook, Whiteman, and Ellington—were among those pointing the way.

In the winter of 1923–24 Whiteman and his chief arranger, Ferde Grofé, checked out Ellington's "Washingtonians," who were playing at the Hollywood (soon to be the Kentucky Club), just two blocks north of the Palais Royal. Ellington's move uptown to the Cotton Club and world fame was three years away. Though they claimed that they "couldn't steal even two bars of Duke's amazing music,"[4] something always rubs off on professionals like Grofé and Whiteman. Ellington recalled Whiteman's visits and how he

FIGURE 10.1
Miguel Covarrubias caricature of Paul Whiteman.
Courtesy of Maria Elena Rico Covarrubias.

"showed his appreciation by laying a big fifty dollar bill on us." He credits Whiteman for leading the country to embrace syncopated music, "which he . . . had made whiter."[5]

Another important black dance-band leader to whom Whiteman and Grofé regularly listened was Fletcher Henderson. Henderson, a Fisk graduate who had played piano in Will Marion Cook's jazzy upgrade of the Clef Club Orchestra, the "Southern Syncopaters," led the house band at the Roseland Ballroom, four blocks north of the Palais Royal. Whiteman and Grofé probably heard Louis Armstrong's electrifying effect on the Henderson band in the fall of 1924.

Inevitably, musical ideas flowed back and forth between bands, within bands, and from soloists to arrangers. Riffs became head arrangements and were soon written down; a collaborative art form was being created en masse. In his pathbreaking book *Early Jazz*,[6] Gunther Schuller writes about Busse cornet licks that found their way into a Don Redman arrangement of "Go 'Long Mule," recorded in 1924 by the Fletcher Henderson band and featuring Louis Armstrong and Coleman Hawkins.

Armstrong's impact on jazz and dance bands was cosmic. His improvisations were no mere ad-libs but, in the words of John Lewis, "compositions-on-the-spot." Much of the vocabulary of jazz was codified for all time by Armstrong. And Redman was among the first to absorb and incorporate Armstrong's licks into his arrangements.

Whiteman maintained his passion for jazz. He wrote a book in 1925 titled *Jazz*, giving full credit to its African American origins: "Jazz came to America three hundred years ago in chains . . . priceless freight destined . . . to set a whole nation dancing." He stayed abreast of its stylistic changes, translating the newest trends into his carefully scripted brand of music — "All I did was to orchestrate jazz."[7] In 1927 Whiteman hired Redman to write special arrangements for his band in the new Armstrong-inspired style and engaged his own improviser, the "hot trumpet man" Bix Beiderbecke. Two years later, Whiteman engaged William Grant Still, another conservatory-trained black composer-arranger, as a full-time member of his arranging staff.

Seeing Whiteman on film, fiddle in hand, fronting his band, suggests yet another, and for me an all-important, reason for his success. From his earliest Hollywood film in 1920 to his last appearances on television in the 1950s, we see Whiteman handling his violin as if he were bouncing a baby on his shoulder. They are totally connected, innocently and infectiously at ease — the fiddle and Paul. "He trembles, wobbles, quivers — a piece of jazz jelly" was how Olin Downes described Whiteman, who was well over six feet tall and weighed three-hundred-plus pounds, in his enthusiastic review of the Aeolian Hall concert.[8]

This was the man who convinced the rich and famous to support his timely "Experiment in Modern Music." In a radio interview, Whiteman later called it "the first jazz concert that was ever given in the sacred halls of a symphonic hall." And about the longhairs who were present, he said, "There was Damrosch, Rachmaninoff, Heifetz and Kreisler and several others [pause] we probably gave them a light haircut."[9]

The program was carefully designed. In recognition of the "first jazz band recording," it opened with "Livery Stable Blues," complete with mock

FIGURE 10.2
Miguel Covarrubias sketch of Whiteman and his Orchestra at Carnegie
Hall, April 21, 1925, repeating their successful "Experiment in Modern
Music" concert, featuring Gershwin playing his *Rhapsody in Blue*
for the sponsors of the American Academy of Rome. Note the profiles
of Oscar Levant and Gershwin in the lower left corner.
Courtesy of Maria Elena Rico Covarrubias.

horse whinnies and chicken squawks in the raucous hokum style of the Original Dixieland Jazz Band. Whiteman then served up his most favored Palais
Royal arrangements. They included two solo turns — one for virtuoso banjo
player Mike Pingatore and one for multiple-reed wizard Ross Gorman —
along with exact renderings of his hit records (he was very proud of this)

"Limehouse Blues" and "Whispering." There were crowd-pleasing "knuck-lebusters" by the dashing novelty piano virtuoso Zez Confrey. Sheet music for Confrey's "Kitten on the Keys" had already outsold Scott Joplin's classic "Maple Leaf Rag," and his player-piano-style novelties were at the peak of their popularity. For all these, Whiteman played his violin while directing the band.

When the audience returned for the second half, they were greeted by a much augmented Palais Royal band. The three reeds, four brass, and five rhythm players were now joined by eight violins, two French horns, and an extra string bass. For the first time in his dance-band career Whiteman put down his violin and took up a baton. He led the twenty-three-piece ensemble as a proper stand-up conductor, dressed, as was the orchestra, in the customary daytime formal cutaway, with striped pants and ascot tie.

Whiteman led newly arranged versions of "standard selections," including Edward MacDowell's "To a Wild Rose" and Rudolf Friml's "Chansonette," later known as the "Donkey Serenade." Then came the ultimate test of the "experiment": two new works by Victor Herbert and Gershwin that had been commissioned especially for the occasion.[10]

Whiteman recognized in Gershwin a kindred spirit. They shared a dream of moving their music out of the dance palaces and music theaters and onto the concert stage, but he had no way of knowing whether Gershwin would produce a winner. While Gershwin's better Broadway songs had been well received in a formal concert setting—an Aeolian Hall recital by the eminent soprano Eva Gauthier in November 1923—Whiteman had witnessed firsthand the failure of Gershwin's operatic scena *Blue Monday Blues*. Zez Confrey was the insurance policy; he would also help guarantee a crowd. Confrey naturally received equal billing with Gershwin. Gershwin was by all accounts an especially winning pianist, and Whiteman's idea that he compose "a jazz piece for solo piano and orchestra" turned out to be inspired.

Virgil Thomson, one of the special few who was at both the original 1924 Aeolian Hall concert and my sixtieth anniversary re-creation, wrote me of his recollections: "My chief memories of that premiere are the clarinet lick, an upward glissando which starts the whole thing off, and the composer's beautiful hands with their lightly fleet fingers, also his singing piano tone."[11]

Whiteman's decision to have Victor Herbert compose a work for the concert was a fitting choice. Despite his Irish birth (1851) and European training, Herbert had by 1924 become a highly respected, beloved, and successful "American" composer, conductor, and solo cellist.[12] The 1911 Metropolitan Opera production of Herbert's opera *Natoma* had been notable: it was the first time a work by an American composer and librettist about American subject matter sung in the English language had appeared on the Met's stage.

Gershwin's Rhapsody in Blue

By accepting the commission, Herbert gave Whiteman's concert the vote of confidence it needed in the eyes of the serious music establishment. It is my guess that the novelty of a Herbert premiere—for a jazz dance band!—helped bring out John Philip Sousa, Rachmaninoff, and possibly Stokowski on that snowy Tuesday afternoon.

The program worked a magic back then and our re-creation of the concert, which since 1984 has toured the United States, Canada, and Europe, still does.[13] The secret of the program's success lies in the artful and inspired way Gershwin transforms the same ragtime and blues harmonies, the fiddle, brass and sax colors, and the banjo and tuba rhythms that the audience had been listening and toe-tapping to throughout the evening into a masterwork with immediate appeal. With his *Rhapsody in Blue* for solo piano and jazz band, Gershwin took a giant leap for American music.

Reconstructing the Aeolian Hall concert gave me hands-on experience with original Whiteman band arrangements, including Grofé's masterful orchestration for the *Rhapsody in Blue*, and I began to understand why Gershwin did not orchestrate this particular work himself. Working from Gershwin's two-piano score, Grofé orchestrated the second (accompanying) piano part for the augmented jazz band he and Whiteman chose for the concert. There were unusual choices of instrumentation to be made, and they were further complicated by the doublings.

The brass and rhythm section doublings were straightforward, but the three reed players covered eleven instruments in all: five different sizes of saxophone, from baritone to sopranino, and every woodwind in the symphonic family except the bassoon but including the rare and exotic heckelphone. Add to this eight violins (divided four ways), another string bass, and two horns. Such a hybrid ensemble would set unusual scoring problems before the most experienced composer. The complex reed doublings were the most obvious—who plays what instrument, how long to get it ready, when to switch.

Furthermore, the scores for the leading jazz bands of the period were hand tailored to fit the skills of the individual players. When Grofé laid out the first page of score for the *Rhapsody in Blue*, he did not write "trumpet 1" or "reed 3," to indicate *what* was to be played on a given staff, but "Busse" and "Ross," to indicate *who* was playing. This practice extended to all bands and was raised to an art form by Ellington, who would switch the trumpet-lead line between "Cootie" and "Rex" (the same for trombone and sax players) *within* a composition because he wanted their particular sound or style for a given passage. The jazz band, being an American invention, places value upon the individual, upon his or her particular instrumental expertise and interpretive contributions. Grofé knew the intricacies of the Whiteman band, player by player and instrument by instrument, but however brilliant his scoring, not one single note of the *Rhapsody in Blue* is his own.[14]

It must be noted that Gershwin possessed a composer's keen ear for instrumentation. There are instrumental indications in the holograph (original manuscript) of *Blue Monday Blues* as well as in the two-piano holograph score of the *Rhapsody*. In fact, his orchestrational skills were about to be put to the test.

Hard on the heels of the *Rhapsody's* triumph came a commission from Walter Damrosch for a new concerto for solo piano and "orchestra"—generic, faceless, European—to be completed in time for the upcoming New York Symphony season (1925). Starting with the Concerto in F, for solo piano and orchestra, Gershwin scored all of his concert works himself even as he continued studying composition and orchestration with every fashionable teacher that would have him.[15]

In preparation for my reconstruction of the Aeolian Hall concert, I consulted several original sources of the *Rhapsody in Blue*: Gershwin's pencil holograph in the Library of Congress (the two-piano score he prepared for Grofé), Milton Rettenberg's 1924 manuscript copy of the same, a photocopy of Grofé's original score in the Whiteman Collection at Williams College, and the June 10, 1924, recording by Whiteman with Gershwin as piano soloist.[16] The short recording time available in 1924—under seven minutes per side—forced Gershwin to make cuts. Nevertheless, the recording, on two sides of a twelve-inch disc, is chock-a-block with details never written down in the score or parts. I have to assume that during the road tour, which immediately preceded the recording sessions, some of the jazz embellishments added by the players or Gershwin became "frozen"—such as the little bundles of turning notes (gruppetti) that flavor a phrase, and klezmerlike whoops and hollers that clarinetist Ross Gorman introduced here and there, not only in the familiar opening.

Milton Rettenberg, who was present at rehearsals for the concert, overheard Ross Gorman suggest to Gershwin that he could play the opening clarinet run with a long lip/finger slur instead of the simple scale that had been written, and Rettenberg claimed that Gershwin loved it. Rettenberg also recalled that Victor Herbert came to one of the rehearsals and gave conducting pointers to Whiteman for his *Suite of Serenades*.[17] Herbert also took the time to help Gershwin, who was having second thoughts about the slow theme of the *Rhapsody in Blue*, the centerpiece of the work, by reassuring him that it was most appropriate. Herbert suggested to Gershwin that he set it up by extending the piano arpeggios that introduce the slow section, giving time for the excitement of the preceding cadenza to cool down. Herbert later turned to Rettenberg and said, in an aside, "I wish I had written that theme. I would know what to do with it."

Victor Herbert's little dig, and Rettenberg's passing it on, is only one of a long line of envious deprecations of the *Rhapsody in Blue*. It pains me to include Leonard Bernstein on this list. Bernstein's overall praiseworthy assessment of the work begins with the disclaimer, "The '*Rhapsody*' is not a composition at all. It is a string of separate paragraphs stuck together with a thin paste of flour and water."[18]

Charles Schwartz, in his well-documented if begrudging biography *Gershwin: His Life and Music*, attacks the *Rhapsody in Blue* for its "lack of musical development in the best sense."[19] Schwartz touts the critic Lawrence Gilman, who found the work "so derivative, so stale, so inexpressive."[20] In his Appendix I, for the most part an essay about Gershwin's "Jewishisms," Schwartz writes: "[His] popular tunes and large-scaled works seem to spring from . . . [a] motley mixture of Jewish melodic characteristics and overt Americanisms." Schwartz then challenges Gershwin as a composer of serious works: "He had loads of *chutzpah*, but practically no grounding in the technique of large scale composition. . . . Mainly by following his instincts, he somehow put together pieces that manage to fall into the serious music category."[21] Schwartz got dangerously close to Constant Lambert's racist and anti-Semitic outburst, with Gershwin as his target, in his book *Music Ho!*:

> In point of fact, jazz has long ago lost the simple gaiety and sadness of the charming savages to whom it owes its birth. . . . The nostalgia of the negro who wants to go home has given place to the infinitely more weary nostalgia of the cosmopolitan Jew who has no home to go to. . . . The importance of the Jewish element in jazz cannot be too strongly emphasized. . . . There is an obvious link between the exiled and persecuted Jews and the exiled and persecuted negroes, which the Jews, with their admirable capacity for drinking the beer of those who have knocked down the skittles, have not been slow in turning to their advantage. But although the Jews have stolen the negroes' thunder, . . . although Tin Pan Alley has become a commercialized Wailing Wall, the only jazz music of technical importance is that small section of it that is genuinely negroid. The "hot" negro records still have a genuine and not merely galvanic energy, while the blues have a certain austerity that places them far above the sweet nothings of George Gershwin.[22]

Rhapsody in Blue has proven itself to be critic-proof and continues to thrive. Like most of Gershwin's music, it generates an immediate resonance in the feet and larynx of anyone who ever thrilled to ragtime licks or Puccini's arching tunes, which, without the genius of inspiration, no master of form can match. The scale of *Rhapsody in Blue* is modest, a sixteen-minute work, 80 percent of which is for solo piano, and conceived with a jazz band accompaniment in mind. Its form is logical and, in my view, coherent.

Gershwin had a plan and carried it out brilliantly. The structure of *Rhapsody in Blue* is supported by a key scheme that revolves around the slow theme. Beginning in the traditional blues key of B-flat, *Rhapsody in Blue* makes its way with ever-developing variants of its two principal motives—the clarinet call and the horn's response—through eleven keys, all the notes of the chromatic scale but F. It arrives midcourse, as far away from B-flat as possible, in the key of E major, for the hauntingly beautiful slow theme. With even more variants the *Rhapsody* works its way back to the key of B-flat for its triumphant restatement of the clarinet motive in the closing measures. Gershwin, a savvy young Broadway songwriter, was confronting in his own way the same challenge that preclassical composers faced. How does a master of the AABA tune create for the first time a sustained, integrated work? Gershwin met this challenge with his tonal arch, working his way to a distant key and back. The structure holds his ever-flowing font of ragtime piano improvisations together, improvisations that rarely lose sight of his two principal motives. Meanwhile, his immense piano chops enabled him to write brilliantly for the instrument.

Gershwin might have taken his lead from one of his favorite composers, Claude Debussy, who challenged the academy and fellow-traveling critics for exalting sonata-allegro form, perfected by Beethoven—with its economy of means and tripartite exposition, development, and recapitulation—as the Olympian model against which all large scale pieces of music were to be judged:

> I should like to see a kind of music free from themes and motives or formed on a single continuous theme.
>
> The development will no longer be that amplification of material, that professional rhetoric, which is the badge of excellent training. But it will be given a more universal and essentially psychic conception.[23]

Almost at the same time, the German straitjacket was being removed from French music by Debussy and Ravel and—coincident with nationalist movements in all parts of Europe—the newly emerging African American music was carving out its own path. Here was a music in which the supremacy of the beat obliges melody and harmony to share center stage with rhythm. American composers such as Copland and Gershwin elevate rhythm where others elevate harmony and melody. Moreover, American composers continued to use traditional harmony—harking back to ragtime, blues, and part-sung spirituals—well past the time that it had been superseded or abandoned elsewhere. Infused with fascinatin' rhythm, this music forms a unique and remarkable strand in the history of twentieth-century art.

Kurt Sachs offered the notion that opera composers write in established and familiar styles in order to make it easier for the listener to absorb the text. Other musicologists have developed a theory of "harmonic rhythm," which posits that there is a limit to the number of harmonies the human ear can absorb in a given span of real time. Mozart, for example, does not change chords on every quarter note of fast-moving music, whereas harmonies change on each beat of a slow-moving Bach chorale. Taken together, these theories suggest a musical "golden mean," perhaps explaining why African American music requires more established, familiar harmony to balance its complex rhythm—a Euro-African symmetry. This was the musical language Gershwin inherited, the language of his *Rhapsody in Blue.*

Until Sam Adler's 1971 recording of the *Rhapsody in Blue* with what was billed as the Berlin Symphony, using parts adapted from the original 1924 Grofé score for jazz band, I had assumed that the only edition available was what I now call the "Hollywood Bowl" version for full symphony orchestra. This is the orchestration I grew up with and first conducted, and it is the last of several expansions that Grofé and others made of his jazz band original. In the full symphonic orchestration, published shortly after Gershwin's untimely death in 1937, the all-important banjo and saxophones are listed as optional instruments. Grofé seems not to have had the heart to discard them altogether. But even when they are included in a live performance, they are swamped in a rich orchestral sea, along with the snappy dance rhythms that distinguish the work.

I began performing the jazz-band orchestration in 1976. But for my re-creation concert, I felt a further responsibility to emulate the "authentic" performance movement, a collaboration between musicologists and those performers who specialize in historic replication by way of original instruments, tempi, size of forces, and especially performance style. I duplicated the exact instruments, mutes, and number of players. Hard to find were the E-flat sopranino saxophone, the heckelphone, and a slide whistle sensitive enough to play the chromatics in "Whispering."

The sopranino saxophone is the smallest of that family, higher in pitch than the more familiar B-flat soprano made popular by Sidney Bechet, and possessing a more sensuous and penetrating sound in the upper register than the E-flat clarinet or, some might say, the flute. The heckelphone extends the range of the oboe family downward into the baritone register, even further than the English horn, and with a weightier and more colorful tone.[24]

My new Paul Whiteman orchestra was assembled by a man who had once worked for Whiteman, the drummer Herbert Harris. Although he grew up with the sounds of the late 1920s and early 1930s dance bands, before he would engage any musicians, Harris refreshed his memory by listening to the Whiteman recordings I had been studying and transcribing. The musicians Harris assembled were not your typical big-band players, but an amazing assortment of fine studio players who were capable of playing in any style. Among them were several 1920s aficionados. Banjoist Eddie Davis was full of information about Mike Pingatore, Whiteman's banjoist and lifelong friend, said to have been in the band longer than Whiteman because "Paul came late to the first rehearsal." Our tuba player and bass saxophonist, Vince Giordano, was an avid Whiteman researcher and the leader of the "Nighthawks," a popular society dance band that specialized in music from the 1920s. We even had a Renaissance music specialist, Allan Dean, a trumpeter with a healthy curiosity for all kinds of good music played on a cup mouthpiece.[25] Dean can listen to a Busse recording and analyze his style, his vibrato, and other subtle nuances such as his peculiar use of rubato—the way Busse rushes a phrase and pauses, waiting for the band to catch up—and come up with an amazing replication. Many of the other musicians did the same on their respective instruments. At the first orchestra rehearsal, I played recordings of the 1920 Whiteman band performing pieces they later played in the Aeolian Hall concert. Musicians took copies home; detailed listening to them was worth more than a thousand words or the most painstaking notation.

For the "role" of Gershwin, we engaged the American pianist Ivan Davis. Ivan had recorded the *Rhapsody* with the Detroit Symphony, but he had never heard the jazz band version, nor was he a jazz pianist. He has an incredible ear and a terrific sense of time. I helped him with the 1920s ragtime style. He contributed his finely wrought phrasing and singing tone. The virtuoso jazz stylist and composer Dick Hyman did the Zez Confrey honors.

As the day of the concert approached, we became something of a media sensation. Hyman and I appeared on the *Today* show. I was interviewed on National Public Radio. All the New York newspapers did feature articles, digging out old Whiteman and *Rhapsody in Blue* stories from the archives. Aeolian Hall had long ago been converted into office spaces, but I was able to hire Town Hall, an acoustically sensitive mid-sized auditorium that was only a block away. By the afternoon of the concert, all 1,495 seats were sold, and more than 600 potential ticket buyers were turned away. Among the notables who attended were Morton Gould, Virgil Thomson, and Lester Lanin. The Gershwin family took a box. Whiteman's granddaughter came with her family. She brought me a blue carnation to wear, as Whiteman had throughout his career. There were three members of the 1924 Whiteman band still around: Milton Rettenberg, housebound in New York; pianist Henry Lange, who was living in a nursing home in Kansas; and eighty-one-year-old Kurt Dieterle, who played violin in the concert of 1924 and was still playing "TV dates" in Los Angeles.[26]

Dieterle agreed to come to New York for the occasion (the Carlyle Hotel had him as a courtesy guest). I suggested he bring his fiddle. Carl Johnson, the curator of the Whiteman Collection at Williams College, called to say he was bringing a gold-clad baton that Whiteman had used. Just before we played the *Rhapsody*, I invited Dieterle to join us on stage and introduced him to the audience. He ceremoniously presented the baton to me and sat in the front desk of the fiddle section. Our concertmaster, Lamar Alsop, graciously turned over the solo violin interlude (in the middle of the slow section) to Dieterle.

I had unwittingly tapped into an astonishing and timely nostalgia. Many of the people mentioned above are no longer with us, and concertgoing days for most of those senior citizens at Town Hall that afternoon have ended. The sixtieth anniversary concert was a triumph, in the hall, in the press, in the buzz that went around New York's tight little music circles and, I am happy to say, at the box office.[27]

After the concert I asked Virgil Thomson if he could compare our performance with the one he heard in 1924. He tried to beg off. I pushed. Finally, he blurted out, "But they all played *lighter* than we do now." This would be in keeping with the quieter sound environment of the 1920s.

Today's singers and instrumentalists are consciously or unconsciously competing with high powered, in-your-face cinematic sound and recordings. Broadway theaters have been turned into veritable sound studios. With body mikes and shotguns (long-distance microphones), the live onstage sound is amplified and "massaged," making the extreme ranges crackle and woof unnaturally. Broadway gypsies hoof their way through complicated steps as they mouth along with prerecorded chorus parts blown up to Mormon Tabernacle Choir size. Pit musicians play into individual microphones; sometimes the "pit" is in another building. And the whole is mixed on a board (by the veritable music director) and piped back *at* the audience through dozens of loudspeakers, and through monitors for the cast on stage. We have forgotten how to sing and play *lightly*.

Three days after the Town Hall concert we were on our way to Rome and the Teatro Sistina for a week of gala performances and a television broadcast. The audiences came dressed in "shimmy" dresses, boas, white silk scarves, and black tie. Within the year would come our recording of the entire program, which won a Record of the Year award from *Stereo Review*.

On our tours with "The Birth of the *Rhapsody in Blue*," we occasionally met folks who were at the original Aeolian Hall event, and some who heard one of the performances during the 1924 tour. In Colorado we met Henry Busse Jr., a television producer. In Los Angeles *two* Ferde Grofé Jrs. came on stage to greet us after the concert; one was an adopted son from Grofé's first marriage, the other his biological son from his second marriage.

When the excitement of the Town Hall concert and the Rome tour subsided, all of the hype I had bought into and passed on to willing audiences and the media began to nag at me. Despite its intrinsic merits as an inspired work of art, and its public acclaim as a breakthrough event, *Rhapsody in Blue* is but one chapter in the American music story. The whole enterprise piqued my curiosity to know more, to pass on more: the African American more. I had tapped in somewhere in the middle of the story, and I knew I would be back. In a few years my muse led me to Dvořák, Will Marion Cook, and Jim Europe.

11

The Clef Club Concert

Jim Europe was the biggest influence in my musical career.
He was at a point in time at which all the roots and forces
of Negro music merged and gained [their] widest expression.
And he furnished something that was needed.
—Eubie Blake, in Lawrence T. Carter, *Eubie Blake:
Keys of Memory*

Thanks to the devoted and thorough research of Reid Badger, James Reese
Europe (1881–1919) is at last being retrieved from the fringes of American
music history.[1] Europe was one of the brightest lights of the African American music world, which he helped guide and shape during the twenty critical years between Scott Joplin and Louis Armstrong—between the publication of the first ragtime hit, "Maple Leaf Rag," and the seminal recordings
of the Hot Five. Europe, a charismatic conductor, founded a unique strumming and choraling "Negro Orchestra," the Clef Club. He formed one of
the first hot dance bands, interpreting the African American rhythms and
moves that fueled the first American dance craze. Just months before his
untimely death at age thirty-nine, Europe's 369th Army Band, "the Hellfighters," was introducing a new music they called "jazz" to amazed musicians and the public of France. James Reese Europe would be the first to
be crowned "King of Jazz."[2] What Europe did not do—and this helps explain his obscurity—was compose a hit. But he was recognized by Sissle
and Blake, close collaborators with Europe in his last years, as the godfather
of *Shuffle Along*, which reestablished black musicals on Broadway and, in
the words of the critic and author Gilbert Seldes, "paid honor to [Europe's]
memory."[3]

　　With some humility I believe that my reconstruction and re-creation of
Europe's 1912 Clef Club concert at Carnegie Hall, the first all-black event

held there, and its broadcast on National Public Radio helped bring Europe's name to the attention of the musical public once again.

It began as a "wouldn't it be fascinating to hear" idea that I broached to Judith Aaron, executive director of Carnegie Hall. It took form as a contract to reconstruct three of the hall's historic concerts—concerts originally presented by Duke Ellington, George Antheil, and Jim Europe. My idea proved timely. The hall was looking for a popular, preferably black, music project, one that would impress the National Endowment for the Arts, which had been chiding Carnegie Hall for its elitism. The Carnegie Hall Foundation could perhaps afford to lose their NEA grants but not the more important prestige and imprimatur the grants then represented in the art world.

The hall's promotional team came up with a title for the series: "Landmark Jazz Concerts." I argued for "Three American Landmark Concerts," preferring not to characterize the music. The Clef Club concert took place before the word "jazz" had surfaced. The Antheil concert, despite its connections to jazz and ragtime, was mostly an avant-garde event from the 1920s. And Ellington, we know, was beyond category. But these were public-relations folks, who lived and breathed labels. They stuck with their title.

The concerts were scheduled to take place in one festival week in July 1989. I had six months to find the music and to hire choirs, soloists, and three very different bands. I incorporated myself, choosing the name "Hold That Tyger Productions" after my mother's maiden name, Tygier. With the odd spelling that referred back to Mom's Polish family, which, with one exception, came to an end in the Warsaw ghetto, the old ragtime title took on a deeper symbolism. Hold That Tyger formed a small but efficient staff. We were off and running.[4]

I began researching the Clef Club concert with a copy of the original May 2, 1912, Carnegie Hall program in hand:

PART I

1. Clef Club March   Jas. Reese Europe
   Clef Club Orchestra, conducted by the composer

2. Song, "Li'l Gal"
   Words by Paul Laurence Dunbar   J. Rosamond Johnson
   The composer [singing and playing]

3. (a) Dance of the Marionettes   Hugh Woolford
   (b) "You're Sweet to Your Mammy
       Just the Same"   Johnson
   Versatile Entertainers Quintette

4. (a) Tout a vous—Valse Petite   Wm. H. Tyers
   (b) Panama—Characteristic dance   Wm. H. Tyers
       Clef Club Orchestra, conducted by the composer

5. (a) Song, "Jean"   Henry [sic] T. Burleigh
   (b) Song, "Suwanee River"   Foster
                Miss Elizabeth Payne

6. Benedictus (from an original Mass)   Paul C. Bohlen
       Choir of St. Philip's Church, NY, Paul C. Bohlen, organist

PART II

7. "Swing Along," a Negro melody   Will Marion Cook
   (See page 10 for words.)
             Clef Club Chorus, Will Marion Cook, leader

8. Piano Solo, Danse Heroique   J. Rosamond Johnson
                   The composer

9. (a) "Hula"—Hawaiian Dance   Europe
   (b) "On Bended Knee"   Burleigh
                 Clef Club Orchestra

10. "By the Waters of Babylon"   Coleridge-Taylor
       Choir of St. Philip's Church, Paul C. Bohlen, organist

11. (a) Dearest Memories
    (b) The Belle of the Lighthouse
    (c) Take Me Back to Dear Old Dixie
    (d) Old Black Joe
               Royal Poinciana Quartette

12. "The Rain Song," words by Alex. Rogers   Will Marion Cook
          Clef Club Chorus, Will Marion Cook, leader,
        assisted by Deacon Johnson's Martinique Quartette

13. (a) Lorraine Waltzes   Europe
    (b) March, "Strength of the Nation,"
        dedicated to the proposed Colored
        Regiment   Europe
                 Clef Club Orchestra

The program encompassed an impressive mix of styles, from banjo-driven vaudeville tunes to liturgical works for men's and boys' choir accompanied by pipe organ. There were formal marches, waltzes, concert arias, a virtuoso piano solo, "traditional" choral selections, and a featured ensemble, the Versatile Entertainers Quintet, which had a style of playing that turned out to be a harbinger of jazz.

This wide-ranging musical palette was the work of the black music elite, yet no one has ever explained why there was not a single work of Scott Joplin's on the program. Joplin was living in Harlem at the time. How could he have been left out, in light of the global spirit with which Europe selected the repertoire for the concert?[5]

I sent copies of the program to scholars and collectors across the country asking them to help me locate the music that had long been out of print. My special connection at the Library of Congress, Wayne Shirley, head of the American Music Division, sent a care package of Clef Club pieces, including the band parts for Europe's "Hi! There! March," for which Wayne went into the chamber of last resort, the Copyright Office file. From the Hogan Jazz Archive at Tulane University, and from Vincent Giordano, who has one of the largest privately owned collections of musical Americana, came sets of parts for the "Clef Club March." Among J. Rosamond Johnson's papers at Yale's Beinecke Rare Book and Manuscript Library I found the unpublished manuscript of his "Dance Heroique," a virtuoso piano solo written in a style that can be best described as "Liszt meets Joplin." Johnson composed it while he was a student at the New England Conservatory and dedicated it to his teacher, Charles F. Deunee, a student of Hans von Bülow.

Another lucky find was the Mass in G by Charles Bohlen. At St. Philip's Church on 134th Street, between Adam Clayton Powell and Malcom X Boulevards—previously Seventh and Lenox Avenues—I met with their music minister, Gerald Morton. A very fine organist and conductor, Morton was, of course, interested to learn that the St. Philip's choir had once sung at Carnegie Hall with the Clef Club—and before that for Dvořák.[6] I asked him if by chance he had a copy of the Mass in G by his predecessor, Charles Bohlen. He pulled open a large metal cabinet. Filed among the Bs was a set of choral parts for the Mass in G, the same ones used seventy-six years earlier. Samuel Coleridge-Taylor's "By the Waters of Babylon," the other sacred work sung by the choir for the Carnegie Hall concert, was there as well.

Coleridge-Taylor was hailed in the United States by Booker T. Washington as "the foremost musician of his race," and, as we know, he was favored by the American Negro Academy.[7] Jim Europe had little interest in Coleridge-Taylor's music. Nevertheless pressure must have been put upon him by his younger sister, Mary, the assistant director and the accompanist of the prestigious Samuel Coleridge-Taylor Choral Society of Washington, D.C., established in 1903.

Mary Europe was the musical equal of her brother. In 1894, when she was nine and Jim was fourteen, they both entered a citywide composition contest. Mary took the first prize; Jim came in second.[8] Mary Europe's influence extended into the theater and jazz world as well. Todd Duncan, the first Porgy, was her student. On the opening night of the Landmark Jazz Concerts, I was sitting backstage in Carnegie Hall with the veteran jazz artist Frank Wess. We were sharing the conducting duties for the Ellington concert, which was being given that evening. Frank had played for ten years with the Count Basie Band as well as with Benny Goodman, Dizzy Gillespie, Billy Eckstine, and Eddie Heywood.[9] Frank was one of the first to introduce the flute into jazz. "I see you are doing the Clef Club concert later this week," said Frank. "I'm from Washington, D.C.; Mary Europe was my music teacher at [Paul] Dunbar High. If it weren't for Miss Europe, I might not have become a musician."

We began engaging artists to sing and play the Clef Club repertoire. I had a lot of explaining to do, for James Reese Europe was unknown to most musicians, as he had been to me before I began my research. The exceptions were the bass-baritone, Bill Warfield; the choral conductor, Jester Hairston; the trumpeter, Joe Wilder, whose father was a Clef Clubber; and a few of the "strummers," the banjo, guitar, and mandolin players.

We engaged the Boys Choir of Harlem. They would join with the men from the Morgan State University Choir of Baltimore to form a men and boys' choir for the sacred works. Following Europe's example, I invited Nathan Carter, the conductor of the choir, to lead them, as Charles Bohlen had done in 1912. I asked William Warfield, who was singing J. Rosamond Johnson's "Li'l Gal," to act as host and narrator where I felt it was needed. And thanks to Walter Gould, Morton Gould's brother and a knowledgeable publisher of American choral music, Jester Hairston, a living legend, came on board to lead Will Marion Cook's "Swing Along" and "The Rain Song," as Cook had done in 1912.[10] Sophisticated and proud of his Negro heritage, the eighty-eight-year-old Hairston made the young singers from Morgan State University comfortable with Cook's dialect song "Swing Along":

Swing along chillun, swing along de lane,
 Lif' yo' head an' yo' heels mighty high;
Swing along chillun, 'taint agoin' to rain
 Sun's as red as a rose in de sky.
Come along Mandy, come along Sue;
 White folks watchin' an' seein' what you do,
White folks jealous when you'se walkin' two by two,
 So swing along chillun, swing along.[11]

The Clef Club Concert

Pianist Leon Bates was engaged to play J. Rosamond Johnson's "Dance Heroique" and to accompany Warfield and mezzo-soprano Barbara Conrad, who sang Burleigh's art song "Jean."[12]

Jim Europe's Clef Club Orchestra was unique. In addition to a salon-sized orchestra with the standard instrumentation of strings, woodwinds, brasses, and percussion, there was the large mass of strumming players who also sang—a combination first exploited on a smaller scale by Will Marion Cook and Ernest Hogan in their Memphis Students' Ensemble (1905), of which Europe was a member.

At an earlier Clef Club "Symphony Orchestra" concert (c. 1910), the program listed sixty-nine strummers in all. There were thirty-seven mandolins and bandoris (a banjo-mandolin hybrid also known as the banjoline), divided like violins into twenty-seven firsts and ten seconds. There were nine tenor banjos and twenty-three harp guitars (a modern version of the Renaissance theorbo, with as many as twelve unfretted bass strings to pluck). According to David Mannes, the Clef Club ensemble had "a beautiful soft sound like a giant balalaika orchestra."[13]

We were able to engage thirty eager strummers in all—ten each on mandolins, banjos, and guitars—but had given up on finding any harp guitarists when one found us. Bob Ault heard about the concert through some guitar-banjo grapevine and offered to drive from Brentwood, Missouri, to take part in it.

Europe's uniquely instrumented Clef Club survives in the lore of the banjo, guitar, and mandolin world. One story still told is that Clef Club strummers played only chords, and by ear. Europe himself hinted at this in a newspaper interview, explaining that his unusual orchestration "gives that peculiar steady strumming accompaniment [of guitars, banjos, and mandolins] and 'ten pianos.' The result is a background of chords which are essentially typical of Negro harmony."[14] Europe also told musicologist Natalie Curtis, "They can catch anything if they hear it once or twice, and if it's too hard for 'em the way it's written, why they just make up something else that'll go with it."[15]

I once asked Marion Cumbo, a former Clef Club cellist born in 1898, whether the strummers did more than just play rhythm. His answer: "All the music they could figure, they put in."[16]

But there has to be more to the story. Why would one divide the mandolins and bandoris into firsts and seconds in symphonic fashion simply to strum chords? Europe was himself a trained violinist who took up the mandolin—which is tuned and fingered exactly like a violin—out of expediency.[17] Some strummers, of course, played by ear. But in order to play the music that Europe's program called for, those who played first mandolin and bandori needed an advanced single-string technique—expert coordination between fast fingered melodies and figures in the left hand and the fluttering pick in the right. The firsts would also need a left-hand technique that could take them into the higher positions. As we will see, there were single-string virtuosos among Europe's banjoists.

Another story I heard from several of our banjoists and guitarists was that many of the strummers in Europe's orchestra were good singers who "ghosted" on whatever strumming instrument Europe needed to fill in the ranks. Lest they make an unjoyful noise in their enthusiasm, their instruments were outfitted with rubber strings. And why not? In the days when nightclub owners wouldn't pay for a mere singer, Bing Crosby and Morton Downey Sr. were fitted out with silent guitars or banjos by Whiteman, as was Noble Sissle by Europe.

For our re-creation the singing was left to the Boys Choir of Harlem and the Morgan State University Men's Choir. They were placed on risers behind the orchestra that fanned out in a long crescent across the Carnegie Hall stage. There were also seven pianos spread about, three on either side and one in the center. The piano strummers, who most of the time chorded along with the rhythm section, were let loose in the ragtime finale of Europe's "Clef Club March," as reported in a review of the 1912 event.

Well before the first rehearsal, urgent requests for parts began coming in from strummers. They wanted to "woodshed," a modus operandi that orchestral players, who pride themselves on their sight-reading ability, would rarely admit to. But we did not find parts for these instruments in any of the published orchestrations we located. So I began writing mandolin, banjo, and guitar arrangements myself, a task that sent me to studying old mandolin society and banjo club publications. And just in case the rumormongers were making a case for themselves and a few "fakers" had slipped in, I wrote many of the chord names onto the guitar and banjo parts as well.

Tom Fletcher explains, in his *100 Years of the Negro in Show Business*, how many, if not most, of the strummer-singers of the Clef Club probably learned their parts:

> When new songs became popular, the musicians would stage a little party and invite Bill Tyers [treasurer and assistant director of the Clef Club]. They would all bring their banjos, guitars and mandolins, and the new songs. Bill would play them over while the gang listened. After he had played the melody two or three times, they would have it fixed in their minds. They would learn the words, an easier matter because they could read and write. After that Bill would teach the boys the harmony and in about an hour or so everybody was up to date.[18]

A week or so before our first full rehearsal, a call came from a cohort of about five or six guitar, banjo, and mandolin players who had gotten together to practice on their own. They serenaded me over the phone: "Is this the sound you wanted?" they asked. I was so choked up I could hardly express my amazement at how beautifully they blended and how steady and even was their rhythm. The best part is the strummers' crescendo. At our section rehearsal, I found that thirty strummers could produce a smooth, swelling tremolo that raises you out of your seat.

Using the "period ear" I developed from transcribing 1920s Whiteman recordings, I did some hard listening to the few Europe and Cook recordings I could find and wrote orchestrations where they did not exist—in particular for Cook's "Swing Along" and "The Rain Song." The most fun was finding, and then orchestrating, Burleigh's "On Bended Knee." In the 1912 Carnegie Hall program booklet, under a section entitled "Words of Songs," a printed text was included for "On Bended Knee," and the caveat, "With apologies to the composer for slight rearrangement."

> Oh, look away yonder—what do I see?
> A band of angels after me.
> Come to tote me away from fiel's all green
> 'Cause nobody knows the trouble I've seen!

I assumed this was a Burleigh song (with a borrowed last line), and that someone, perhaps William Tyers, had arranged it for the Clef Club's unusual combination of singer-players. I contacted all of my sources to be on the lookout for a vocal or choral work by Burleigh titled "On Bended Knee" and based upon the old spiritual "Nobody Knows the Trouble I've Seen." By 1912, more than fifty of Burleigh's songs and choral arrangements had been published—his lifetime total would top four hundred—but no one came up with "On Bended Knee." After some sleuthing I discovered the elusive title in a collection of Burleigh's piano pieces, *From the Southland*, published in 1910.[19] Each piece is introduced with an inspirational poem by Louise Alston, Burleigh's wife—thus the inclusion of a text, her poem, in the program booklet.

As one might expect, "On Bended Knee" ends with a musical quotation of the familiar spiritual "Nobody Knows the Trouble I've Seen," for which Burleigh devised the most delicious Dvořákian harmonies. The familiar and moving phrases cry out, if not for words, for hummed support. I was drawn to the unusual palette made available to me. And the combination of delicately strumming mandolins, choral humming, and a cornet warmly singing the tune produced a fresh "made in America" sound.

One final challenge: Europe's "Clef Club March" was described in the reviews as a rousing opener, with the strummers "bursting into singing" at the trio and masses of ragtime pianists playing away at the end.[20] But neither Henry Creamer's words nor Europe's rag piano parts appear in the published versions. So I supplied them—wrote some appropriate words and a piano-rag variation—making sure to add my own caveat: "apologies to the composer for liberties taken."

The conservative style of most of the Clef Club music surprised even aficionados, who, upon hearing about our reconstruction of an all-black concert from the early years of the century, expected a lot of ragtime syncopation. But the marches are right out of Sousa, the waltzes from Victor Herbert. A few hotter numbers are ragtime inspired: William Tyers's boisterous havanaise "Panama," Will Marion Cook's showstopper "Swing Along," and the pieces played and sung by the Versatile Entertainers Quintet.

The search for the music of the 1912 Clef Club Concert was gratifying: out of a total of twenty-one compositions, only five substitutions had to be made. For example, the songs performed by the Versatile Entertainers—the "Dance of the Marionettes" and "You're Sweet to Your Mammy Just the Same"—had not come to light, neither on recordings nor as sheet music. Moreover, I didn't have a clue as to how the group might have sounded. Were they singers, players, or both, and if players, on what instruments?[21] The day of the concert was fast approaching and I was about to give up when Frank Driggs, a jazz historian, came up with a recording of a Versatile Entertainers Quartet (also known as the Versatile Four) that was recorded in Great Britain in February 1916 (His Master's Voice, C-654). Three of the four musicians on the recording were members of the Versatile Entertainers Quintet at Carnegie Hall in 1912—! They were Anthony Tuck, vocalist and "banjoline" player; Charles Wenzel Mills, pianist and vocalist (who was heard playing on New Orleans riverboats as early as 1907); and Charles Wesley Johnson, who played cello and drums.

In the summer of 1913, Tuck, Mills, and Johnson were members of a band sent to France by Jim Europe to play for Irene and Vernon Castle at Café de Paris and the Casino in Deauville. The three Versatiles remained abroad and established themselves as "household names in England"[22]—thus the HMV recording, which provided me with an authentic example of their singing and playing style.

What I heard on the HMV recording was an electrifying virtuoso single-string plucking technique. No chording strummers these. The Versatiles' banjo playing was wild and "jazzy," as was their singing, and at a time when the word "jazz" was yet to be officially introduced to New York. Resenweber's

Cafe on Eighth Avenue off Columbus Circle had been featuring hot black bands, including the Versatile Four, for some time when in 1917 they brought up from New Orleans—irony of ironies—an all-white band with a name catchy enough to match its music, the Original Dixieland Jazz Band.

But the Versatile Entertainers Quartet I heard on the HMV recording could hold its own against the ODJB. If we could match the Versatile's performances—a devilishly difficult task—we would demonstrate that there was an ensemble at Jim Europe's historic and wide-ranging concert that played a style of syncopated music that would soon make a place for itself under the rubric jazz. Admittedly, it is hard to equate banjos with the ODJB's cornet, clarinet, and trombone. But the aggressive drumming of Wesley Johnson, in particular, reminds one of ODJB's Tony Sbarbaro.

Hanging over a tape copy of the old HMV 78s for hours, I transcribed, note for note, the Versatile Quartet's performance of "Winter Nights," by Schwartz, and Wilber Sweatman's "Down Home Rag." I gave not a second's thought to the fact that these songs were different from those performed at the Clef Club concert in 1912, or that there was one less Versatile Entertainer. Our four musicians—banjoists Martin (Aubert) Ayodele and Eddy Davis, pianist Frank Owens, and trap drummer[23] Chuck Spies (there was no cello on the HMV recording)—had the necessary skills and caught the just-before-jazz sounds dead on. At the concert, the audience went wild. I found myself at the microphone saying, "Eat your heart out, ODJB," an invidious comparison that has since been independently taken up by a team of British jazz researchers:

> When the Original Dixieland Jazz Band arrived in England in April 1919, they brought with them a new style of music with a new name, jazz. In all other respects, however, they were merely continuing a line of American artists playing syncopated music who came to England from the end of the nineteenth century, many of whom were black. Of these groups that preceded ODJB one obtained truly national popularity . . . the Versatile [Quartet] Four.[24]

Our new Versatile Quartet rehearsed five or six times over a two-week period. But I had less than a week to turn the New Clef Club Orchestra of sixty-three players and fifty-two singers into an early-twentieth-century vernacular band that could play waltzes, marches, characteristic pieces, and ragtime.[25] The musicians we assembled—from mandolin societies, pizza parlors, Broadway pits, and the rich pool of New York freelancers—easily played their way through the marches and waltzes at the first reading. But it took several passes before the ragtime tunes began to click into the "eight to the bar" frame.[26]

One might think that playing in ragtime style would be second nature for the average American musician. But for those brought up on swing, or on bebop and rock, not to mention the classical repertoire, the playing of ragtime and the related dance music of the 1920s is particularly difficult. Swing playing is distinguished by a rolling triplet "twelve to the bar" inner beat. And as swing bands and combos moved into the smaller clubs, where they were listened rather than danced to, swing and bebop players devised ever-looser time and phrase structures. Lagging behind (playing off) the beat became the thing to do.

To play in ragtime, we have to relearn the way ragtimers supported the nervous dancing style of the 1920s, how they respected and constantly re-iterated, reinforced, and landed squarely *on* the beat "eight to the bar," not twelve.

"Eight to the bar"[27] denotes that there are eight pulses in a normal four-beat measure (whether they come on four quarter notes or, as with Scott Joplin, four eighth notes); and that every pulse, or subdivision, is present and accounted for. Joplin illustrates this in his "Ragtime Primer," lining up the notes of a ragtime phrase with vertical dotted lines from bass clef to treble, from left hand to right, to show how to keep the eight pulses steady and

SCHOOL OF RAGTIME
BY
SCOTT JOPLIN
Composer of "Maple Leaf Rag."

REMARKS – What is scurrilously called ragtime is an invention that is here to stay. That is now conceded by all classes of musicians. That all publications masquerading under the name of ragtime are not the genuine article will be better known when these exercises are studied. That real ragtime of the higher class is rather difficult to play is a painful truth which most pianists have discovered. Syncopations are no indication of light or trashy music, and to shy bricks at "hateful ragtime" no longer passes for musical culture. To assist amateur players in giving the "Joplin Rags" that weird and intoxicating effect intended by the composer is the object of this work.

Exercise No. 1.

It is evident that, by giving each note its proper time and by scrupulously observing the ties, you will get the effect. So many are careless in these respects that we will specify each feature. In this num-ber, strike the first note and hold it through the time belonging to the second note. The upper staff is not syncopated, and is not to be played. The perpendicular dotted lines running from the syncopated note below to the two notes above will show exactly its duration. Play slowly until you catch the swing, and never play ragtime fast at any time.

FIGURE 11.1
From Joplin's *School of Ragtime*, self published in 1908.

locked together. Only then can the desired "weird and intoxicating effect" be achieved.

A simple shifting of accent within the motor pulse of ragtime creates a striking effect. For example, an unsyncopated measure "eight to the bar," has a natural stress accent on the first of every pair of pulses:

dada-**da**da-**da**da-**da**da; dividing the bar 2222.

If we displace the natural accent of the second pair, we get the havanaise or habañera effect:

dadada-**da**-**da**da-**da**da; dividing the bar 3122

If we displace the accent of the first and second pairs we get a variant, the Turkish "belly dance" rhythm Cook talks about:

da-**da**da-**da**-**da**da-**da**da; dividing the bar 12122

Finally, if we go back to the habañera and remove the accent of the third pair, we get the magical ragtime syncopation:

dadada-**da**-dada-**da**da; dividing the bar 332

Joplin loves to combine or even further displace these syncopations. The second strain (measures 9–16) of "Maple Leaf Rag" is an eye-opener:

dada-**da**da-**da**da**da**-**da** / dada-**da**dada**da**-dada /
dadada-**da**da-**da**dada / da**da**-**da**da-**da**da-**da**da;
dividing the phrase 223333 / 323 / 2222

By accenting the last (off-beat) pulse of the first measure and not accenting the first two pulses of the second measure, the bar line is displaced or obliterated.

This displacement of the bar line, I am convinced, caught the keen ear of Stravinsky. I have often performed the "Ragtime Dance" from his *L'histoire du soldat* (1918) as an example of the influence of African American music on European masters. The work is scored for a prototypical ragtime ensemble—violin, cornet, trombone, clarinet, drums, double bass, and one interloper, a bassoon—but it has become clear to me that the entire work derives largely from Stravinsky's fascination with ragtime's motor rhythms and mixed meters, a game of displaced accents where the eighth note is king. The respected twentieth-century music critic H. H. Stuckenschmidt concurs: "The polyrhythms we observe in *L'histoire du soldat* would be unthinkable but for the jazz records which [conductor Ernest] Ansermet brought Stravinsky from America during the First World War."[28]

In ragtime, the "weird and intoxicating" Joplin effect comes from playing or improvising off-beat, "displaced" accents over a steady and heady beat of eight pulses per measure. Our bodies, following our ears, take off, defying gravity. "Swing" ups the ante, offering more places for displacement over a steady beat of twelve pulses per measure. And the pulses can be real or implied, for in jazz—African American music—everyone is a drummer.

Listening to vocal and jazz band recordings of the 1920s has led me to believe that "swing" entered our consciousness and overtook ragtime through the blues. At a time when the most popular bands, such as those of Fletcher Henderson and Paul Whiteman, were playing uptempo, two-beat dance tunes with a straight eight-to-the-bar pulse, blues singers such as Ma Rainey were already rocking and swinging the slower blues tunes, tentatively on some, like "Lucky Rock Blues" (1924), but with full-out tripletizing in "Ma Rainey's Black Bottom" (1927). I even hear some swinging on earlier instrumental blues recordings that W. C. Handy's Memphis Blues Band made in 1922. One back-up band for Ma Rainey included the all-star saxophone section from the Fletcher Henderson Band—Coleman Hawkins, Don Redman, and Buster Bailey—and Henderson himself playing piano. It was only a matter of time before bands would swing uptempo tunes twelve to the bar as well.[29]

The notation of the new swing music did not follow suit. Swing arrangements, sheet music, and eventually bebop "charts" were written with even eighth notes! This practice continues today. The music *looks* like "eight to the bar," but players automatically produce the long-short "twelve to the bar" rhythm of swing unless specifically told to "play straight eighths." There is a practical side to this. To notate the long-short rhythms as they are really played requires a more complex musical arithmetic, either groupings of quarters and eighths with triplet brackets or writing out the whole thing in 12/8, both of which are tiresome when everyone *knows* how to do it as if by second nature. Sometimes composers and arrangers who want a swing effect resort to dotted eighths and sixteenths, which is not only rhythmically inaccurate but tedious to notate as well.[30]

Here lies the danger of putting a sheet of ragtime music in front of jazz or symphonic musicians who are used to swinging the eighths or tripletizing. I have heard this anachronism intrude into a performance of Gershwin's *Rhapsody in Blue* by the Berlin Philharmonic under Simon Rattle and *An American in Paris* by the New York Philharmonic under Leonard Bernstein. Both should know better.

Swing lost its hegemony over popular music when Chuck Berry, Fats Domino, Elvis Presley, and the Beatles brought back the "eight to the bar" feel. We were due for a change. It seems that a fundamental rhythmic shift, the way we feel our bodies in space, occurs about every thirty years. Ragtime emerged around 1895, swing began taking over in the late 1920s, and in the mid-1950s, right on schedule, came rock and roll.

Jazz musicians became paranoid. Rock and roll wasn't just another new dance craze they could master. Many asked themselves whether this was the death of swing, of jazz itself. According to Ruth Ellington Boatwright, Duke Ellington's sister, he thought his world had been undermined. The story he tells in his opéra comique *Queenie Pie* is not so much about an aging millionairess fighting off scheming young beauties trying to move in on her territory as it is about Ellington's bewilderment at the sea change that his music world had undergone, and his quandary over how to go on with his work. (Ellington never revealed how it would end for Queenie.)

At about the same time as the deaths of the principal keepers of the flame, Ellington (1974) and Louis Armstrong (1971), a jazz repertory movement sprang up to revive and document the recent past and to reaffirm jazz as art. The first shot across the bow came in May 1972 when Gunther Schuller, a national treasure, launched a Scott Joplin revival with a period performance of "The Entertainer" to top off an all-American orchestral concert at the New England Conservatory's Jordan Hall.[31] Within two years Chuck Israels founded his National Jazz Ensemble and George Wein sponsored the New York Jazz Repertory Company under the direction of Dick Hyman.[32]

In the decade following, Vince Giordano and his circle attracted audiences hungry for the acoustic delights of Paul Whiteman and Luther Henderson into New York's fancier cabarets and bars, and I found myself with some of these same fellow-travelers on the stages of Town Hall and Carnegie Hall, conducting Gershwin, Ellington, and Cook where once I did Mozart.

When we were rehearsing for the Clef Club re-creation, it was with a strict "eight to the bar" approach that I was able to breathe life into much of the Clef Club repertoire. But Will Marion Cook's "Swing Along" was the inevitable exception that proved the rule.

"Swing Along" was first heard in 1903 as a new curtain-raiser for the London production of *In Dahomey*.[33] It stopped the show at the 1912 Clef Club concert and again at our re-creation in 1989. And although it is subtitled "ragtime march," "Swing Along" contains elements of blues and swing, anticipating styles that would not be fully established for several decades.

During rehearsals, I tried to make sure that no rhythmic anachronisms seeped in. Nevertheless, "Swing Along," for which Cook also wrote the text, seemed here and there to do exactly what it said. The words "*swing*along *chill*un" (*da*dada *da*da), though written in even eighth notes, insinuated a subtle, long-short, tripletlike inner lilt into the reading. Toward the end of the song, the strutting and joyous mood turns dark and pensive, the music slows, and a harmonic-melodic-textual juxtaposition that we usually associate with the blues appears: a four-bar phrase turns to minor as the text is repeated, the tune leans on lowered thirds and sevenths (blue notes), and a tonic-seventh chord resolves toward the subdominant (Cook uses a diminished seventh on the raised-fourth scale step). The blues form, whether twelve, sixteen, or eight bars in length, invariably begins with repeated strains going from major to minor and with this order of harmony.

The "first" blues, W. C. Handy's "Memphis Blues," was composed in 1909 and published in 1912. Cook's bluesy coda in "Swing Along" indicates either that he was ahead of his time—as early as 1898 or 1903 when it was put into *In Dahomey!*—or that he added this hint of an emerging form into the final strains for the 1911–12 Clef Club performances and the song's subsequent publication by G. Schirmer in 1914. We tried playing this bluesy passage straight, but the section began to make sense only when I asked the band to bend the notes as the harmonies changed. And of course I let the straight eighths swing.

Jon Pareles, who reviewed my re-creation of the 1912 Clef Club concert in the *New York Times* (July 17, 1989), remarked that our "rainbow coalition . . . brought to life a fascinating moment in American music." Noting that "the most memorable pieces were by Will Marion Cook . . . dialect songs that maintained their tuneful directness," Pareles saw Cook's line "White folks watchin' to see what you can do," from "Swing Along," as "slyly appropriate to the original concert." Pareles summed up the evening by pointing out that those black musicians who, like Jessye Norman, had triumphed in the classical tradition, those who had passed it by completely, and those who, like Wynton Marsalis, had conquered it "as a sideline" have "proved themselves in different ways since 1912 . . . [and that] all those ways for members of a minority to make themselves heard in the majority's musical culture were foreshadowed at the Clef Club."[34]

12

Will Marion Cook

I have been intrigued by Will Marion Cook, a catalytic figure and an angel of black music who seems to show up for a short yet efficacious time at every notable African American music event, from the 1890s to World War II, from Dvořák to Duke Ellington.

The conservatory-trained Cook and his association with symphonic music was on Ellington's mind when he was preparing for his first appearance in Carnegie Hall: "[Cook] was a brief but strong influence . . . Some of the things he used to tell me I never got a chance to use until . . . I wrote the tone poem *Black, Brown and Beige.*'"[1] "Doc" Cook was mentor, guide, and/or adviser to countless American artists besides Ellington. Among them were Eva Jessye, music educator and original choirmistress for *Porgy and Bess* and *Four Saints in Three Acts*; the composer Harold Arlen; and the jazz saxophonist Sidney Bechet, whom Cook discovered in Chicago. Cook is the central character in Josef Skvorecky's historical novel *Dvořák in Love*,[2] and articles and radio broadcasts spring up every time he is rediscovered.[3] A full biography of Cook is long overdue, but here are some highlights.

After the success of *Clorindy*, Cook rode out the wave of black musicals through the early 1910s, directing and arranging for choruses, composing songs for shows, and conducting. He also tried his hand at musical dramatization. The last of the Williams and Walker musicals,[4] *Bandanna Land* (1907), featured Cook's scena "T'Ain't Gwine Be No Rain," with words by Alec Rogers. In it, four men (a male quartet) drop in on Simmons's house, sit around the wood stove, and have a sung debate about signs of impending rain: "Any time you hear de cheers an' tables crack / An' de folks wid rheumatics dey jints is on de rack / 'Look out fu' rain, rain, rain' . . . !" (the last words in four-part harmony). The scena, retitled the "Rain Song," was also performed at the 1912 Clef Club concert and was warmly received at our 1989 re-creation.

Cook's theatrical sensibilities, and in particular his marriage of black vernacular text and music, are evidenced in some of his other works from around the same time: "Exhortation: A Negro Sermon," again with words by Alex Rogers (1912); and "An Explanation: The Scene, the Charge, the Explanation," a trial scene with words by James Weldon Johnson (1914).

These dramatic settings were as close as Cook would get to the Negro opera he was never able to complete. Besides "Uncle Tom's Cabin" and "Saint Louis 'Ooman," mentioned by Cook in his memoir, he was working with his son Mercer on an opera about the Haitian revolutionary Toussaint L'Ouverture in his last years. I cannot help but wonder what inner conflicts Cook and Mercer must have suffered when Cook's wife and Mercer's mother appeared in the world premiere of Gershwin's "American folk opera," *Porgy and Bess*. Abbie Mitchell brought her sophisticated musicianship and a lifetime of stage experience to the role of Clara, whose sublime rockabye aria "Summertime" marks the opening moments of the opera.[5]

No doubt the highpoint of Cook's career was the London production of *In Dahomey*. In an unpublished memoir, "A Negro Invasion of Buckingham Palace in 1903," Abbie Mitchell tells how Cook and other members of the *In Dahomey* company went off to Buckingham Palace to perform for the birthday of nine-year-old Prince Edward, the future Duke of Windsor, while she remained behind at their London lodgings with Mercer, their newborn baby, disappointed and confused that she had not been included.[6]

At the palace, King George V inquired, "Where is 'She ain't no violet'?"—referring to Mitchell by the first line of the song, "Brownskin Baby Mine,"[7] which stopped the show on opening night—and sent his liveried footman and a private carriage to fetch her. "His Majesty, the King . . . held up the performance until I arrived," wrote Mitchell.

The show had another devotee in twenty-two-year-old Percy Grainger, newly arrived in London, who was moved to compose what he called his "Cakewalk Smasher *In Dahomey*" for solo piano (completed in 1909), in which "Brownskin Baby Mine" is freely quoted.

During this time Cook had a chance meeting in London with his old violin teacher, Joseph Joachim. In response to Joachim's inquiry "Wo ist die Geige?" (Where is the violin?), Cook proudly told him he was now a composer and was conducting his own music at the Shaftesbury Theatre.[8] Cook and Mitchell returned to New York for the 1904–5 season still high on their London success. This might explain why he felt it safe to take on his next, controversial, project: music director of *The Southerners: A Study in Black and White*, which opened that spring at the same theater where *In Dahomey* had only recently triumphed. Principal roles were played by whites in black-face, but *The Southerners* bravely employed an all-black chorus. The *New York Times* reported:

> When the chorus of real live coons walked in for the cake last night . . . mingling with white members of the cast, there were those in the audience who trembled in their seats. . . . The Negro composer of the score Mr. Will Marion Cook . . . succeeded in harmonizing the racial broth as skillfully as he had harmonized the score.[9]

Cook's triumphs at the 1912 Clef Club concert led to a contract with G. Schirmer for the publication of his dialect choruses and scenas. In 1918 he organized the Southern Syncopated Orchestra, a jazz orchestra with a large string contingent that anticipated Whiteman's hybrid orchestras by almost a decade. The Syncopators also sang spirituals *a cappella*. In the spring of 1919 Cook and his orchestra set out on a European tour. I'm sure he expected to take up where James Reese Europe left off, introducing the newest American jazz styles, this time with Sidney Bechet as the leading soloist. Bechet also bought his first soprano sax while in London. The Syncopators opened at the Royal Philharmonic Hall, impressing the Swiss conductor Ernest Anser-met—"the astonishing perfection, the superb taste, the fervor of its play-ing"—and garnered a second command performance for Cook at Bucking-ham Palace featuring Bechet and members of the band. Internal bickering and a tragic boating accident literally scuttled much of the tour, but many of the players, Bechet included, remained in Europe to form small bands on their own. A reorganized Syncopators appeared in Montmartre at the Apollo Theater in 1921. Back in the United States, Cook formed a Clef Club Orchestra that toured with a musical show that included the singer and actor Paul Robeson.[10]

Cook's furiously guarded self-respect seems to have suffered a setback in 1927. In a letter published in the *New York News* on October 29, Cook chastises Carl Van Vechten for his controversial book *Nigger Heaven*[11] and reveals a broken spirit:

> Men like you can stop our habit of weak imitation. The fault is yours, not ours. You tell us that Anglo-Saxon civilization is the best perhaps the only right one. You tell us that all white is good, all black, bad and evil. Then you expect us to be proud of and develop something that

we have been taught is inferior. Help us to develop a race conscious-ness, a pride of things Negroid.

Cook then names Negro artists who have "reached the heights" and those "unfinished artists who need heaps of study." In a closing paragraph Cook gives vent to his bitter disappointment:

> Too much praise and too easily earned money kept me for thirty-five years from becoming a master. Now it is too late. Your job as a lover of humanity, of the Arts and as a critic, is to see that my great genius race does not fail as has . . . Will Marion Cook.

I came across a series of letters that Cook wrote in the 1940s, toward the end of his life (he died in 1944).[12] Cook was apparently quite ill, mostly alone, and struggling to maintain his pride. He lashed out at publishers, whites, and Jews, and wrote pathetic letters to the American Society of Composers, Arrangers, and Publishers trying to keep some royalty money coming in. AS-CAP responded with a special grant. The letters remind me of an uncharac-teristic remark made to me by John Lewis: "Our country drives many African Americans into madness."

Cook's disillusionment seems a far cry from the Clef Club Concert of May 2, 1912, when he was the hero of Carnegie Hall, which is how I intend to remember him.

> There were a great many representative white musicians and the en-tire New York musical press present, and there was a stir when the or-chestra started to play the fascinating rhythms of Cook's "Swing Along," . . . and all the musicians, while playing their fiddle or jerking their banjos, joined in singing this rousing tune in good four-part har-mony, lilting, swelling, thunderously bursting forth on the big fermata, and winding up in a frenzy. When it . . . had ended, followed by a storm of applause, there was no one in the audience that did not feel for once that he had heard the "real thing," the true Southern Negro Idiom, worked out with clever musicianship and genial verve into a truly artistic manifestation.[13]

13

George Antheil's *Ballet Mécanique*

The scene is a beautiful theater of the Champs-Elysées, filled
with an audience of more than 2,000 people among whom one
can distinguish James Joyce, Serge Koussevitsky, Ezra Pound,
Darius Milhaud, Nadia Boulanger, Marcel Duchamp, Alfred
Knopf . . . each and every one buzzing with the excitement
and expectation of hearing for the first time anywhere . . .
George Antheil! who proceeded to outsack the "Sacre"
with the aid of a Pleyela.
—AARON COPLAND, in Aaron Copland and Vivian Perlis,
Copland: 1900 through 1942

When I set out to re-create George Antheil's 1927 Carnegie Hall concert, I
was in no small way intrigued by his avant-garde signature piece, the "notorious" *Ballet Mécanique*, which started riots in Paris at the Théâtre Champs-
Elysées in June of 1926 and laid an egg the following year, April 10, 1927, in
New York's Carnegie Hall. Few American music histories and contemporary
memoirs by musicians as well as others fail to mention the *Ballet Mécanique*
—and for the most part, derisively: Deems Taylor, "as a comedy hit it was one
of the biggest successes that ever played Carnegie Hall"; Gilbert Chase, "Antheil made the headlines and reaped the ephemeral rewards of a *succès de
scandale*"; and Richard Franko Goldman (son of Edwin Franko Goldman)
"The greatest public sensation of the time."[1] Now that I have studied, performed, and recorded the immensely complex, original *Ballet Mécanique*,
it pains me to see how the music, in my view a fascinating work of genius that
represents yet another strain in our jazz-age lineage, was eclipsed by the
hoopla surrounding it.

New York's half dozen daily papers were fed stories about the riots the
Ballet Mécanique caused at its Paris debut. Cartoons and provocative headlines began to appear: "'Ballet Mécanique' To Din Ears of New York / Makes
Boiler Factory Seem as Quiet as Rural Churchyard"; "Seeks a Technic [*sic*]
to Express Skyscrapers and Subways in Tone"; "A Riot of Music." An ad
placed in the fashionable *New Yorker* magazine unblushingly declared it

FIGURE 13.1
Miguel Covarrubias
sketch of George Antheil.
Courtesy of Maria Elena
Rico Covarrubias.

would be "an event no New Yorker can afford to miss—the first appearance in America of George Antheil in a concert of his own works."

Antheil was apparently determined to attract as much publicity as possible, good or bad—it didn't seem to matter—even at the expense of his most ambitious and revolutionary work. The musical public and the critical press were forewarned. They were being invited to witness and participate in a Dadaist cause célèbre.

A stellar array of artists was assembled for the concert. The first half opened with a new string quartet performed by the Musical Arts Quartet. This was followed by the Second Sonata for Violin, Piano and Drum, played by violinist Sascha Jacobsen—immortalized in the Gershwins' party song "Mischa, Yascha, Toscha, Sascha"[2]—with Antheil presiding at the piano and on the Arab drum. W. C. Handy's "all-negro" orchestra, under the direction of Allie Ross, closed the first half with another premiere, A Jazz Symphony, again with Antheil as piano soloist. The entire second half was taken up with the Ballet Mécanique, which employed an unusual ensemble of multiple pianos and sundry percussion instruments, including a so-called "aeroplane propeller," under the direction of the British conductor Eugene Goossens,

Dvořák to Duke Ellington

with Antheil presiding over an especially constructed Welty-Mignon player piano.

Antheil's erstwhile concert manager, the publisher and Broadway producer Donald Friede, carried the jazz- and machine-age metaphors even further by commissioning set designer Joe Mullens to create two backdrops — for Carnegie Hall! In his book *"Flop Mécanique": The Mechanical Angel*,[3] Friede describes the scene at the concert. For the first half of the concert, the entire back of the stage was covered by a painted drop that showed

> a gigantic Negro couple dancing the Charleston, the girl holding an American flag in her left hand, while the man clasped her enthusiastically around the buttocks. . . . For the *Ballet Mécanique* there was suspended a cyclorama with a futuristic city of skyscrapers as the background. In the foreground was a series of enormous noise making machines.

Add to this the unwieldy, overblown version of the *Ballet Mécanique* that Antheil assembled. There were ten "live" pianists, eight more than had appeared in Paris, engaged at the urging of the Baldwin Piano Company, which provided nine-foot concert grands for all. Among them were two young American composers, Aaron Copland and Colin McPhee. They were joined by eight xylophonists and four bass drummers from the New York Philharmonic, and at least four "mechanical effects" persons (who probably didn't read music) who were assigned to a battery of electric bells, a siren, and "aeroplane propellers."[4] Front and center sat Antheil overseeing his piano rolls, which produced an amazing variety of disembodied, wild, machinelike sprays of sound, ragtime licks, long ostinatos, and thudding clusters. Goossens, who came to America to lead the Rochester Philharmonic and teach at the Eastman Conservatory, was known for his performances of new and difficult music. He led this ungainly collection standing atop a table at the edge of the stage.

Mayhem followed, on and offstage. This must have been anticipated by Goossens, to judge by his description of the rehearsals:

> The moment the percussion instruments were added much of the detailed teamwork [between the "live" pianos and the player piano] was lost, and when the aeroplane propellers joined the fray, near pandemonium ensued. I tried to temper this at the final rehearsal, but accomplished only a tolerable balance.[5]

According to some accounts of the concert, the "aeroplane propeller" blew the audience into disarray. Some responded in kind by making paper airplanes out of pages torn from their programs and floating them at the stage.

The Nerviest Opened
Umbrellas
as a Protection
Against the Snow
of Paper

Drawn for the Herald Tribune by T. S. Tousey

FIGURE 13.2
Cartoon of *Ballet Mécanique* concert. Drawing
for the *New York Herald* by T. S. Tousey, April 12, 1927.

An out-of-control siren continued wailing away well after the piece ended, and the dignified critic Deems Taylor raised a white flag on the tip of his walking stick. The reviews that followed treated the whole affair as a bad joke, and so began the legend, which persists.

Sixty-two years passed before my restaging of the 1927 concert and the real *Ballet Mécanique* was heard again. Two years later came the first CD of what is arguably the most revolutionary American work of the twentieth century.[6]

The American filmmakers Man Ray and Dudley Murphy had been shooting lengths of film in Paris in 1923–24, preparing a satirical Dadaist mon-

FIGURE 13.3
Photograph of a Picabia sculpture entitled *Ballet Mécanique*

tage with the intended title of *Ballet Mécanique* after an abstract sculpture by Francis Picabia. The sculpture, which appeared as a photo on the cover of Picabia's Dadaist magazine 391 ("Dessin de Machine," August 1917), was made out of axle supports from a Model-T Ford that, when formed into a ring, resembled a circle of curvaceous ballerinas leaning out and backward.[7]

The filmmakers ran out of money, but Ezra Pound came to the rescue by getting the French painter Fernand Léger into the act. Léger lent his all-important name and a Chaplinesque sculpture that was animated for the film and—to the dismay of Man Ray and Murphy—also got involved in the film's editing. At the same time Pound proposed that Natalie Barney, an American heiress and patron of the arts, underwrite a musical score for the film, to be composed by his new young protégé, the American composer George Antheil.

Born in Trenton, New Jersey, July 8, 1900, Antheil was the first American composer of avant-garde music to be taken at all seriously in Europe. He established himself as a singular concert pianist and composer in Berlin, Budapest, and Vienna during the 1922–23 season—"he comes from the dance and becomes, with the dance rhythms, electrical."[8] He then moved to Paris. In addition to his mainstays—Chopin, Debussy, and Bach—his own pieces, *Sonata Sauvage*, "Mechanisms," and the *Airplane Sonata*, which exploited his demonic technique, provoked welcome demonstrations among the riot-prone Dada set. With Ezra Pound's help, he became "notorious," a darling of the intellectual, literary, and visual arts circuit.[9]

The practice of accompanying silent films with piano music had long been established, and ragtime was often the vernacular music of choice. It was a short logical step for Antheil—who played for the "silents" in his youth—to compose music for a player piano, or a Pianola,[10] some of it in ragtime, for this "American" film.

The Pianola is an instrument—some might say a machine—that can convert any normal piano into a "reproducing" player piano. Its cabinet is about the size and shape of a small spinet but it has no keyboard or piano works. At the back of the Pianola are eighty-eight levers that, when positioned and secured in front of a normal concert grand or upright, convert it into a player piano. The front of the Pianola contains a player-piano mechanism, powered by foot pedals, with the usual spools and tracker bar exposed. It is fed "digital" information, punched out on paper rolls, that pneumatically sets the piano keys in motion. For our purposes, the terms player piano, Pianola, and the French Pleyela are interchangeable.

Antheil's player-piano score was transferred onto rolls, punched out by hand, at the Maison Pleyel factory and made available commercially in a three-roll set for player-piano enthusiasts who collected new music, such as Pleyel's version, in nine rolls, of Stravinsky's *Rite of Spring*.[11] Since film projector and Pianola speeds are adjustable, an exact coordination between image and sound was theoretically possible, and to this day contemporary prints of the "silent" film *Ballet Mécanique* retain the title credit "Synchronisme Musical de George Antheil."

The collaboration between the filmmakers and Antheil was short lived. The film and the music had already assumed separate lives by the fall of 1924, when they were premiered independently within five days of each other.[12] "*Ballet Mécanique*, a film by Léger," was presented in silence at a Musik und Theaterfest organized in Vienna by the architect, sculptor, painter, and stage designer Frederick Kiesler on September 25.[13] *Ballet Mécanique*, the Pianola music, was "played" (foot-pedaled) by Antheil on a single player piano, at a private hearing in Salle Pleyel on September 16, before an audience that included the James Joyces, the Hemingways, Natalie Clifford Barney, and other Paris intellectuals. Benoist-Mechin wrote an ecstatic *revue* for *La revue european*. Janet Flanner summed it up, "Good but awful."

Antheil soon began searching for ways to expand his score. At first he hoped to attach sixteen pianos to a single player piano or Pianola mechanism. Like several other of his ideas, this proved to be beyond the reach of the available technology. He then wrote additional parts onto the player piano score for electric bells and "aeroplane motors," noisemakers that would accompany the player piano: a version that was never performed.

Finally, in 1926 Antheil wrote out a new score, 399 densely packed pages carefully scratched out in pen and ink. Above the old Pianola music—the driving force of the work which remained intact—he created parts for a percussion ensemble: two "live" pianos, three xylophones, and four bass drums. The noisemaking machines were now clearly identified as eleven electric doorbells (of specific pitch) and three airplane propellers—"small wooden," "large wooden," and "metal"—to which he added a fire engine siren. This was the scandalous score performed in Paris in 1926 and in New York the following year.

The story does not end there. The Paris–New York player-piano version was radically recomposed by Antheil when he finally had it published in 1952–53. By dispensing with the player piano and long stretches of silence—the work's most original and novel concept—Antheil made the new version far more practical to perform. The extent of the revision—the rolls contain twenty-seven minutes of music, the revised version sixteen—was, for obvious reasons, not dwelled upon by Antheil or his publisher. It would be better not to disturb any publicity value the 1950s revision might inherit from the "scandalous" work of the 1920s. One reviewer, who did not have the original score with which to compare, wrote that with the creation of the new version, "'Ballet Mécanique' . . . now sounds like an ebullient and lively piece that is actually pretty in places."[14]

In the spring of 1988, a West Coast tour of "The Birth of the *Rhapsody in Blue*" concert made it convenient for me to visit the Antheil Archive, set up in an abandoned church in Berkeley, California, where the holograph scores of the *Jazz Symphony* and the 1926 Paris–New York player-piano version of the *Ballet Mécanique* were stored. It was also the home of Charles Amirkhanian, avant-garde composer, Pacifica Radio new music host, and Antheil's musical executor.

I had naively assumed that gathering together the music for my re-creation of Antheil's concert would be simple compared with the search for the Clef Club concert music, or the transcribing of old recordings for the Aeolian Hall concert. The revised score of the *Ballet Mécanique* could be found in any good music library, and parts were available for hire from Antheil's publisher, as was material for the other works on the program. All it would take was a telephone call.

After only a cursory thumb-through of the *Ballet Mécanique* holograph score, I realized that the published revised score was but a distant relative of the original before me. We would of course have to play the 1926–27 Paris–New York player-piano version at our forthcoming concert.

The archive had neither a matching set of orchestral parts nor a set of the all-important player piano rolls that corresponded with the wild music meticulously laid out in the score. New parts for the "live" instruments could be extracted from the score, but the player-piano rolls were another story.

Locating an original set of rolls and a proper player piano became my top priority, a search that soon had me floundering in a netherworld of player-piano enthusiasts, piano roll collectors, piano roll suppliers, and piano roll copiers—the pirates and the legal ones. This arcane community was of course divided into warring camps. It was not until Amirkhanian put me in touch with Rex Lawson, a professional British "Pianolist," and his partner, Dennis Hall, president of the Friends of the Pianola Institute of England, both of whom live and breathe Pianola history, science, and repertoire, that I stopped being spun one way and another. I was particularly fortunate in being led to Lawson, because he could coordinate piano roll performances with a conductor.[15]

When Rex Lawson "plays" the Pianola, he actually humanizes what was designed to be an automaton. He uses foot pedals to work the bellows, and with his knee he guides a speed controller. He also works a series of levers that make it possible to bring out particular passages in the high, medium, or low registers of the piano at hand. During rehearsal breaks for our Carnegie Hall concert, Lawson entertained, and exasperated, our eight "live" pianists with well-realized performances from rolls of the most difficult Chopin études, adding expression and rubato with real artistry.

I learned that there was a set of original *Ballet Mécanique* rolls at the Curtis Institute in Philadelphia. They had been presented by Antheil to his principal American sponsor, Mary Louise Curtis Bok. But the Curtis Institute librarian would not allow the rolls to leave the premises in the mistaken belief that they were fragile and that once played on a Pianola they would be compromised.[16]

The Antheil gods were watching over us. Marc-André Hamelin of Canada, one of the "live" pianists we engaged to play for our re-creation, also collected piano rolls. He had only recently bought an original set of *Ballet Mécanique* rolls—for fifty cents!—at the annual deaccession sale held by the Music Division of the New York Public Library and was happy to lend them for the concert. I immediately sought to have a set of back-up rolls made, which led me to a whole subset of piano roll copiers: digital computer copiers, photographic copiers and mechanical-transfer copiers, each one insisting that theirs was the only reliable system. I had digital copies made and sent them off to Lawson in London with a photocopy of the full score so he could prepare for the concert.

Lawson drew horizontal lines on the rolls to correspond with the bar lines on the score, thus enabling him to follow my beats and find his place in the middle of a roll during rehearsals. By performance time I had learned how to catch the ends of tricky runs by peeking over at the moving roll as it glided past the brass tracker bar, which is not very different from watching a pianist's hands to bring in the orchestra at the end of solo piano runs in the Beethoven Fourth Piano Concerto.

Vince Giordano had connections in the Pianola world and arranged to have Randy Herr, a restorer of player pianos, run through the rolls—he worked up quite a sweat—on his foot-powered Steinway concert grand player piano while I made a cassette recording for study purposes.[17]

I was not prepared for the startling music the rolls produced, a futurist music of a complexity beyond the playing capabilities of two, or even four, human hands that stemmed from Antheil's unique "time canvas" concept, which separates it from most music yet composed by 1924. This was the Pianola music that captivated the Joyces and the Hemingways in Salle Pleyel. As a "Synchronisme Musical," it would have overwhelmed Man Ray and Dudley Murphy's film.

Now that I have come to know the *Ballet Mécanique* in all of its manifestations, I understand why both Virgil Thomson and Aaron Copland held Antheil in awe. In his autobiography Virgil Thomson quotes from a letter he wrote about Antheil from Paris in the winter of 1926–27:

> My estimate of him as "the first composer of our generation" might have been justified had it not turned out eventually that for all his facility and ambition there was in him no power of growth. . . . The Ballet Mécanique," written before he was twenty-five, remains his most original work.[18]

Copland described his reaction to the Paris premiere in a 1926 letter to his friend Israel Citkowitz: "I am honestly bound to repeat my unshakable conviction—the boy is a genius. Need I add that he has yet to write a work which shows it."[19]

Despite the disclaimer, Copland carried his enthusiasm back from Paris to New York that same year and, ever the supporter of patronage for his fellow composers, talked up the idea among friends of bringing Antheil back for a concert. I called Copland in 1989 to invite him to our re-creation, meanwhile hoping that he would be a font of information. He said he had but "little memory of the Carnegie Hall event," but he did remark that "Antheil had Paris by the ear!"

At the archive I was also able to examine the holograph score of Antheil's piano concerto, titled *A Jazz Symphony*. I was already familiar with it through a photocopy I had used for an earlier perfomance[20] and recognized the dedication that appears on the title page: "To Evelyn Friede [wife of Donald, Antheil's Carnegie Hall concert manager] with appreciation and affection." But with the actual manuscript in hand, I saw that this dedication was pasted over an earlier one. By holding it up to the light I discovered the work's original title and dedication: "Americana for Paul Whiteman and his orchestra, Paris, October 1925."

Antheil evidently composed his *Americana* for Whiteman's second "Experiment in Modern Music," which was held in Carnegie Hall on December 29, 1925, hoping to follow, if not overtake, Gershwin's success at the first "experiment." It can be no coincidence that within a year after the news of the enthusiastic reception given the *Rhapsody in Blue* reached Paris, both Copland and Antheil began composing their own jazz-inspired piano concertos. Antheil's *Americana* was scored, as was the *Rhapsody in Blue*, for solo piano and a hybrid jazz orchestra.[21]

For reasons unknown, *Americana* was not included on the Whiteman concert; the big new piece of the evening was a revised version of Gershwin's *Blue Monday Blues* under a new title, *135th Street*. *Americana* went on the shelf, only to be brought out for Antheil's own 1927 Carnegie Hall event under its own new title, *A Jazz Symphony*. To go Whiteman, and Gershwin, one better, W. C. Handy's "all Negro" orchestra was engaged to perform it, with Antheil as piano soloist.

Handy evidently found the mixed, Stravinskyesque rhythms of the work too complex and enlisted Allie Ross, associate conductor of the Harlem Symphony, to take over. Ross was a musician after my own heart. He played in Tyers's and Jim Europe's Clef Club dance bands, appeared as a classical violin soloist with the Harlem Symphony, and led a hot jazz band good enough to follow Louis Armstrong at Connie's Inn in 1929.[22]

Ross and Handy's orchestra were allowed unlimited rehearsals, twenty-five in all. Most of the later ones were held in the ballroom of the mansion of Harlem millionairess Madame A'lelia Walker, daughter of C. J. Walker, the hair-care entrepreneur, Ellington's model for the title role in his opéra comique *Queenie Pie*.

From all reports, Ross and the orchestra made the piece their own. Antheil noted on the holograph that "'A Jazz Symphony' received an ovation at its premiere—a fact usually forgotten because of the scandal of the *Ballet Mécanique* which followed it."[23]

During the intermission of the premiere performance, Samuel Chotzinoff, critic for the *New York World*, interviewed Gershwin and others about *A Jazz Symphony*, which they had just heard. Gershwin remarked, "I really can't compare Antheil's jazz with mine. He deals in polytonalities and dissonance . . . follows Stravinsky and the French. His music has moments of humor." The unusually gifted actor and singer Paul Robeson said succinctly, "The jazz was fine." Gilbert Seldes was the most enthusiastic: "The jazz symphony was simply grand. It is better jazz than Gershwin and better music than Stravinsky."[24]

The loose use of the word "jazz" was typical of the time. "Jazz" was fast moving from verb to noun, and it was being tacked onto every sort of music for dance band or symphony orchestra that had the slightest hint of ragtime or blues. Louis Armstrong had only recently, in the fall of 1924, introduced New York to the sort of open-ended improvisation for which we now reserve the word jazz.

A Jazz Symphony posed no unusual challenges to Ivan Davis, our virtuoso solo pianist, nor to our excellent orchestra of freelance jazz musicians and studio players who played for our re-creation concert. It opens with a joyous maxixe played by the full orchestra and punctuated by raucous glissandos on the slide trombones; it could easily be mistaken for a work by Gershwin or Ellington. But the piece quickly turns toward parody, quoting from Joplin's "Entertainer" and Stravinsky's *Rite of Spring* and *L'histoire du soldat*, as well as a long-forgotten rag tune that, according to composer Benjamin Lees, former student and friend of Antheil, was "George's favorite . . . 'Oh My Baby.'" Lees was right about Antheil's obsession with "Oh My Baby." This tune shows up in three of the four works offered at the Carnegie Hall concert: it provides the principal motive for *Ballet Mécanique*, it makes a strong showing in the *Jazz Symphony*, and it can be heard buried in the final brutal cadenza of his Second Sonata for Violin, Piano, and Drum.

Toward the middle of *A Jazz Symphony*, Antheil writes a would-be jazz solo over a steady (four-four) beat—not, as would be expected, for the featured solo piano, but for a (jazz) trumpeter, calling upon the player to "employ all the tricks of the trade." This gesture toward authenticity is probably what Antheil was referring to in his 1927 program notes when he described his work as "an expression of the American Negro in symphonic music, a reaction towards Negro jazz as away from 'sweet jazz' which in a few years will sound . . . like 'In [By] the Shade of the Old Apple Tree.'"

What Gershwin, Robeson, and Seldes called "Antheil's jazz" really boils down to whatever "tricks of the trade" Handy's trumpet player came up with that night, plus a few collages and quotes, anthropological stuff gathered in the jungles of North America and cleverly mounted up for display. Antheil had his sights on Picasso and Stravinsky, not Sidney Bechet.

A Jazz Symphony does not deconstruct the rhythmic and tonal elements of jazz, as does Stravinsky in L'histoire du soldat, nor does it lovingly recast jazz's blues gestures, as does Ravel in his Piano Concerto in G Major (1931) and Sonata for Violin (1923–27). Like most European composers who enjoyed a brief affair with My Lady Jazz, Antheil trivializes African American music, finding it useful as parody and as a symbol of low life, exotic primitivism, or the noble savage. I include Claude Debussy, Darius Milhaud, Erik Satie, and Ernest Krenek in this category.

Antheil winds up A Jazz Symphony with a delightful caricature of a Viennese waltz to be played mit Schwung, which literally means "with swing," but of a far different variety. The last sound we hear is a snarling, augmented "joke" chord.

It was for Ezra Pound's significant other, the American violinist Olga Rudge, that Antheil composed the Second Sonata for Violin, Piano, and Drum. The work was premiered at the Salle du Conservatoire in December 1923 and bears the dedication "For Ezra Pound, best of friends." Copland describes how Pound "with his striking red beard much in evidence, passionately turned pages." Pound was said to have played the drum part in the coda, although the latter claim is probably apocryphal.[25]

According to Charles Amirkhanian, the Second Sonata is written in what Antheil called his "synthesized jazz idiom," a style of composition reminiscent of the work of the then-unknown Charles Ives that quotes other works.[26] Violinist Charles Castleman and pianist (and drummer) Randall Hodgkinson opened our Carnegie Hall concert with the Second Sonata.[27] The "quotations" that I am able to identify include "By the Shade of the Old Apple Tree," Debussy's Rêverie, "Come Back to Sorrento," "Silver Threads among the Gold," and the aforementioned "Oh My Baby."

The work ends quietly with an evocative reference to the tune that made an enormous impression on the thousands who flocked to the Midway Plaisance in the summer of 1893. Over a haunting havanaise drum rhythm (dada-dada-dada-dada), the violin plays scraps of the pervasive "Hootchy Kootchy," transporting us not only back to the fair, but also to the veiled danse du ventre of Tunisia in North Africa, one of Antheil's favorite vacation spots.

Antheil also brought to Carnegie Hall his String Quartet no. 1. It was first performed at a private concert titled "Musique Americaine (Declaration of Independence)" and presented by "M. et Mme. Ezra Pound" at the Salle Pleyel on July 7, 1924. Olga Rudge (presumably Mme. Pound) was the first violinist on the quartet. Also on the program was a repeat of Antheil's

Drum Sonata and two pieces by Pound, "Fiddle Music" and "Strophes de Villon."

At our re-creation concert, the Mendelssohn String Quartet[28] played Antheil's quartet most earnestly. Like myself, they must have been greatly confused by the music, which struck me as parody—a work that had been composed by an ungifted academician trying to impress his colleagues, tongue-in-cheeky, mildly modern, and frankly boring, unlike any other work of Antheil's I have ever heard, seen, or read about. In a letter to his American patron Mary Louise Curtis Bok,[29] founder of the Curtis Institute in Philadelphia, Antheil explained the idea behind his new quartet:

> It is very radical—and it will surprise and perhaps offend you by its desperate banality. But it is the banality of Picasso I hope, or a Matisse. It sounds exactly like a third rate string orchestra in Budapest trying to harmonize . . . mongrel Hungarian . . . themes—but doing it with a . . . brilliant success. (November 15, 1924)

I visited with Olga Rudge in June of 1987 at her home in Venice. She was then spry and lucid at ninety-three years of age. Rudge's small two-story house, located in the "English" district, off the Guidecca Canal, was a veritable museum, archive, and shrine to Pound, who had died there in 1972. A larger-than-life-sized plaster head of the poet, a copy of the white marble "Hieratic Head" by Henri Gaudier-Brzeska, dominated the sitting room.

I asked about the violin sonatas Antheil composed for her. "Why, they're around here somewhere," she replied. Without a second's pause she jumped up on the daybed and began opening overhead drawers and pulling down valises; I was encouraged to sort through stacks of paper in the attic. Holographs of the Second and Third Sonatas did turn up, as well as one for unaccompanied solo violin, and some Antheil letters and reviews. She kindly allowed me to have them all photocopied.

I found no music in the attic, only a pile of old newspapers emblazoned with anti-Semitic and anti-black headlines. They had been mailed to Pound in Venice from America. Apparently Pound's reputed remorse over his pro-Axis broadcasts during World War II was for public consumption. The editor of T. S. Eliot's poem *The Waste Land* had comforted himself with racist trash in his last days.

Rudge described Antheil in the 1920s as "too funny, very small, with a well scrubbed face . . . looked like a virgin choirboy or schoolgirl." She quoted then dismissed what must have been an Antheil epithet, "'Young American in Montparnasse'—a good piece of advertising set up by Ezra," poking fun at Pound's characterization of Antheil as "America's answer to Stravinsky."

Rudge preferred talking about her own career and the famous people she knew: the Russian aristocrat Madame Boulanger, who "kept those two girls [Lily and Nadia] in order"; playing Schumann sonatas with the American heiress De Polignac in Venice ("she sent her gondolier around to carry my violin case . . . Stravinsky entered to turn pages"); playing Beethoven, Mozart, and Veracini for Mussolini in Rome on the via Rasella ("he liked to talk English").[30] To my surprise, Rudge had little memory of Antheil's *Ballet Mécanique* and its glamorous Paris premiere even though Pound was its godfather.

I would have better luck back in New York that fall (1987) interviewing three octogenarian pianists who had played in the *Ballet Mécanique* performance in 1927. With the Manhattan phone book and an old Local 802 union directory, I located them in a matter of minutes.

Madeline Marshall, age eighty-seven, remembered "a lot of nonsense" and the audience throwing paper airplanes toward the stage. I pressed her for more, but she dismissed me as she did the music.

Stephanie Shehagovitch, age ninety-one, remembered dancing with Paul Robeson at the party following the concert. Antheil's music "was foreign to us . . . we grew up on Bach and Beethoven. . . . It was unwieldy, it was difficult for the aeroplane [propeller] people to find their entry." Her remark confirmed my impression that the "mechanical effects" people were not reading musicians. "There were strange lapses . . . an unholy mess." Shehagovitch remembered that the renowned pianist Walter Gieseking came to the Baldwin Piano Factory during a rehearsal. After listening for a few moments, he commented, "I wish you much pleasure," and left.

Marion Morrey (Mrs. Adel Richter), age eighty-four, had the most vivid memory of all:

It was easy [rehearsing] with Goossens, not with Antheil. Gieseking and Hindemith visited rehearsals. . . . The battery was from the Philharmonic. Antheil played "in the pit [*sic*]." But I could not hear the Pianola. There are influences from "The Rite of Spring" . . . boiled down. It was played well. [There was] no disturbance or laughing during performance. We played to the end with a flourish!

Marion Morrey on the aftermath:

It was a one-time stunt. . . . The piece dropped from sight. The *New York World* called it "a quiet day in any Russian family." We all went to the Deauville nightclub afterwards. There were many celebs . . . brilliant blacks, Paul Robeson, and Madame Walker. It was spectacular!

She told me she had once given a talk at Cornell University and was able to play excerpts from memory. I could have kissed her when she sang to me the rag theme, "Oh My Baby." Madeline Morrey and her old beau, Richard P. Snow, who attended the 1927 performance, sat in aisle seats at ours.

The *Ballet Mécanique* takes twenty-seven minutes to perform, too long for a single piano roll. It is perforce divided into three sections by short pauses—while the spent roll is rewound from off the receiving spool and a new roll is inserted. "Oh My Baby" (**Dah Dah** da **Dah**) dominates the first roll, but another jaunty ragtime tune, for solo Pianola, interposes itself shortly after the opening rush of glittering sounds. "Oh My Baby" appears again in roll two and at the beginning of the third roll, where the ragtime tune is transformed into a demonic solo cadenza.

A series of "minimalist" ostinato passages appears at the end of the first roll. These were apparently meant to accompany looped images in the film, an idea of Murphy's. The film shows a washerwoman gaining the top of a tall set of Paris street steps, then "cuts back" repeatedly, and we see her climbing again and again. Another loop shows a girl on a swing. Antheil's music cuts back as well. During several of these minimalist ostinatos, Antheil subtly shifts the time frame for a subgroup of instruments, an orchestra within the orchestra, sending it off on its own metric voyage, a device we normally associate with Varèse and Ives.

In a letter to the music critic and encyclopedist Nicolas Slonimsky on July 21, 1936, Antheil proffered an unusually clear description of his conception:

> I personally consider that the *Ballet Mécanique* was important in one particular . . . that it was conceived in a new form, that form specifically being the rolling out of a certain time canvas with musical abstractions and sound material composed and contrasted against one another with the thought of time values rather than tonal values. . . . I used time as Picasso might have used the blank spaces of his canvas. I did not hesitate, for instance, to repeat one measure one hundred times; I did not hesitate to have absolutely nothing on my piano rolls for sixty-two bars [Antheil is referring to 62 eighth-note rests, over twenty seconds in real time]; I did not hesitate to ring a bell against a certain given section of time or indeed to do whatever I pleased to do with the time canvas as long as each part of it stood up against the other.[31]

Antheil complains that he "was completely misunderstood by those morons who listened to the *Ballet Mécanique* in 1927," meaning the Carnegie Hall critics, conveniently forgetting his own collusion in the circus atmosphere that prevented serious listening. Yet there could have been method in his madness.

I for one find it hard to imagine that the composer would have invested so much care and thought into a work that was simply to be sacrificed for a brief, if blazing, moment of fame. There are those who would admire a revolutionary aesthetic that requires such elaborate sacrifice; for such people the event is the work of art. On the other hand, here I am more than seventy years later still studying, performing, and writing about the man and his music. I am intrigued by Antheil, and so were Morton Gould and John Cage, who attended our dress rehearsals.

In fact, an elaborate sacrifice *is* dramatized in the closing moments of the piece when, after a fiendish cadenza, the Pianola—the machine—breaks down. Antheil may very well have borrowed this notion from his Third Piano Sonata, *Death of Machines* (1923). The Pianola stutters and becomes stuck on a single phrase repeated over and over again: a trill and leaping clusters, followed by a moment of silence. As the "machine" winds down, the phrase is stretched out even more, and Antheil introduces increasingly longer silences. According to Slonimsky, this is the first time in the history of Western music that silence is used as an integral part of a musical composition. Antheil did offer his own explanation in a letter written to Ezra Pound the very month of his Carnegie Hall concert:

> The *Ballet Mécanique*: here I stopped. Here was the dead line, the brink of the precipice. Here at the end of this composition where in long stretches no single sound occurs and time itself acts as music; here was the ultimate fulfillment of my poetry; here I had time moving without touching it.[32]

To my relief, our audience got the idea and did not interrupt the twenty-second-long silence with applause. *Ballet Mécanique* ends with a final paroxysm. The ensemble builds to a huge climax. The siren peaks, and the last sounds we hear, a final burst of the ragtime lick "Oh My Baby" hangs in the air like spent fireworks.

Once I had the piano rolls in hand and had found Rex Lawson, the re-creation of the 1926–27 Paris–New York *Ballet Mécanique* went quite smoothly. The Baldwin Piano Company was happy to provide us with nine concert grands (one for Lawson's Pianola), especially after I told them that Baldwins were used in 1927. Our eight pianists and six xylophonists were given their parts in advance, and we came together for section rehearsals that went without a hitch. Lawson flew in from London with his Pianola (made c. 1911 in Meriden, Connecticut) crated safely in the cargo bay, and as soon as he was squared away we had a maestro-soloist rehearsal.

By this time I had learned to follow the Pianola music from the Randy Herr tape, but it was like holding on to a kite in a hurricane. With Lawson able to control speed and nuance, the Pianola music became far more coherent, and when we rehearsed with the rest of the orchestra, the piece quickly came together.

Different challenges were posed by the eleven pitches of electric bells and the enigmatic "aeroplane propellers." It seemed impossible to assemble electric bells with the specific pitches that the score called for; then I came across a 1927 newspaper photograph of Antheil demonstrating his electric bells before the concert. He had settled for a rack of six randomly pitched doorbells of different sizes, each with its own button—about all one can still find in a well-stocked hardware store—and I had them replicated. That left the "aeroplane propellers."

How does a propeller sound? The best propeller substitute Antheil could devise in 1927 was a huge hand-cranked ratchet the size of a beer barrel and a whirring electric fan with a leather strap held across its blades. (His 1952 revised version calls for recorded airplane sounds.) For our re-creation, the electric fan and strap idea was vetoed by the Carnegie Hall staff as too dangerous. I was not about to disappoint the critics and those who read about Antheil's "aeroplane propellers" in the history books. So we had a scenic shop design a mount for a huge, *real* wooden propeller that activated a ratchet. This contraption was twirled at appropriate points in the score by our prop man and percussionist, Ted Sommer, for its visual effect. Meanwhile Ted concentrated his efforts on an assortment of hand-held ratchets according to cues in the music.

Several of the ideas Antheil conceived for his *Ballet Mécanique* were ahead of their time. For example, his first notion, to have sixteen pianos playing simultaneously from one set of rolls, can be accomplished today with computerized player pianos.[33] When it came time to record, I was finally able to fulfill Antheil's unusual requirements for "aeroplane propellers" and pitched electric bells thanks to Gordon Gottlieb, a master percussionist with computer-age skills. He digitally "sampled" several electric bells, then connected—the new verb is "MIDIed"—them to a keyboard. Gordon did the same for the aeroplane propellers again by sampling recorded sounds of vintage aircraft. We could start and stop the propeller sounds instantly, and they could be produced in three pitch ranges. At the mixing sessions I played, via the keyboard, onto open tracks—they ran parallel with the "live," already-recorded instrumental tracks—the exact pitches of electric bells and fistfuls of idling asthmatic aeroplane motors, or an entire airfleet cruising and climbing. With the passage of more than fifty years, computer technology made possible Antheil's machine-age conceptions.

Antheil, who came to New York fully expecting he would repeat the triumphs of his concerts in Europe, never fully recovered from the disappointment of his Carnegie Hall debut. He returned to Paris "heartsick and broke." He began to see himself as the "bad boy of music"[34] and in time moved to Hollywood, where he wrote film music and did magazine articles — endocrinology and lonely-hearts letters were among his areas of expertise — but he also taught composition privately.[35]

Antheil's iconoclastic ideas and music furnish an unforeseen counterpoint to the "Dvořák to Duke Ellington" story. It was the brilliant and brittle instrument of ragtime, the piano, not the intoxicating effect of syncopation against a steady beat nor the seductions of jazz harmony, that occupied his genius. In ragtime Antheil found the material for one of the most unusual works of the century; meanwhile he developed on his own an aesthetic that links him with Ives, Cage, and Morton Feldman rather than with his contemporaries Gershwin and Ellington.

I wish I could say that my disinterment and exact realization of the original Paris–New York *Ballet Mécanique* led to a revised evaluation of the work. The critics who attended wrote differing opinions. Bill Zakariasen's impression: "Whether 'Ballet Mécanique' is music or not is debatable, but it's certainly fun" was countered by Tim Page's: "One of those works of art that is more fun to hear *about* than they are to actually hear." Allan Kozinn in the *New York Times* found it derivative of Stravinsky and Varèse, yet "not without sequel; its angular, mechanistic and repetitive xylophone and piano lines foreshadow some of Steve Reich's music." Susan Elliot, writing in the *New York Post*, agreed: "The work's use of pulsation, its slow harmonic movement and ever-so-subtly shifting meters would suggest that it was Antheil, not Reich or Terry Riley, who invented minimalism."[36]

For now though, the "happening" continues to eclipse the music.

14

Bernstein's *Mass*

My most vivid image of Leonard Bernstein is a 1956 film clip of him conducting the New York Philharmonic in the old Lewisohn Stadium, accompanying Louis Armstrong in W. C. Handy's "Saint Louis Blues"—two happy souls swinging in perfect harmony before the sweltering masses of New Yorkers who completed the equation. The Stadium Concerts took place on a Harlem hillside surrounded by the campuses of City College and the High School of Music and Art. It was a time when all three exuded optimism and opportunity.[1] The stadium could accommodate 7,500 people, and there were many more who "listened for free" while leaning on pillows from their tenement windows. Through the power of music, Bernstein and Armstrong turned that disparate human mass into a congregation, a transformation I have sensed most particularly in jazz clubs. In the words of the black social historian Gerald Early, "where else have the races really come together, really syncretized their feeling?"[2]

A like melding almost always occurs when I conduct one of Bernstein's love-in finales, what he once described to me as "a Jewish ending . . . everyone gets a girl." No matter the cruel, unpredictable world of earthquakes, autos-da-fé, and betrayals that constantly greet Candide's optimism; the meaningless murder of Tony in the insane, unending gang wars of *West Side Story*; the Celebrant/Priest of *Mass* driven mad by the very same community that loved and exalted him; the destruction of innocence in the *Chichester Psalms*—in each instance Bernstein ends a tragic tale with a paean of hope:

"Make your garden grow," "There's a place for us," "Almighty Father incline Thine ear," "Hi Neh Maatov voo ma nahim" ("How good it is when we live together as brothers"). In each instance he calls forth the power of music on behalf of universal peace.

Bernstein changed my life. When I first met Bernstein, I was in no way even remotely heading toward the musical career I have since enjoyed. He became for me, over the next two decades, my model, my mentor, and my friend. When he heard about my father's death, Lenny sent a telegram in phonetic Hebrew: "Y'heh sh'meh rab-bo m'vorach. . . ." It was the congregational response to the mourner's kaddish. He would symbolically be by my side when I recited this prayer reaffirming my faith in the face of death.

I was naive enough to think I could count on this kind of concern forever. In time I realized the impossibility of his ever being a "father" to my "devoted son." My real father gave me the gift of music on his Arabic oud. Lenny, who often referred to me as his "without whom," could depend on my energizing any project he assigned. In turn, he opened the door to a musical world I grew up believing beyond my reach.

Lenny was in his Fairfield, Connecticut, studio working on his *Kaddish* Symphony, which was originally intended to honor his father ("while he's still alive!") when the awful news came about the assassination of the president in Dallas. He immediately changed its dedication to John F. Kennedy. The Bernsteins knew the Kennedys. Miss Helen Coates spoke of play dates between their children, and I remember Lenny's mischievous story about a dinner party at the Kennedy White House: "Stravinsky fell asleep in his soup, and we all went upstairs to dance the twist!"

In the spring of 1964 I traveled up from my post in Texas to attend Lenny's rehearsals, performances, and recording sessions of his *Kaddish* Symphony with the New York Philharmonic.[3] The work was huge and complicated: two choirs, extra-large orchestra, soprano soloist, and narrator. I left fired up with the idea that my Texas orchestra and Texan choirs must perform the work on, or close to, the first anniversary of the Kennedy tragedy.

I hoped that Felicia Montealegre, who narrated the New York performances, would do the same in Corpus Christi, but according to her manager at Columbia Artists, she was "unavailable." My guess is she was probably skeptical about what might happen in the wilds of south Texas. And so we engaged, in her place, Patricia Neway, who had made a distinguished career as a singer—she created the role of Magda Sorel in Menotti's opera *The Consul*—but by that time she was appearing more often as a dramatic actress. The work required a big concert choir, and ours came from North Texas State University, near Dallas. I formed and trained a children's choir in Corpus

Christi. Like the city, it was a vibrant mix of brown-skinned Mexican and "Anglo" kids and included my daughter Lorca. Hearing them sing the complicated rhythms, in Hebrew, by heart, their trusting eyes never leaving me, is one of my treasured memories. The performance, on November 16, 1964, was our own Texas kaddish for Kennedy, and it was transcendent.

Lenny and Felicia were, for obvious reasons, curious to hear the tape of our performance. We listened to it together while lying on rugs in front of the fire in the library of their Park Avenue penthouse apartment.

My tenure as assistant conductor with the New York Philharmonic had been shared with the impressively solid and steady John Canarina, who charmed everyone with his droll sense of humor and impressed even Bernstein with his encyclopedic knowledge of repertoire and conductors, and Seiji Ozawa, a doll-like, young, and brilliant talent from Japan who captivated everyone. It was hard to be noticed. But my Texas performance of *Kaddish* got Lenny's undivided attention. He began to call on me to conduct his music—*Candide* in Chicago, *West Side Story* at Lincoln Center. He also recommended me for the co-directorship of a fascinating music and dance pilot project for the Bureau of Indian Affairs. And eventually, he asked me to be his assistant conductor for the world premiere of *Mass*.

In the early spring of 1971 I was passing through Vienna on my way to Regensburg for a guest conducting stint. Lenny was conducting *Der Rosenkavalier* at the Vienna State Opera. I visited him at the Hotel Sacher, where he was staying in a suite that Gustav Mahler is said to have used. The sitting room was dominated by a huge Bösendorfer piano. On its rack was some manuscript paper. A double window looked out over the Kärntnerstrasse and the opera house where, in the love-'em-and-leave-'em scenario that Vienna thrives on, Mahler triumphed and crashed.

It was Passover eve, April 9, and while Lenny was on the phone in the next room, trying to get me a place at the Israeli Consulate's seder table, I started quietly singing and playing from the manuscript. It was a song about a tree, delicate and sad.[4] "That's beautiful!" I said when he came back. He crossed his fingers, revealing a Lenny I had not yet known—afraid, unsure, curious about this thing he wrote, as if it had a life of its own. He said he didn't know if it was lovely as of yet. "We'll see. I'm writing a Mass . . . for Kennedy."

A few months passed. Lenny asked me to direct another *Candide*-to-end-all-*Candides* production, my fourth.

The saga of *Candide*, a score in search of a libretto, is summed up in a remark made to me by Virgil Thomson. I spent a memorable evening alone with him at a little French restaurant in the West Thirties. He was close to ninety. Nevertheless he insisted on walking back home to Twenty-third

Street, tripping over what seemed to be every curb on Eighth Avenue and catching himself just in time. The conversation got around to *Candide*, and I mentioned that the poet John Latouche had worked on it. Virgil stopped his teeter-tottering long enough to cackle, "*Everyone* worked on *Candide*. It didn't help."

Candide, the musical, has stubbornly remained in limbo ever since Lillian Hellman withdrew her book following the show's short run on Broadway. She believed the hard-hitting political satire she adapted from Voltaire had been turned into a soft tits-and-ass entertainment. The optimism and hope of the grand finale, "Make Your Garden Grow" (and grow . . . and grow . . .), was the final straw. She read Voltaire's message quite differently; for Hellman, "Make Your Garden Grow" meant: Go off, find a quiet place, and don't expect too much from a world that is inevitably going to disappoint and push you down, yet again. Yes, Lenny's music was ravishing, his best to date, but Hellman would not be swayed beyond allowing the few lyrics she had contributed to stay. Lenny had a master score and no book.

There were some concert performances and a tour "package"—a narrator telling the Voltaire story while a small cast, accompanied by two pianos, sang the delicious send-ups of Rossini, Puccini, and Gilbert and Sullivan. Meanwhile the "Overture to *Candide*" became one of the most frequently performed American works for orchestra. This was the status of *Candide* when Gordon Davidson and I found a way of putting it back on stage in 1966.

Gordon and I met on Broadway a few years earlier. I was playing trumpet in a stage band, and Gordon was second assistant stage manager for Norman Corwin's *The Rivalry*, a dramatization of the Lincoln-Douglas debates.[5] We struck up a friendship and became a director-conductor team, mostly doing operas together: *The Barrier* in New York in 1961 (libretto by Langston Hughes and music by Jan Meyerowitz, both of whom attended the performances), and *Carmen*, *La Bohème*, and *Così fan tutte* in Corpus Christi.

I had permission from Lenny to do a concert staging of *Candide* in Corpus Christi for the 1965–66 season. Gordon was of course going to direct. But the Corpus Christi Symphony was going through a down phase in the usual feast-or-famine cycle that most small American orchestras experience. The prospective *Candide* was canceled, but fate stepped in and more than made up for our loss.

Gordon had been engaged to direct a summer season of plays at the University of California, Los Angeles. We went to Bernstein for permission to do *Candide* in Los Angeles instead of Texas. No sooner did he give us his blessing than he blurted out, "Don't tell Uncle Lillian."

Lenny was genuinely excited. He presented us with his "Pandora's box" —music written for *Candide* that had not made it into the Broadway show.

Perhaps some of it would help flesh out our "concert version," which is what the first Los Angeles *Candide* would officially be called, even though it was tacitly understood that Gordon intended to let the piece "evolve." There would be some dancing and a unit set.

It was a miraculous summer—a grownup version of Mickey and Judy putting on an instant musical. Carroll O'Connor, for whom the character of Archie Bunker in *All in the Family* was still in the future, played the three roles of Pangloss, Martin, and the Narrator—optimist, pessimist, and Voltaire himself. O'Connor and the stage designer, Peter Wexler, worked with Gordon on a new script based upon Voltaire. They tried to work around Hellman's book but inevitably a little slipped in, especially some left-leaning in-jokes. Wexler's wife, Connie, did the costumes.

The "Pandora's box" contained several treasures, in particular the aria "Nothing More than This," which would strengthen the role of Candide. Candide searches endlessly for a world of peace and harmony and for his childhood love, the beautiful and pure Cunegonde. (Like those of Pangloss and Candide, her name is wordplay reflecting her true character, in this case, a "grand vagina.") When Candide finally realizes that he has been chasing a dream, the aria "Nothing More than This" expresses his anger and bitterness. Everyone was doing three jobs at once. I orchestrated and copied the new material myself, including "Nothing More than This."

Lenny flew out a few days before the opening. I picked him up at the airport. He was dressed in a white linen suit. As we drove to the hotel, he reminisced about his Hollywood days working on the film score for *On the Waterfront*, his time with "Bogey and Bacall" (Humphrey Bogart and Lauren Bacall). He insisted on serving me my "last supper" before the dress rehearsal, putting on the room service waiter's apron and a Russian accent.

The first Los Angeles *Candide* was a big success.[6] At the time, planning for the Los Angeles Music Center was underway, and our *Candide* production played no small part in Gordon Davidson's appointment as the artistic director of its resident drama company, the Center Theater Group at the Mark Taper Forum. He has since made an immense contribution to the American theater.[7]

Five years (and three *Candides*) later, in the summer of 1971, I was back in Los Angeles working on a new *Candide*-to-end-all-*Candides* that was scheduled for a cross-country tour. If this lavish production, with a new book by Sheldon Patinkin and choreography by Michael Smuin, passed muster with New York producers, *Candide* would continue on to Broadway, its first reappearance there since its short-lived but glorious succès d'estime in 1956.[8]

Bernstein was also in Los Angeles, ostensibly to oversee the new *Candide*, but he was mostly hard at work in what he called his "*Mass* factory," set up in two poolside cottages at the Beverly Hills Hotel. What had been mostly an idea only six months earlier, when I spied one of Lenny's sketches on the piano rack in Vienna, was about to go into production.

Gordon Davidson was on the *Mass* team, as were the composer and lyricist Steve Schwartz and his partner, the writer John Michael-Tebelak, who together had created *Godspell*. Alvin Ailey flew in to discuss becoming the choreographer. Various candidates for musical assistant to Lenny came and went. And there I was doing another *Candide* and green with envy.

Just before the opening, we held a private run-through of the new *Candide* for Bernstein, followed by a production meeting with the directors and staff. Lenny gave us notes until well past two in the morning, mostly about the script. His few musical comments were about diction; his favorite "fix" was the introduction of an "OO" sound before "W," producing "OOWhere" instead of "air." Lenny grabbed me at the elevator: "We must talk." I had been up for hours getting the show scrubbed clean. "Lenny," I whined, "it's almost three a.m." "I need you on *Mass*," he whispered.

A week or so after *Candide* opened in Los Angeles, the musical direction of the show was turned over to my assistant conductor, Ross Reimuller, and I began working full time on *Mass*. Lenny explained my role: "We will be the two sides of a two-headed coin." We would share rehearsals, and I would take over after he conducted the opening gala performance in Washington, D.C.

No work of Bernstein's expresses his passion for universal reconciliation more dramatically than does *Mass*, composed for the grand opening of the John F. Kennedy Center for the Performing Arts in Washington, D.C., at the behest of Jacqueline Kennedy. The form is from Roman Catholic liturgy; the music is a kaleidoscopic voyage from Harlem to the Rhine.[9] In *Mass*, folksong, blues, marches, rock songs, black gospel, and jazz scat stand cheek by jowl with Mahlerian meditations for orchestra, Hebrew prayer, chamber music, Arabic dances, and a Chilean folk ballad. The characters are "street people," liturgical and children's choirs, rock and blues singers, and dancers and musicians of every stripe and style. The story follows the rise and fall of a young priest, a beloved leader—a metaphor for the ecstatic elevation and tragic death of the first Catholic president, John F. Kennedy. The time was "Vietnam."

I quickly learned the music Bernstein had already composed—it was mostly in sketch form—and went through it with Gordon. Even after several sessions with Lenny talking and playing through the work, Gordon was still searching for a dramatic line that would thread its way through the formal set pieces mandated by the Roman mass liturgy. John Michael-Tebelak, who had recast the Gospel of St. Matthew into *Godspell*, was there to help Bernstein as he searched for ways to transform the ancient ritual into musical theater. Bernstein sought out liberal Catholic scholars as well, including Daniel Berrigan, seeking information about obsolete or lesser-known elements of the mass, such as the kiss of peace, and additions, known as tropes, that could help fulfill his narrative.[10]

Once, after a long "listening" session, in exasperation and confusion one of us ventured the inevitable question: "What are three . . . four . . . nice Jewish boys doing, writing and working on a mass?" Lenny welcomed the question and took us through his own reasoning process: his search for an appropriate vehicle to inaugurate a new arts center named after our first Catholic president; the universal appeal of the mass, with its Roman, Greek, and Hebraic roots; and the possibilities it offered for dramatization. The choice, he said, seemed inevitable. Several times he said he was comfortable with not being able to find an explanation for everything—that one must accept, on faith, that there are mysteries that cannot be understood.

Bernstein outlined his dramatic concept for us. Like President Kennedy, the Celebrant—the central character and priestly leader of the mass—holds out hope for peace, yet he is struck down by his own followers. During the "Dona nobis pacem" section, which grows from ceremonial chant into an orgiastic rock-blues, all the well-established walls—between the rock and blues bands and the symphonic wind and brass players, between the street singers in blue jeans and the robed liturgical choir—are breached, and the stage is filled with a roiling mob. A pack of protesters corners the Celebrant, threatening and shouting, "Dona nobis pacem"—"Give us peace now, not later. Don't you know you were once our creator?"

Bernstein painted a picture of the final scene. The Celebrant shrieks "Pa-a-cem" ("Peace") and throws down the holy vessels. He is at once Christ being crucified and Moses smashing the tablets before the idolators. The frenzied dancing, the blues shouting, the instrumental wailings, and the attacking protesters are stopped cold. All fall to the ground, petrified. They watch in horror as the Celebrant goes mad. He dances on the sacred altar, stripping himself of all the encrustations of power his followers had heaped upon him. Pared down to his jeans and guitar strap, he goes to the rear of the bare stage and slams the door of the Kennedy Center as he shouts, "Fuck you and your War!" Lenny envisioned the scene on opening night for us: "the cast spread about the stage, and the audience, Nixon and the entire Congress of the United States, left sitting there, abandoned, stunned. And that's how the piece ends."

I knee-jerked, "Lenny, you can't do that!" He only smiled. And for the next two months I labored on *Mass* with blind faith, knowing no more of the story than what we had been told. I was convinced that Bernstein, not one to be behind the trends, would ask Alan Titus (cast as our Celebrant) to bolt out of the set stark naked, nakedness having invaded the opera world at the time.[11]

I went to Tanglewood to audition young musicians for the stage band. We needed no fewer than thirty-three players. They would enter from the audience as a brilliant marching band, playing, of all things, a strutting, happy Kyrie ("Lord, have mercy"). Over the next hour and a half they would subdivide, as the need arose, into blues and rock bands, a gospel street band, woodwind sextets and trios, churchy brass choirs, and/or big-band brass sections, all the while being integrated into the drama and never leaving the stage.

Putting only a few instrumentalists on stage for even a short scene means trouble. They have to be positioned so they can see the conductor and must somehow be provided with music stands and lights. They also need to be outfitted with costumes. I was expected to come back from Tanglewood with a list of young, attractive instrumental virtuosos of all races who moved well on stage. Bernstein had this recurring anxiety about a make-believe musician he named "Burt Silverman" schlepping across the stage with his trombone wearing one white and one brown sock. "Don't bring me back any Burt Silvermans," he admonished.

The elaborate stage band remains a challenge to be overcome. Two years after the Washington premiere I did a production of *Mass* for the Cincinnati May Festival. A few days after I arrived, I was told that the musicians' union had met and decreed that "there would be no marching, no lyres [with which to carry music], and no costumes." My response was, "Then there will be no *Mass*." The town was already in an uproar. A pastoral letter had been read in all of the area's Catholic churches the previous Sunday declaring the piece blasphemous and calling for a boycott. The Cincinnati Symphony, of course, sold out every ticket. I assumed that Nick Webster, the general manager, would find a way to solve the ministrike. But by some coincidence, he was out of town.[12]

By this time I had more than once experienced the emotional impact of *Mass* on its performers. I awaited the first *all' italiana* reading of the piece, when the various choirs and orchestras, all of whom were prepared and rehearsed separately, would come together for a first musical run-through. When the run-through ended, the members of the stage orchestra—the wind and percussion players of the Cincinnati Symphony—now surrounded by weeping choristers and street people, were themselves visibly moved. They agreed to march, carry lyres, and wear simple costumes. The first clarinetist even freed himself from his lyre, scratching out the notes for an important solo onto the stage floor so that it would appear to the audience as if he were making it up.

The "Mass factory" was moved from Los Angeles to New York for final casting. The company we were about to assemble would encompass a musical and human palette as diverse as America itself. We auditioned dozens of opera singers and Broadway belters for our Street Chorus. One day a young man, Tom Ellis, arrived wheeling along a speaker-amplifier. He plugged the power cord into a wall socket and pulled out a microphone. I grinned at his naiveté, thinking, "How does one make a Street Chorus out of 'mike' singers?" Bernstein was delighted. "After all," he said, "that's his instrument."

In our first production of *Mass* the Rock Singers, who come out of the Street Chorus, used hand-held, wire-cabled mikes for their solos, an image one associates with early rock singers. Ellis got the job. Like Ellis, every other singer in the Street Chorus had a solo turn somewhere in the show. One of our Street Singers, Louis St. Louis, serenaded us during lunch breaks with his gospel piano magic. That's probably how we discovered that Carl Hall, a member of the tenor section, was also a male falsettist, with the highest and most piercing soprano voice in the entire ensemble. Bernstein wrote a solo descant for him in the Confiteor (confession) sequence.[13]

Alvin Ailey's company of superb dancers, mostly African American, was spread throughout the cast. Seven Ailey dancers were cast as ceremonial "acolytes," led by Judith Jamison in the role of the High Priestess. The rest joined the Street Chorus. We soon had some of the Ailey dancers in the Street Chorus singing as well, thus creating an ensemble with a look and movement seldom seen on Broadway.

The Street Chorus carries the bulk of the nonliturgical vernacular text of *Mass*. They ask questions and make commentary and are the heart of the show. From mid-July to early August, the Street Chorus of twenty-two singers and sixteen dancers, the thirty-three-member stage band (with its subsets), the seven acolyte dancers, and the Celebrant, Alan Titus, rehearsed independently and together using several rooms and one huge ballroom in the Masonic Hotel, around the corner from the Ansonia on West Seventy-third Street.

Time was flying, and Lenny was still composing. He was forced to engage people to help orchestrate. One of my jobs was to distribute his sketch scores to various arrangers, principally Hershey Kay and Jonathan Tunick. I myself scored much of the Gloria before Bernstein took over.[14] I kept a check on the stage logistics for the various instrumental groupings before sending the orchestrations off to Arnold Arnstein, the master copyist. Lenny or Arnstein would send us a new section at the end of one day, and we would have it learned and "on its feet" the very next.

Arnstein was a beloved, respected, and feared character in the working lives of composers of Bernstein's generation, in particular Gian-Carlo Menotti,

Samuel Barber, and William Schuman. He had a foul mouth and loved catching these giants of American music in mistakes. Arnstein's "shop," where he supervised the copying of musical parts for *Mass*, was the modern equivalent of a medieval monastery. In the hushed, smoke-filled room, scriveners, bent over their inkpots, scratched out with Pennypoints on semi-transparent vellum paper the piano-vocal scores for the singers, dancers, and rehearsal pianists and the parts for the musicians in the pit, and, in the case of *Mass*, those onstage.

I was rarely able to get away from a visit to Arnstein's without his pulling down, from an endless shelf of oversized scores, some work by a celebrated living composer—Menotti was his victim of choice—and with his favorite epitaph, "How dumb can you get?," demonstrating how he, Arnstein, alone had rescued the piece from disaster and oblivion. He would also slip me pre-publication copies of works that I was interested in.

Arnstein distributed the music for *Mass* among the various forces that were spread about, now more than one hundred and fifty strong. The twenty-four members of the Berkshire Boys' Choir were learning their parts at their summer camp. The sixty-voice Scribner Chorale was hard at work in Washington. The New York contingent of seventy-eight dancers, singers, and musicians, three rehearsal pianists, and a large production staff gathered daily on Seventy-third Street. We all assembled in Washington the last two weeks of August to begin rehearsals on the stage of the Kennedy Center's new Opera House. Arnstein followed the caravans as well, setting up shop in the Howard Johnson Hotel, across from the Watergate, where he finished copying the parts for the Washington-based freelance pit orchestra of thirty-one string players, a harpist, five percussionists, and two organists—playing "Little Al" and "Big Al," Allen electronic organs—that would complete the musical forces for *Mass*.

Even with the help he was getting from the orchestrators, it became increasingly clear that Lenny couldn't be in two places at once. He had little time to spend with the larger company, but he did coach several of the soloists himself, in particular Alan Titus, the high baritone whose tall good looks, Prince Hal hairstyle, innocent demeanor, and sweet, unforced voice destined him to sing the role of the Celebrant.

Lenny once told me that his ideal heroic male voice was a baritone, closer to the range of the natural speaking voice and capable of producing clearer diction than the artificially extended and cultivated tenor voice. But there is a catch. Lenny's baritone, like Alan Titus, must be capable of delivering a ringing high note, such as the Celebrant's high A in *Mass*, or Tony's B-flat in *West Side Story*.[15]

Besides finding time to coach Titus and others, Bernstein still had the final scene to complete and the orchestrations for all of the Sanctus, the Dona nobis pacem, and the final scene, which he had reserved for himself. With a work so large and complex, the conventional wisdom that the composer of a new music-theater work, no matter how skilled as an orchestrator or conductor, remain "in the house" during the final stages of production was bound to prevail.

When I was given the awesome, delicious task of conducting this massive structure on opening night, of being its heartbeat, of being Lenny,[16] I surely felt prepared. *Mass* had been filtered drop by drop into my ear, brain, and body. My journeyman days were over. I was about to enter the world stage. "Somebody, quick! Break a glass! My fifteen minutes of fame are about to begin!"

The announcement that I would conduct appeared on the front page of the *New York Times* on Labor Day. We were opening on September 8. Lenny was now free to fine-tune the lighting, diction, and especially the sound balance during our final rehearsals.

We were constantly mixing live and amplified sounds. The Celebrant and all the solo singers wore wireless body mikes, newly introduced on Broadway. And there were the ubiquitous hand mikes for the rock singers who sang along with the rock band, which had its own highly electrified sound system.

Once something or someone on stage is amplified, every other aural element is at risk, and *Mass* was, for all intents and purposes, a sound-enhanced production. Transitions from enhanced to acoustic sound hopefully went unnoticed, and both were perceived as "live." But sometimes the contrast between live sound and patently electric sound was used by Lenny to make a dramatic statement, as, for example, in the opening sequence, which had musical-political overtones.

Mass opens with the house in total blackness. Disorienting sounds begin to spew from four speakers that surround the audience.[17] Running at painful levels, each speaker in turn blasts out a different twelve-tone Kyrie for voice and percussion. When all four Kyries are going full force, lights pierce the blackness to reveal the Celebrant, who, with a single stroke on his folk guitar, wipes out the mad cacophony. Following this acoustic miracle, the Celebrant sings the gentle "A Simple Song": "Sing God a simple song / Lauda, Laude" to the accompaniment of muted strings and harp, with quiet comments from his guitar and a magical solo flute.

At once Bernstein silences the enemy—overamplified twelve-tone aleatoric (chance) music—with live folk-rock song. Decadent art, replicated by Bernstein with mocking mastery, is vanquished by the even more skillfully conceived and crafted rock-based "simple" song.

At the last New York run-through, Bernstein and Alan Titus unveiled a surprise. I was looking forward to showing Lenny how well we were doing. But he had been holed up for days in his studio, composing away with his favorite Blackwing pencils, and could not wait to get his hands on his piece. And so, he took over the rehearsal, rather abruptly, I felt. Fortunately, John Corigliano Jr. was there and, sizing up the situation, took me for a quick walk to cool me down. Lenny turned the stick back over to me as the Dona nobis pacem approached, the moment when everything is about to come apart and the Celebrant is threatened. Soon the room was ablaze, and the cast was singing and dancing their protest to the band's ten bar rock-blues:

We're fed up with your heavenly silence,
And we only get action with violence,
So if we can't have the world we desire,
Lord, we'll have to set this one on fire!
Dona nobis, Dona nobis.

We reached the end of our music and Alan Titus, the Celebrant, cried out "PA . . . CEM! PA . . . CEM!! PA . . . CEM!!!" and feigned throwing down the holy vessels. Lenny was at the piano. He told the cast to drop to the floor where they stood, and for the first time all of us—singers, dancers, musicians, staff, directors—heard and lived through Fraction, the mad scene, which Lenny and Alan had been rehearsing in secret. The Celebrant roars at and pleads, with the cast members lying closest to him, with God. He exhausts himself completely in a dazzling cadenza, a collage of fragments from all the music we have heard, ranging over two and a half octaves and ending in a babble of Latin, Hebrew, English, and solfeggio wordplay: "ad Dominum, ad Dom...Adonai—don't know—I don't no-bis . . . Miserere no-bis . . . Mi-se . . . mi [this on the note E—mi in solfeggio] . . . Mi alone is only me . . . But mi . . . with so [on the note G—sol]. . . ."

The Celebrant has lost his mind, his voice, and his soul, and with his last breath he keens a dirge: "Oh, I suddenly feel every step I've ever taken / And my legs are lead . . . Oh . . . How easily things get broken." Lenny struck the final deep polychord (A major and C minor), which slowly faded into silence as the Celebrant, our own Alan Titus, walked out of the rehearsal area and left us all splayed on the floor. Like the others, I asked myself, "What have we done? What now?"

We found out in Washington, when Bernstein began, almost grudgingly, to part with the final section of Mass, his "Secret Songs," which breathed a bereft, leaderless, and fractured community back into life. In retrospect I realize that this manipulation of the company was Bernstein's way of protecting his message of peace from the inevitable criticism of the pessimists, the Voltaires and Martins, of this world.

In the theater, at the end of Fraction the Celebrant makes his catatonic descent into the orchestra pit—no slamming of doors or flinging of curses at Congress—and the deep polychord fades ever so slowly into silence. Lenny implored me to hold the silence as long as I dared—"You'll know when!"

A querulous flute breaks the silence, recalling an earlier moment: the mirror image of the desolation we feel, the moment of Epiphany, when the entire *Mass* community had first assembled and, pleased with itself, sang together the "Almighty Father . . . Bless us and all who have gathered here . . ." and then listened as a solo oboe, from everywhere and nowhere, sounded (over the four speakers) a cadenza, an Epiphany.

This time the music of Epiphany is sounded by a lone flutist, who raises himself from where he was lying on the lip of the stage. The flute's last note is picked up by a child soprano: "Sing God a secret song / Lauda, Laude." It is the first of the "Secret Songs," symbolizing the kiss of peace. A harp joins the flute. The child passes the "kiss" in turn to a bass-baritone, thence to a woman. Chains of "Lauda, Laude" canons begin to form. The orchestra too begins to filter in. The cast joins, helping each other up, joining the "Lauda, Laude," one by one, two by two. Their rebirth gathers energy and power. As the music subsides, bassoonist and dancer, French horn player and Street Singer are massed together downstage before the audience, forming a rainbow of humanity. We hear the last "Lauda, Laude" sung from one side of the rainbow by the unseen Celebrant and echoed from the other by an unseen child. The mantle has been passed. The cycle can now begin anew. Bernstein puts forth the hope that one of these voyages of faith will transport us to true peace and redemption. As the final notes of the child and the Celebrant float away, the cast sings, "Almighty Father, incline thine ear: / Bless us and all who have gathered here— / thine angel send us— / Who shall defend us all; / And fill with grace / All who dwell in this place. Amen." The lights dim and we hear a voice, Lenny's voice (on tape): "The Mass is ended; go in Peace."[18]

The first bringing together of all the elements of the production—the onstage cast, choirs, and bands, and the pit orchestra with costumes, sound, and lights—was at a dress rehearsal for an invited audience that included members of the United States Congress. At the end of the first-ever *Mass*, the members of the company, and many in the audience, were shattered, in tears. The sadness and sense of loss—for the Celebrant, for our innocence, for John Kennedy—was palpable. That night Ted Kennedy came down the aisle to the pit to thank us. He was deeply moved.

Every one of the six productions I have worked on has produced this emotional reaction. *Mass* proves to be greater than the sum of its parts. Because the elements are perforce assembled only for an actual performance, the cast itself has no idea how deeply they will be affected. A large part of the power of *Mass* comes because the audience witnesses those onstage discovering their loss and confusion and giving themselves to the kiss of peace.

Lenny wanted to pass the kiss of peace into the audience. The choirboys were told to fan out, touch a few of those sitting on the aisles, and say, "The kiss of peace, pass it on." The conceit was that the kiss of peace would pass through the audience and hence into the world. We tried it during one of the previews. I can still see Lenny, who had gradually become possessed by *Mass*, a huge Coptic cross dangling from around his neck, as he showed the boys how to "pass it on." Many in the audience shrank from their touch. His final gesture toward universal redemption was abandoned.

President Richard Nixon, though invited, did not attend the opening night. According to columnist Jack Anderson, it was J. Edgar Hoover who enjoined Nixon not to attend:

> On July 12, 1971, Hoover wrote to White House major-domo H. R. Haldeman and Attorney General John Mitchell, warning of "proposed plans of antiwar elements to embarrass the United States Government." Composer Leonard Bernstein, Hoover correctly reported was composing a mass. . . . Daniel Berrigan had been asked to write the Latin verse to be sung to Lenny's music. "The source advised the words will follow an antiwar theme," he said. "Important Government officials, perhaps even the President, are expected to attend this ceremony and it is anticipated they will applaud the composition without recognizing the true meaning of the words." The source said the newspapers would be given the story the following day that "the President and other high ranking Government officials applauded an anti-government song." Possibly because of Hoover's hysterics, President Nixon missed what the audience and critics thought was a superb performance.[19]

Was the poolside cottage of the Beverly Hills Hotel bugged when Lenny pronounced the Celebrant's so-called exit line, "Fuck you and your War!"?

Mass calls for the literal massing together of a universe of music and musicians in the cause of peace. Its sheer size is mesmerizing. Yet in 1973 Gordon Davidson and I did a scaled-down version at the Mark Taper Theater in Los Angeles. We dubbed it "Mini-*Mass*." And for some cast members, the magic, the message of universal peace, faded after several performances. In this more intimate format—eight instrumentalists onstage, three offstage, twelve singers, three dancers, small children's choir, and liturgical choir—it was more play than pageant.

Actors ask questions, and when Bernstein came to see it, he had a sit-down with the company. Several of the performers expressed their frustration with the ending. There was a leap of faith that some of them, in good conscience, could not take. And they found themselves having to *act* the emotion at the end. They still hungered for peace in our time, but not a big hugfest. Bernstein listened. Hard. He came up with an alternative ending: an expression of doubt, a fragment borrowed from the Epistle section, "The Word of the Lord," which was to be sung by one of the doubters in the cast just before we hear Bernstein's voice intone the "go in Peace" benediction. One night we put it into the show, but it felt awkward, like an "add-on," and was dropped. I have Lenny's holograph sketch. The text reads:

> So we wait in silent treason until reason is restored
> and we wait for the season of the Word of the Lord.

15

Duke Ellington

There will one day come a black Beethoven, burned to the
bone by the African sun.
—WILL MARION COOK, from interview of Mercer Cook
    by Josef Skvorecky

For my teenage dance combo, the Starlighters, I wrote arrangements of Duke
Ellington's "Mood Indigo" and "Caravan," trying to imitate the voicings I
heard on my 78 r.p.m. records. It was the late 1940s, and I was a fan of Ellington's music, along with that of other big bands. I didn't have a recording of
Black, Brown and Beige, which had been premiered only a few years earlier,
in 1942. But I might have heard at least some part of it somewhere, for in my
unconscious the provocative title was stored away, together with a sense that
it was an important, serious work.

Duke Ellington and his *Black, Brown and Beige* entered my life in the
summer of 1965. I was settling in as music director of the Corpus Christi Symphony. I was also "covering"—working as an assistant conductor for—the
New York Philharmonic summer concerts and conducting for the Joffrey
Ballet whenever they could afford to work with an orchestra. In June of 1965,
the Joffrey Ballet was invited to represent American dance at a White House
Festival of the Arts, hosted by President and Mrs. Lyndon Baines Johnson,
and in July, the New York Philharmonic held a French-American Festival at
Lincoln Center. Duke Ellington appeared at both.

For one jam-packed day, June 14, 1965, the White House was transformed into a museum, sculpture court, theater, and concert stage. On the
walls of the public rooms hung paintings by Franz Kline, Ben Shahn, and
Marc Rothko, among others, and photographs by Stuart Eisenstadt, Man
Ray, Edward Steichen, and Alfred Stieglitz. There were sculptures by Alexan-

der Calder, Louise Nevelson, and Isamu Noguchi. Many of the artists themselves were in attendance.

The daytime performances began with an event titled "Prose and Poetry." Mark Van Doren introduced readings by Saul Bellow, Catherine Drinker Bowen, and John Hersey. Robert Lowell, who declined to appear, was outside leading a protest against the festival because it was being held while the nation was in the grip of the Vietnam War. American music, set apart from jazz, was represented by a short afternoon concert given by the Louisville Orchestra and introduced by Marian Anderson. We heard instrumental pieces by Ned Rorem and Robert Whitney and vocal works by Gershwin and Bernstein sung by Roberta Peters. A program of drama followed, with scenes from Tennessee Williams's *Glass Menagerie* and Arthur Miller's *Death of a Salesman*, introduced by Helen Hayes. The daytime presentations ended with film clips from Elia Kazan's *On the Waterfront* and Alfred Hitchcock's *North by Northwest*, introduced by Charlton Heston.

I recall the prevailing mood of that marathon day as stiff and formal. The many luminaries appeared self-conscious, in awe of one another. There were polite exchanges all around, little more. But that was about to change.

The evening's entertainment took place upon a stage erected on the White House lawn. Gene Kelly was the host. Jazz was to be the culminating event for the entire festival, but first came American dance. The Joffrey Ballet performed *Gamelan* to music of the same title by Lou Harrison and *Sea Shadows* to the second movement of Ravel's Piano Concerto in G; Gilbert Kalish was the piano soloist. I conducted an orchestra recruited from members of the United States Marine Band. Polite applause covered our exit; then Kelly began reading his next introduction:

> It's a long road from Congo Square to Carnegie Hall, and a longer musical way still. But jazz made it. Riding on the well-tailored coat tails of Duke Ellington some twenty-two years ago, he and the great artists of his ensemble, took lady jazz out of her off-the-racks cotton dress and put her in a long velvet gown. Ladies and Gentlemen, if there had never been a Duke Ellington, jazz would have had to invent him. And so it's with pride that I present the "Duke."[1]

A wall of applause rose in greeting as Ellington stomped out the tempo. The band kicked off with "Take the A Train," and the motley crowd of artists and poets, actors and dancers, politicians, and glitterati melted into one. Ties were loosened, shoes and jackets came off. I remember smiles and dancing. We were caught up in the delicious, delirious embrace of Ellington's music. Ellington followed with "one of our latest compositions": selections from the *Far East Suite*. He then introduced portions of the featured work from the historic Carnegie Hall concert that Kelly referred to: "our tone parallel to the history of the Negro in America, *Black, Brown and Beige*." I *listened* to the work for the first time. The band still featured Ellington veterans Johnny Hodges, Ray Nance, Lawrence Brown, and Harry Carney. I was in orbit, carried along by the audience's obvious pleasure in Ellington's music, in particular the haunting alto saxophone and violin solos of Hodges and Ray Nance in "Come Sunday."

Having spent considerable time since that magical evening studying, scoring, and performing *Black, Brown and Beige*, I now realize that in choosing to place his "tone parallel" alongside the other American masterworks performed and displayed at the Festival, Ellington was reaffirming his faith in the work, no matter its less than enthusiastic greeting by most critics and fans when it was first presented.

After the Ellington Orchestra finished its set, Lady Bird Johnson, the real force behind the festival, thanked all the performers and artists and invited everyone to enjoy refreshments and view the art and sculpture on display. But the audience would not let Ellington and his orchestra go. The band remained onstage to play many of his celebrated compositions, including, of course, the "Mood Indigo" and "Caravan" of my youth.

I was fired up, wondering how a symphony conductor like myself could take part in this important music — music that spoke to me as profoundly as any other, music that reached out and embraced everyone. Later that evening I met Ellington's collaborator, Billy Strayhorn, at a reception in the East Room. To my pleasant surprise, Strayhorn had heard of me as a conductor with some jazz in his soul. I asked him if Ellington or he, himself, had ever thought about scoring *Black, Brown and Beige* for symphony orchestra. "Why don't you ask him yourself?" Strayhorn responded, and proceeded to introduce me to Ellington. When I repeated the question, Ellington countered, "What's wrong with it the way it is?" I explained how I loved his music and jazz and that I was now conducting my own symphony orchestra and wanted to play some of his bigger works. He was charming but had no more to offer.

I met Ellington again six weeks later, on July 29, 1965, when he came to direct the New York Philharmonic in his work *The Golden Broom and the Green Apple*. Here was the hero of the White House Festival of the Arts conducting his own music *for symphony orchestra*! This time, however, I found the experience disappointing. The orchestration was four-square.[2] Jazz licks — "oo-shoo-bee-doos" that any musician of my generation could scat with ease — were blurred by awkward bowings. And despite having the master jazz drummer Louie Bellson at his side, Ellington seemed uncharacteristically uncomfortable in front of the New York Philharmonic. Louie Bellson still tells the story of "playing a piece I never heard with Duke and the New York Phil, and there was no part for me!"[3] Louie of course knows that Ellington never wrote out drum parts, giving total freedom to his drummers to improvise their own. But this, he was saying, went too far. I never figured out what *The Golden Broom and the Green Apple* was doing on a French American concert, but his tonal essay (about an encounter between two women, one worldly-wise and citified, the other a fresh *naïf* from the country) enjoyed no more than a lukewarm reception. I was frustrated for Ellington and for his music, with which I strongly identified. I began planning a symphonic jazz program for the Corpus Christi Symphony with the Modern Jazz Quartet as guest artists, the first of many collaborations to come.

The MJQ was a very disciplined group with a repertoire of highly organized pieces created by the erudite composer and swing and blues pianist John Lewis. Behind the formally structured settings, John's sparse yet intensely rhythmic urgings at the keyboard, in combination with the swinging, crystal-clear string bass and percussion work of Percy Heath and Connie Kay, gave the MJQ one of the all-time great rhythm sections in the history of bebop. The beneficiary of all this, their star soloist, was the vibraharpist and jazz genius Milt Jackson. The dramatic tension between John's formal designs and Milt's fighting to break free, with swinging flurries and leaps and perfectly placed punctuations, is what made the group so singular and attractive. I knew that the MJQ would work well within the more rigid confines of a large symphony orchestra and that John had already composed pieces for the quartet with orchestra.

Their earliest availability was for the 1967–68 season. Billy Strayhorn agreed to compose a new orchestral work for this concert as well. Around February 1967, I tried reaching him by phone to see how the piece was coming and was given a forwarding number—at a hospital. I had no idea how sick he was when he apologized to me for not being able to finish the MJQ piece. "Blood Count," Strayhorn's musical commentary on his illness, composed in the hospital for the Ellington Orchestra, was to be his last work.

Around the same time, I decided to tackle *The Golden Broom and the Green Apple*. I felt it deserved far more symphonic justice than it had received from the New York Philharmonic and decided to present it at one of the Corpus Christi Symphony's Young People's Concerts during the 1968–69 season. When I went to pick up the score and parts at Ellington's library/ office, set up in an elegant town house on Riverside Drive near 110th Street (since designated Ellington Place), I met Ellington's sister, Ruth, who was running his publishing company.

In February 1970, with Ruth's help, I tracked down Duke and his band. They were doing a one-nighter at a college on Staten Island.[4] I went backstage during intermission and announced myself as "the conductor who wants you to orchestrate *Black, Brown and Beige*. We met at the White House and I have just performed your *Golden Broom!*" This last bit of information unlocked the door, and Duke invited me into his dressing room. He was wearing only a towel and a stocking cap.

Ellington was, of course, interested in hearing how *The Golden Broom and the Green Apple* went over. I told him that I cleaned up the bowings and touched up the scoring in a few places, and that it had come off beautifully. "But why," I asked, "did you give such a high solo to the French horn? It's in nosebleed territory and might more easily be given to a saxophone." He was ready for the question. "Yes, it is very high but there is a way around it." I was all ears. "When I rehearsed the work in Cincinnati," Duke explained, "I told the orchestra that we would start the second section at measure 17, knowing that if the horn player had worked up the part, he'd raise his hand or come to the podium during a break and ask me why I cut out his solo. On the other hand, if the part is too difficult, no one is embarrassed."

I never found out what happened in Cincinnati, but the notion that a musician's feelings could be more important than the music itself wasn't exactly in the maestro tradition. The logic was Talmudic. I had found a new guru. There was so much to learn. Duke went on to explain that he did not want to introduce the saxophone into his symphonic works since the orchestra had so many wonderful colors of its own. The saxophone question would come up again, and sooner than I thought.

Ellington gave me a ride back to Manhattan. I sat next to the driver: baritone saxophonist Harry Carney, who had been in the band since the 1920s. Duke was in back with Joe Morgan, his publicity man. The conversation was light. I remember Duke's bantering with Joe about making such a big deal over Duke's seventieth birthday: "No chick wants to share her favors with a seventy-year-old man." As I was getting out of the car on the corner of Sixty-sixth and West End Avenue, Duke said, "You do it." "What?" I asked. "You orchestrate my *Black, Brown and Beige*."

About a week later, we met at Duke's apartment to discuss the orchestration. His trusted assistant Tom Whaley sat in. Whaley, who joined the Ellington organization in 1941, had recently taken over some of the scoring responsibilities that once were Strayhorn's. Ellington talked about the music. He told me the story behind the second section, "Come Sunday," about black people standing outside a white church they could not enter and harmonizing with the beautiful music they heard from within, realizing that they all shared the same God. He supplied me with a tape of the January 23, 1943, Carnegie Hall concert, an archival "location recording," and a set of seven full scores for *Black, Brown and Beige*, published in 1963 by Tempo Music, his own company.[5] These were the only full scores (jazz band orchestrations) of his music that Ellington allowed to be published in his lifetime. Ellington composed almost exclusively for his orchestra of hand-picked players, and, like most big-band leaders, he guarded his scores from peering eyes. *Black, Brown and Beige* was the rare exception.

Duke suggested that I orchestrate the same three sections I had heard the band play at the White House Festival of the Arts: "Work Song," "Come Sunday," and "Light." These three sections made up the original first movement, *Black*. Our conversation turned to the scoring of "Come Sunday." Ellington balked at the idea of using alto saxophone for the haunting solo that brings "Come Sunday" to a close. This time his reasoning had nothing to do with using the available symphonic colors. Duke did not want "to tempt anyone" into imitating the extraordinary original performance of Johnny Hodges. Hodges had an uncommon, bluesy, conversational way of bending and sliding through a melody, reaching the true center of a pitch only at the resting point of a principal note or phrase. If Hodges ever left the band, Duke told me, he would assign the solo to an instrument other than the alto saxophone, in order to encourage a new and fresh interpretation.

We met again a few weeks later when Duke attended a performance of *La Bohème* that I was conducting for the Washington Opera Society. The superb cast included Alan Titus as Marcello and the soon-to-be movie star Madeline Kahn, who all but stole the show with her comical interpretation of Musetta. At the after-performance reception, Ellington was a center of attraction. When it came time to leave, I was still keyed up by the performance. The evening was young as well for Duke. We ended up in the apartment of Barbara Kheen, a friend of his who was a ballet consultant for the National Endowment for the Arts. High on Puccini and wine, we talked through the night. I felt the evening brought me and the Duke closer together. My later work with Ellington on *Queenie Pie* had its roots in that *La Bohème* night.[6]

While my orchestration of a *Symphonic Suite from Black, Brown and Beige* was still in the planning stages, an engagement to conduct the Chicago Symphony at the Ravinia Festival in July 1970 came through. The festival management welcomed the idea of an Ellington premiere (my new orchestration) on a program that would include music by Bernstein, Copland, and Gershwin. With this deadline now staring me in the face, I was bound to finish the score.

The Chicago Symphony played the new orchestration amazingly well. My trumpet-playing days were not that far behind me, and I was particularly aware of how stylishly the orchestra's legendary principal trumpeter, Adolph Herseth, led the brass section, swinging the phrases and working away with his plunger mute in the final measures of "Light."

Ellington, I am happy to report, approved of my orchestration. He listened to a private taping of the Ravinia performance, which took place on July 5, 1970, and made no fuss over my orchestrational decisions, nor did he object to my using the alto saxophone in "Come Sunday." His one caveat, drilled into my memory—take a more deliberate tempo, especially for the opening of "Work Song"—I have respected ever since.[7]

Not long after, Duke called upon me to work on his ballet score, *The River*,[8] and *Queenie Pie*. I was becoming one of Ellington's "symphony men."

Duke Ellington

16

Ellington's *Queenie Pie*

In the late fall of 1970, at Ellington's insistence, I was engaged by Peter Herman Adler, director of the National Educational Television Opera Company, to help Duke prepare a piano-vocal score and eventually orchestrations for *Queenie Pie*, what he slyly referred to as his "opera comique," for television. I did this periodically for the next three years, through the last summer of Ellington's life.

NET Opera had given Ellington a commission, and the requisite cash advance, after hearing him sing, play, and tell the story of *Queenie Pie* while sitting at the keyboard—the Duke at his most charming self. But the vocal score and script were slow in coming. Ellington was busy, on the road, keeping his orchestra working in a shrinking market. He was getting ready to focus his creative energies on the *Third Sacred Concert*. Perhaps he knew he was running out of time. My task was to bring Ellington back to *Queenie Pie* and pry a score out of him.

I caught up with Ellington and the band in January 1971 while they were playing a two-week engagement at the Shamrock-Hilton Hotel in Houston, Texas.[1] I arrived early in the afternoon and went up to his suite. The scene looked somewhat contrived, as if Duke had said, "Quick, get out the *Queenie Pie* set-up." Betty McGettigan, his traveling companion and secretary, was typing away at the script. Duke was on the bed, surrounded by sheets of manuscript. He showed me where he stood with the score and handed me a half-dozen or so parodical television jingles he had composed about Queenie's beauty products (for Queenie was a highly successful businesswoman as well as a celebrated beauty queen). It was Ellington's idea to "interrupt" his television opera with commercials and news bulletins about Queenie's life and times:

> If you are agreeable to the eye
> Of your favorite guy
> You can make him hit the sky . . .
> Just apply some Queenie Pie . . .
> And try, I mean, BUY.

The most intensive work on *Queenie Pie* took place during the summer months of 1972 and 1973, when Ellington was appearing at the Rainbow Grill, an art deco heaven on the sixty-fifth floor of the NBC Building in Rockefeller Center. Ellington's band was scaled down: a full (five-man) sax section, one trumpet, bass, drums, two vocalists, and the maestro at the concert grand.[2]

I set up shop in the Duke's dressing room, and we had a small piano brought in. Pinned to the wall, where he couldn't miss it, was my long checklist of the tunes we had already committed to paper and those yet to be done. I would write as he played: the tune, the "dummy" lyric, the chords, and sometimes his ideas for counterthemes and orchestration. We worked between sets and into the wee hours. Duke was one of those "night creatures" drawn so winningly in his symphonic tone poem of the same name. Once, around three o'clock in the morning, Ellington decided we should take a break and go to the Stage Deli, then an after-hours gathering place for show-business people. When we got to the street, I went into my New York taxi-waving act. Ellington told me to relax and quietly walked to the curb. In a matter of seconds three cabs careened over, vying to pick us up.

It was a heady time. I was in the catbird seat, backstage with the Duke. Once the word got around that I passed unchallenged in and out of the great man's dressing room, women—old flames and wannabe flames—began pressing notes on me to pass on. Miles Davis was among the many musicians, both humble and high, who came to pay their respects. More than once I watched as Duke signaled his son, Mercer, to give "a taste" to some down-at-the-heels cat. Mercer, who was then managing the band, would discreetly peel off a bill from a large roll he carried and slip it to him. Out front in the Rainbow Grill, Duke unobtrusively initialed table checks for his friends.

One August night in 1973, Richard Burton came to the grill with his teen-age daughter, whose birthday was being celebrated. Ellington coaxed him up on stage, and he began to recite Shakespeare while the band played. "I usually get a big fee for this," quipped Burton.[3] The audience wanted more. Burton finished with an "improvisation," a talking blues poem of praise for Duke and the band. During the break Burton came backstage. Duke explained my presence and all the music paper strewn about. "It's for a new opera comique, *Queenie Pie*," Ellington told Burton. "Here's a number you could sing." Ellington pulled out "Women," a bluesy, slow, swinging ballad, and before he could think, Burton was reciting to Ellington's piano:

Women
B'eautiful Women
Comin' on like crazy
Will she stay or go?

Ellington began envisioning his plans for *Queenie Pie*. Lena Horne was his choice for Queenie. Duke himself would narrate. I would conduct Ellington's orchestra, which was to be supplemented with French horns, a harp, and a small string section. *Queenie Pie*'s fantasy scenes would especially benefit from a broader orchestral palette:

Synopsis: The first scene opens on a beauty pageant being held on a street in Harlem. Mendelssohnian hymns of praise, sung by an assemblage of dignitaries, are being offered in Queenie's honor, and there is an immediate response of affirmation, in jazzy New Orleans prance style, by "second-line" street people.

We soon learn that Queenie barely scraped through as the winner. Clearly her days on the beauty queen's throne are numbered.

The scene shifts to her boudoir. As she studies herself in the mirror, the reassuring voice of her paramour, Big Daddy, is heard: "Oh Gee, You Make that Hat Look Pretty." But Li'l Daddy, her trusted houseman, reminds her, "Those little girl competitors are comin' too close." Li'l Daddy has a solution. He conjures up a vision, "My Father's Island," where, on "Full Moon Midnight," a singing tree unfolds its arms and releases a magic potion.

Here Ellington takes his inspiration from Madame C. J. Walker's celebrated Hair Straightening Cream. Li'l Daddy confides in Queenie:

Li'l Daddy: There's a thing that grows in the heart of the tree, and this thing someday will be the basic ingredient for every modern product—medical, cosmetic, industrial and physical energy. And all it needs is for someone to go and get it. It's called the NUCLI, and it's yours for the taking.

QUEENIE: Li'l Daddy, this NUCLI? Will it make hair grow?
LI'L DADDY: Two inches a day.
QUEENIE: Will it make freckles go?
LI'L DADDY: Just wipe 'em away.
QUEENIE: Will it remove a wrinkle?
LI'L DADDY: A touch in a twinkle.
QUEENIE: What about a blister?
LI'L DADDY: She'd think her sweetheart kissed her.[4]

Queenie Pie boards her speedboat and lands on the island. It is full moon midnight, and a trio of tree sirens sings "Smile As You Go By." Queenie and the boat crew dash off with the NUCLI and sail into the sea. Queenie strut-sings, "Hey Now, I Don't Need Nobody Now," but they are shipwrecked as the first act ends.

The second act opens on "another uncharted island." We meet the hip Harlemites from Act One. They have just turned off their air conditioners, changed into skins, and grabbed their spears and drums as they head down to the beach to see what has washed up on shore. Queenie wakes up to the poke of a spear and the eerie chanting of "Eenuff, Iinoof, Angalong, Dangalong. . . . " They sing a war song:

STICK IT IN
    JAB IT
PULL IT OUT
    GRAB IT
AND STICK IT RIGHT BACK . . . IN AGAIN
DON'T BE AFRAID TO WEAR WAR PAINT
GOTTA LOOK MEAN, EVEN THOUGH YOU AIN'T
(End of first part of the synopsis)

Harlemites "going native" had already surfaced in Ellington's plan for a 1940s musical he called "Air Conditioned Jungle," and again in *Jump for Joy* (1941).[5]

These ironical send-ups of nativist clichés have a long history in black minstrelsy, as well as in early black Broadway theatricals—as already noted, there is a similar scene in full jungle regalia in Cook and Dunbar's *In Dahomey*—and one can find a parallel in the whooping and feigned scalping in American Indian Wild West shows.

At the end of our second summer's work on *Queenie Pie*, I put together a progress-report-*cum*-audition for Ellington and the NET Opera folks (Peter Herman Adler and his assistants), which took place at Duke's summer sublet on West Fifty-eighth Street. Betty McGettigan provided an up-to-date script.

I prepared a vocal score of lead sheets. With a few of the singers from *Mass* and myself chording at the piano, I prepared a rough-and-tumble demo tape of some of the best songs.

I assumed that Adler and his assistants, all opera pros, would fill in the gaps as they listened to the tape while following the music, but Adler did not have a jazz bone in his body. They sat stone-faced, mumbled a few awkward words of the "keep up the good work" variety, and left. I was mortified in front of Duke. How could they, despite the unpolished performances, not hear the beauties in this score—the exotic moonlight and magic tree music, the swinging sexy struts for Queenie and Big Daddy? Duke was very kind. All he said was, "Remember, Maurice, there is no such thing as a demo tape!"

I soon headed back to my orchestra in Texas. Ellington left for London, where he gave his *Third Sacred Concert* in Westminster Abbey before the royal family on October 24, 1973. In midwinter the NET Opera people approved a budget for a "serious" demo tape. By this time Ellington had checked himself into the Columbia Presbyterian Hospital. I was not on the short list of permitted visitors. We spoke by phone a few times, and I sent him seventy-five blue irises (blue being his favorite color) for his birthday on April 29. In the late spring I engaged three wonderful singers—Robert Guillaume, Lee Hooper, and Ernestine Jackson—and a terrific jazz trio, with Tom Pierson at the keyboard, to make the new demo tape. Duke died on May 24, 1974, before we could schedule the sessions.

I was in Kansas City, being introduced as the new music director for the Kansas City Philharmonic, when the news came. The Modern Jazz Quartet was there as well, and we all took the same flight back to New York to attend the funeral, held at the Cathedral of St. John the Divine.

The cathedral, located uptown just south of Columbia University and on the edge of Harlem, has become the ecumenical heart and soul of creative New York. I attended several of David Amram's magical American Indian Thanksgiving concerts at the cathedral and have since attended funerals and memorial services given there for Virgil Thomson, Alvin Ailey (Max Roach's African drum processional was awesome), Leonard Bernstein, and John Lewis; but it was for Duke Ellington that I made my first pilgrimage.

The huge crowd of mourners overflowed into the streets. Ruth Ellington arranged a place for me near the family. I carried a rose in Duke's honor. As the casket was taken out, Alice Babs's soprano soared to the highest reaches of the cathedral, and I broke down.

I made a vow to help get Duke's symphonic works published and on their rightful journey. I couldn't imagine what would happen to *Queenie Pie*.

A few months after Duke's passing, the NET Opera directors had a big meeting at which they decided that *Queenie Pie* without Ellington was not a good idea. Fortunately, I had gone ahead and recorded the new demo tape. There was no way I could know it at the time, but the tape would ultimately lead to a full stage production. It would take twelve years.

In 1985, on the strength of my Aeolian Hall re-creation, I was engaged by the American Music Theater Festival of Philadelphia to help reconstruct Gershwin's 1929/31 Broadway musical *Strike Up the Band* and to serve as music director and principal orchestrator. It was while working on that project that I brought the demo tape and TV script of *Queenie Pie* to the attention of the theater festival's artistic advisor, Eric Salzman. The tape and script remained as they were in 1973, a work in progress, and it was my hope that the AMT Festival would be interested in a workshop production, along the lines of what they were doing at the time for Anthony Davis's opera *Malcolm X*.

Salzman was quite taken with *Queenie Pie*, and the notion of presenting a new work by Ellington was extremely tempting. The workshop idea was scrapped, and the AMT Festival set out to expand the one-hour narrated television script and score into a full stage production. A young unknown writer, George Wolfe, was given responsibility for the book. I would again be music director and orchestrator, but my first task was to compile additional music from the huge body of Ellington's work to flesh out the score. After long and difficult negotiations, a deal was struck with Mercer Ellington giving the production full access to Ellington's published and unpublished works, except for those in the Broadway show *Sophisticated Ladies*. Mercer also relinquished artistic control over *Queenie Pie*, with the proviso that the pit orchestra be the Duke Ellington Orchestra, which he was then leading. He did allow me to add a French horn and a synthesizer but balked at including strings for the projected orchestrations.

Mercer provided me with photocopies from a huge cache of sketchbooks and loose sheets of music manuscripts that Duke left, in the hope I could find "new" music for the expanded *Queenie Pie*. At first, given free access to the composer's hideaway, I felt discomfited, then boozy, afloat in a wondrous sea of sketches, scraps, phone numbers, and more-or-less completed compositions. There were countless melodies to blues changes and dozens of Duke's idiosyncratic scores, complete arrangements for the band, written out in his peculiar shorthand system, ready to be copied.

Ellington laid out his scores in concert pitch on four staves. Four of the saxophones, two alto and two tenors, are grouped together on the top staff, often with particular players' names attached. Harry Carney's baritone sax line stands alone on the second staff, in treble clef, one octave higher than it sounds. On the third staff is the music for four "cors," the trumpets. Three trombones, in bass clef, share the fourth and bottom staff. The brass players are also frequently assigned by name. Sometimes Ellington adds a string bass

FIGURE 16.1
Ellington's orchestra score. Courtesy of Mercer Ellington.

FIGURE 16.2
Ellington anagrams on hotel stationery.
Courtesy of Mercer Ellington.

line to the trombone staff. Rarely are there any indications for the drummer or for himself at the piano.[6]

There were some surprises in the sketchbooks: a score for a full symphony orchestra—something Ellington was never known to do himself;[7] a double column of anagrams, printed in block letters on Detroit Hilton hotel stationary, represented an evening's worth of tunes Ellington was planning to have the band play—KLOP stands for "Polka," UWIZ" for "University of Wisconsin."[8] On another sheet of hotel stationery (the Shoreham Hotel and Motor Inn of Washington, D.C.) Ellington scribbled out an entire tune using but one line for a staff: the E, or bottom, line of the treble clef. It was typically Ellingtonian—maximum expression through minimal means. I was amazed at how well it worked. There were poems, some quite personal.

FIGURE 16.3
Ellington one-line staff on hotel stationery.
Courtesy of Mercer Ellington.

I did find interesting material for *Queenie Pie* among the sketches: a soaring ballad for Queenie to sing at the end of Act One titled "Beautiful"; three blues choruses that worked in counterpoint with one another that I recast into a canonic song called "Style"; and a blues lick that Barry Lee Hall, former trumpeter with Ellington and a brilliant composer and arranger, developed into a show-stopper, "Blues for Two Women." The lyrics for these "new" songs were by George David Weiss. Using what I learned from *Black, Brown and Beige*, I also established a Queenie leitmotif that I laced throughout the work as transitional music and in dream sequences.

The producers felt there still remained a problem with Ellington's non-ending. Ellington had never really resolved Queenie's dilemma of how to retain her title as Queenie Pie, the reigning beauty queen of Harlem.

When we left the story of *Queenie Pie*, Queenie was lying on the shore of "another uncharted island":

> *Synopsis (continued)*: She wakes up on the beach to find herself surrounded by "natives" and quickly sizes up the situation. Queenie se-

duces the King with a trilly Mozartian parody, "Come into My Boudoir, Your Majesty," only to emerge minutes later announcing her triumph with a growling, funky, enigmatic shout, "Blow the Horn and Ding the Gong, His Majesty's at, where the King's belong."

Queenie sings a soliloquy, the story of her life. It begins again in a breezy operatic style—"Just lucky, I guess, just lucky"—and builds to a false climax with the ironic, "Then fate decided I should be a real Queen with all the pomp and circumstances thrown in-n-n-n." Queenie holds the last note. The mask comes off, and "in-n-n-n" turns into "n-n-if I were to tell you, what I really mean, I wouldn't know where to begin." Queenie then pours out her soul in a heartachingly slow, slow, confessional blues, "I Don't Wanna Be the Lonely-est Woman in Town."

For both of the above examples Ellington employs a two-part form, a parody of a classical aria transformed into jazz revelation.

A rescue boat arrives but Crown Prince, the King's son, intercedes: "Sorry, Madam, but the Supreme Constitutional Document of Decision says, 'No Crown Head must EVER leave this Island!!!'"

Ellington ended his "opéra comique" with Queenie imprisoned on the island. She would never return to Harlem to face the inevitable.

George Wolfe was brilliant. His book incorporated most of Ellington's characters, conceptions, and choice pieces of dialogue, and he reimagined the ending. Wolfe has Queenie wake up from her magic-island "dream" to find herself still in her boudoir in Harlem. Queenie has acquired wisdom. She accepts the truth of her situation and turns over her crown to her new competitor, Cafe O'Lay, taking comfort in the idea of living out her life with Big Daddy, the storyteller and Queenie's paramour. Big Daddy, a composite invention of Wolfe's, serves throughout the play as the Ellingtonian figure.

Garth Fagin's dance troupe was incorporated into the company and provided movement that drew a fine line between Broadway cliché and precious vernacular art. In a matter of months we delivered an opera comique that received critical acclaim everywhere except in the eyes and ears of the tough Broadway oligarchy that decides what shows book space in their theaters. *Queenie Pie* was moved to Washington, D.C., by one enthusiastic producer, Roger L. Stevens, chairman of the board of the Kennedy Center, where again it was well received. By that time, the winter of 1986–87, both George Wolfe and I had left for other projects. Garth introduced some changes, hoping to please the Broadway crowd, but *Queenie Pie* closed in Washington, D.C., to a full house in early 1987, the same year I returned to *Black, Brown and Beige*.

17

Ellington's *Black, Brown and Beige*

My first hands-on experience with *Black, Brown and Beige* had been the orchestration of the *Symphonic Suite*, the extraordinary music I heard Duke and his band play at the White House Festival in 1965. Over time I would become a proponent of the work in its original form, for jazz orchestra, but back then I suffered no doubts when I plunged ahead to make at least a part of the work available for symphony players and audiences.

The *Symphonic Suite*

As with a literary translation or a screen adaptation, recasting a jazz band composition for symphony orchestra raises several issues, some philosophic and aesthetic, some practical. For many jazz purists, a symphonic adaptation of a jazz work is a contradiction in terms. Some Ellingtonians reject any kind of re-creation, believing that the Ellington Orchestra died with him, and only the archival location recording or Ellington's later studio recordings and air checks of excerpts can represent *Black, Brown and Beige*.

Nevertheless, Ellington conceived his large-scale programmatic work for the concert hall, and he had it published in 1963 so that others could play it. Moreover, Ellington gave his blessing to the idea of a symphonic version. Perhaps he remembered the review of its 1942 premiere by Irving Kolodin, who wore two hats for the occasion, critic for the *New York Sun* and program-note annotator for Carnegie Hall: "One can only conclude that the brilliant ideas [*Black, Brown and Beige*] contained would count for much more if scored for a legitimate orchestra, augmented by the solo instruments indicated for certain specific passages."[1] Kolodin's encouraging review among the many naysayers leads me to suspect that he got closer to the work than his fellow critics and gained respect for it by attending rehearsals and interviewing Ellington in preparation for writing the program notes.

What, then, are some of the challenges I faced? The handling of improvised passages is the first to come to mind. But *Black, Brown and Beige* has no purely improvised passages. In Ellington's autograph score of the work, now in the collection of his music at the Smithsonian Institution, the "improvised" solos, even the celebrated ones for tenor saxophonist Ben Webster, are written out by the composer! Most of these solos can easily be transferred to symphonic instruments, and I rarely come across modern orchestral players who cannot reproduce the improvisatory flavor of the original.

In my orchestration, I leave most, but not all, of Ellington's brass parts intact. The parts for saxophones—which whisper countermelodies and blend rich harmonies so magnificently, and can "call and respond" toe-to-toe with the brass—I freely reworked for the string, woodwind, or French horn sections. I also keep intact the unifying jazz rhythm section—a single lightly amplified jazz bassist (the other basses remain part of the string section) and a jazz drummer—but I drop the all-but-inaudible rhythm guitar. As we know, Ellington rarely wrote out a drummer's part. But I transcribed Sonny Greer's playing, on traps and timpani, from the 1943 location recording throughout, and I found many opportunities for other percussion instruments as well.

My single greatest challenge was to capture the inflections, phrasing, and coloring of Duke's own magnificent orchestra. Informed by a living performance tradition, these sonifications cannot be adequately conveyed through notation. Nevertheless, I carefully transcribed dynamics, durations, and rhythms, turning swinging eighth-note passages into triplets where necessary. And I added bowings that make it possible for a large string section to swing.

Common sense tells us that an ensemble of seventy or more players spread out on a big stage cannot be as rhythmically tight as a fifteen-piece jazz band gathered around a swinging drummer. On the other hand, harmonically rich, sweeping music such as that of "Come Sunday" profits from the delicacy and sheen of massed strings.

For "Come Sunday," I went against Ellington's wishes and used a solo alto saxophone. This decision was not made lightly.[2] In the original jazz-band version, the alto saxophone makes a dramatic entrance after a heaving, train-like musical figure—a splendid example of Albert Murray's favorite Ellington metaphor, "locomotive onomatopoeia"—to which Ellington adds a few church-piano chords.[3] In my symphonic orchestration the train music fades into the distance, and the ensuing silence is broken by the entrance of the alto keening its song over a humming thirteenth chord. To deny ourselves this perfect confluence of moment, melody, and instrument, an essential part of Ellington's genius, would in my view be a sacrilege.

One exchange I had with Ellington gave me a glimpse of the loose boundaries between composer, performer, and arranger that Duke seemed comfortable with. I brought to his attention my feeling that "Light," the last section of the new suite, ended abruptly. Duke agreed and blithely told me to write a bigger ending. When I protested that I wasn't a composer, he simply said, "Use 'Come Sunday.' That tune should have made more money than it did." When I sang and played my ideas for a new ending to him over the phone, Ellington encouraged me to stretch out and go even further, empowering me to outdo myself. Was this scenario in its own way similar to what happened between Ellington and Strayhorn? Duke's inclusive way of introducing his music to audiences—"one of our latest compositions"—is not purely self-effacement.

In the fall of 1987 John Lewis asked me to conduct the original jazz-band version of *Black, Brown and Beige* with the American Jazz Orchestra, a New York–based repertory ensemble founded by Lewis and the author and critic Gary Giddins. I had not forgotten Duke's response at the White House reception twenty-two years earlier, when I suggested that the work be rescored for symphony orchestra: "What's wrong with it the way it is?" And I took on the assignment with a large measure of curiosity and as an act of personal redemption, for having ignored Duke's original conception.

Original Jazz Band Version

Ellington shied away from playing *Black, Brown and Beige* in its entirety after its Carnegie Hall premiere. He might have been intimidated by its mixed reception: "brilliant, complex, highly original, but much too long."[4] The 1943 audience and critics seemed unprepared for so serious and extensive a work: three large movements—the first two comprising six shorter sections, the last an unbroken twenty-minute essay—from a master of short forms. Ellington did, however, continue to perform all or parts of the first two movements, *Black* and *Brown*. Of *Beige* he played only excerpts: the opening jungle-style music under the title "War" and an evocative slow dance, "Sugar Hill Penthouse."[5]

With the rise of the jazz repertory movement in the early 1970s came a renewed interest in *Black, Brown and Beige*. Alan Cohen, a British jazz saxophonist and arranger, edited Ellington's Tempo Music score—the same one he had provided me with—and performed and recorded it in London in 1972. Dick Hyman presented the same version with the New York Jazz Repertory Company at the Smithsonian Institution in the mid-1970s. Jazz audiences were becoming more accustomed to hearing their music in concert halls, and in symphonic proportions; Ellington's "tone parallel to the history of the Negro in America" is over forty-four minutes long, as lengthy as Beethoven's *Eroica* Symphony.

The American Jazz Orchestra performance of the original *Black, Brown and Beige* took place in the historic Great Hall of the Cooper Union Foundation Building. It was the first of five such engagements, plus a recording, that I would direct over the next decade.[6] Dizzy Gillespie listened to the performance from backstage. He was brought to the concert by his protégé, John Faddis, the orchestra's "power lead" and high-note trumpet specialist, who literally and figuratively elevated the AJO trumpet section. Bobby Short read Ellington's spoken introductions, which I had retrieved from the archival location recording of the 1943 Carnegie Hall premiere. A year later, in 1989, I re-created that entire concert.

Ellington's Carnegie Hall Concert of January 23, 1943

I began by poring over a copy of the original program booklet. Ellington's concert took place on a Saturday, sandwiched between a pair of New York Philharmonic subscription concerts led by Bruno Walter. And just to mock my disbelief in coincidence, the featured soloist was the Philharmonic's concertmaster, John Corigliano Sr., in Dvořák's Violin Concerto.

The evening was billed as a "Twentieth Anniversary Concert, Proceeds to Russian War Relief," which seemed to imply there had been an earlier appearance in music's mecca. But Ellington was purposely conflating his Carnegie Hall debut with the first time New Yorkers heard his music and his "Washingtonians" orchestra at the Hollywood nightclub.

The "Proceeds to Russian War Relief" is harder to explain. Like most musicians of his generation, especially musicians of color, Ellington made sure he was perceived as apolitical. His fiercely held political concerns were expressed in his music, not with speeches. The (United States) Russian War Relief, a nonprofit corporation that would collect over $50 million by 1944, was a broad-based organization that included highly politicized garment workers, black civic and political organizers, churchmen, and other unionists.[7] Many of these were old lefties happily back in the fold after Stalin's pact with the Nazis wore out its usefulness and the USSR joined the Allies. There may have been jazz devotees among them, but Russian War Relief supporters were more apt to enjoy singing workers' songs such as "Joe Hill" (by Earl Robinson and Alfred Hayes) or tunes from the old country while strumming on mandolins and guitars. On the other hand, Ellington had every right to expect that his frankly political work, a musicalization of the "history of the Negro in America," would fall on sympathetic ears.

Besides the war-relief activists, there were also musical notables in attendance—among them Benny Goodman, whose presence was meaningful. Goodman had hoped to have the Ellington orchestra start off the evening for his landmark "Sing, Sing, Sing" concert, which had been held in Carnegie Hall six years earlier, on January 16, 1938. Instead, Ellington sent a few of his best players: Johnny Hodges, Harry Carney, and Cootie Williams. Duke was wise to wait, and his sense of propriety won out. When Ellington and his band finally played Carnegie Hall—"practically a social obligation these days," according to the *New Yorker*[8]—the "King of Swing" was seated among the "honored guests" in a box with John Hammond, as were Count Basie with Marian Anderson and Jimmy Lunceford with Jack Mills.

The program listing ran for three pages, starting with the members of Ellington's sixteen-man orchestra and his two vocalists. Ellington is listed as "pianist-leader" and Billy Strayhorn as "ass't arranger."

PROGRAM

I.

Ellington-Miley	*Black and Tan Fantasy*
Ellington-Carney	Rockin' in Rhythm
Mercer Ellington	Blue Serge
	Jumpin' Punkins

II.

Ellington	Portrait of Bert Williams
	Portrait of Bojangles
	Portrait of Florence Mills

III.

Ellington	*Black, Brown and Beige*

(A Tone Parallel to the History of the Negro in America)

Intermission

IV.

Ellington	The Flaming Sword

Ellington's *Black, Brown and Beige*

Billy Strayhorn	Dirge
	Nocturne
	Stomp

V.

Ellington	Are You Stickin'
(Chauncey Haughton, clarinet)	
Tizol	Bakiff
(Juan Tizol, valve trombone; Ray Nance, violin)	
Ellington	Jack the Bear
(Alvin Raglin, string bass)	
Ellington	Blue Belles of Harlem[9]
(Duke Ellington, piano)	
Ellington	Cotton Tail
(Ben Webster, tenor saxophone)	
Ellington-Strayhorn	Day Dream
(Johnny Hodges, alto saxophone)	
Warren-Gorman-Leslie	Rose of the Rio Grande
(Lawrence Brown, trombone)	
Ellington	Trumpet in Spades
(Rex Stewart, cornet)	

VI.

Ellington	Don't Get Around Much Anymore
	Goin' Up
	Mood Indigo

Performing this epochal list, veritably Ellington's musical autobiography, took over three and a half hours; the concert ended at midnight. Where was I to find parts and scores for all this music? I had the materials for *Black, Brown and Beige*. For the rest, I went to the Ellington Collection, held in the Smithsonian Institution archives in Washington, D.C.

In a truly important and generous act, and with the help and support of the Congressional Black Caucus, Duke's son, Mercer, had worked out an agreement with the Smithsonian Institution's archives during the late 1980s. He turned over to their care the vast library of autograph scores, manuscripts, arrangements, and other materials that his father had saved and collected over the half century of his career (the sketchbooks I perused for *Queenie Pie* were not included), thus making them forever available to scholars and musicians. The Smithsonian's Duke Ellington Collection contained a little over half the music I needed. Some pieces were incomplete. The rest would have to be transcribed.

Fortunately, Carnegie Hall had installed a recording studio by the time

Ellington played there, and acetate discs of the concert were made. The equipment was low-fidelity by today's standards, and the single microphone employed was often overwhelmed by a booming bass drum; nevertheless, this location recording made possible transcriptions of the missing material and brought to light several deviations from the printed program.[10]

Transcribing, whether of a single-line jazz solo or of a complete arrangement, has long been a cottage industry in the jazz and big-band community. Paul Whiteman acknowledged transcribers as early as 1926:

> Many conductors and arrangers can adapt an orchestration from hearing a record played. I am told that when a record is made by certain Eastern orchestras, arrangers of orchestras in the West and Middle West gather for the first playing with paper and pencil. I have heard [bands playing] some of our arrangements obtained in that way.[11]

Young arrangers-to-be learned their craft by transcribing and getting deep inside the work of Bill Challis, chief arranger for Whiteman, or Fletcher Henderson, and, of course, the Duke. Some transcribers used a piano and could wear out an old 78 with repeated listenings. Others sat at a desk. Not much has changed. The accuracy of a transcription still depends upon the quality of the recording and the good ears, listening skills, and musicianship of the transcriber.[12]

Our masterful transcriber was tenor saxophonist Mark Lopeman. I took additional passes at the recording and wrote phrase markings, dynamics, and expressive details into Mark's transcribed scores before the parts were copied. After hours of close listening, I began to realize how much jazz phrasing and instrumental coloring had changed in the fifty years that passed since the 1943 concert, and how subtle was the artistry of Duke and his band.

Almost every long, sustained note that Ellington wrote at the end of a phrase was snipped off in perfect unison by his players, who knew exactly when and where to edit. Duke's sax, trumpet, and trombone sections phrased as one, shaping melodic lines with nuanced rises and falls; they breathed together and blended. The sax and clarinet players knew where to add little lilts and lifts and when to add *portamento* (tiny slides) between notes. And, as Virgil Thomson lamented, the world was softer back then. Ellington's guitarist and bass player were the only band members using "light amplification." These days everyone gets a microphone, even in Carnegie Hall. Modern sax mouthpieces and reeds are "set up" to match the power and cutting-edge sound of modern brasses. But in the 1940s the saxes used hard rubber mouthpieces and softer reeds, which enabled them to produce a humming "subtone."

Ellington's players were working together fifty weeks a year in the 1940s.

Ellington's Black, Brown and Beige

They learned the long and complicated *Black, Brown and Beige* from scratch. But the rest of the program was out of their current "book," which they could play practically from memory. For the Carnegie Hall re-creation I had a band of New York freelancers facing three hours' worth of manuscript music, only a small amount of which was familiar. I was able to engage several old-time Ellingtonians and younger aficionados who purportedly knew the style, among them Ellington's clarinetist, Jimmy Hamilton, flown up from the Caribbean; Milt Hinton, rock-steady bassist and jazz photo historian; Sir Roland Hanna, a swinging virtuoso pianist who had made a study of Ellington's keyboard style; Frank Wess, master big-band saxophonist; and John Faddis, trumpet genius.[13] We were about to visit holy ground. I provided the players with copies of the location recording, and the results were gratifying.

"Trumpet in Spades," one of Duke's eight mini-concertos, exploited Rex Stewart's unique "half-valve" technique. Normally, when a player depresses a trumpet or cornet valve to its full depth, the air stream is redirected through an extra length of pipe. But someone somewhere in our rich, still uncharted jazz history discovered that by depressing the valve less than its full depth an entire vocabulary of buzzes, bends, groans, and rusty whispers can be coaxed out of the horn.

Stewart was the undisputed master of the half-valve. He humanized his solos with "ghost" notes that seemed to come from deep inside the instrument. John Faddis, best known for his pyrotechnical *altissimo* (piccolo range) trumpet playing, came down to earth and recreated Stewart's solo. It was obvious he had spent long hours studiously analyzing with which valve, and at what depth, he would find a given sound.

I asked Frank Wess to share the conducting and rehearsing duties with me, partly to avoid my being cast in the role of Duke Ellington, but more important to have the input of a highly respected veteran. Wess led most of the swinging jewels like "Cottontail," and "Jack the Bear," Duke's homage to the legendary stride pianist which enigmatically features the bass; our soloist was Milt Hinton. I conducted the opening and closing sequences and of course *Black, Brown and Beige.* Frank also played the iconic Johnny Hodges "Come Sunday" solo using Johnny's horn, which he had purchased from Hodges's widow. Ours was a reverent, if reserved, re-creation.

With the approach of the fiftieth anniversary of *Black, Brown and Beige,* I proposed that Music Masters make a digital recording of the jazz-band original. Unbeknownst to me, the master drummer and composer Louie Bellson had been talking with Music Masters about recording his *Ellington-Strayhorn Suite,* written while he was playing in Duke's band in the 1950s. We were brought together and our projects merged. Louie's big band was augmented with Ellington alumni, among them trumpeters Clark Terry and Barry Lee Hall and trombonists Britt Woodman and Art Baron.[14] As an added bonus, Joe Williams agreed to sing his interpretation of "The Blues."

For the American Jazz Orchestra and the Carnegie Hall re-creation, I had used the score and parts that were prepared by British arranger Alan Cohen. Since Ellington had published only a fragment of *Beige* (a truncated version of "Sugar Hill Penthouse") the rest of the movement—over fifteen minutes of music—was painstakingly transcribed by Cohen. This necessitated a great deal of educated guesswork on his part, trying to hear around the bass drum on the location recording.[15]

By good fortune, Ellington's sketches and his autograph score for *Beige* had come to light at the Smithsonian Archives just as I was getting ready to record. The highly respected and sorely missed Ellington scholar Mark Tucker helped organize the collection and kindly provided me with a copy of the autograph, enabling me to correct the Cohen parts in time for the recording.

I was particularly gratified by the reception given, by audience and critics alike, to a performance I did with John Faddis's Carnegie Hall Jazz Band at the hall on January 21, 1999 (later broadcast on National Public Radio). I privately considered this "full circle" return the ultimate test. "Did *Black, Brown and Beige* have the wherewithal to perpetuate itself as a fertile work of art and not just a historic oddity?" The circumstances could not have been better. I had the time and the resources to revisit the score and parts and make what I now consider a definitive edition, beautifully rendered by a computer engraver.[16] The Carnegie Hall Jazz band, a superb ensemble of musicians, led by John Faddis, who know their jazz history and revere Ellington, could not have been more dedicated. And by this time Ruth Ellington Boatwright had introduced me to an amazing document, a thirty-three-page double-spaced typescript by Duke Ellington titled "Black, Brown and Beige": a narrative poem that evidently preceded the music and gave me considerable insight into his thinking about the piece.

George Wein, the jazz warrior impresario and producer of the Carnegie Hall Jazz series, warned me that he remembered *Black, Brown and Beige* to be overly long and suggested that I consider some cuts. Of course I did not cut one measure. When we finished he came running backstage wild with pleasure, as was most of the audience, which rose as one at the end of *Beige*.

The critics—all five—concurred: "'*Black, Brown and Beige*' brims with gorgeous music and should be played more often." "The Carnegie audience jumped to its feet and cheered. . . . That's the sign of a living piece of music." "Would have made the Maestro's eyes moisten with gratitude . . . 'Beige,' the third and least performed segment, offered more mysteries and far more rhythmic complexities than the others. A near-frantic welter of motifs and themes . . . handled with unflagging authority and crispness by the Carnegie band." "The dark familiar colors were beautifully reconstructed, and the band approached the musical narrative with reverent unity." "Peress and the Carnegie Hall Jazz Band proved [*Black, Brown and Beige*] deserves to be heard on concert stages throughout the world, during [Ellington's] centennial and for many years to come."[17]

Black, Brown and Beige—"as it is"—has "legs." I had grown ever closer to the music and Ellington's fascinating poem. And I believe that by consciously following the "program" in my mind as we played, the band, and in turn the audience, intuitively felt the signifiers in the work.[18]

The Poem

The poem is divided into three sections, titled *movements*: "Black" takes up the first half while "Brown" and "Beige" together share the remainder. Mark Tucker writes that the poem was finalized in the early 1940s, although an earlier handwritten draft may date to the mid-1930s.[19] The poem traces the life of Boola, a mythical African, through three centuries, beginning with his enslavement and painful crossing to America on a slave ship. It tells of his bondage on a plantation and how he regains strength from music and faith. It follows Boola the soldier, fighting against America's enemies, even while enslaved; and Boola the newly freed man, as he experiences emancipation and learns about the blues. "Beige," the last part of the poem, describes life in Harlem, the "Black Metropolis," during World War II. To convey this saga in music alone was the immense task Ellington set for himself.

Ellington had been planning to compose a significant concert work about the history of Africans in America for at least a decade before his first Carnegie Hall appearance. It was known that he had an opera in mind. In a *New York Times Magazine* article just before the 1943 Carnegie Hall concert, Howard Taubman wrote: "Ellington's most elaborate composition is an opera, still unproduced, called 'Boola.' . . . He has taken some of the music from this opera and turned it into a half-hour tone poem for his band."[20] Did Ellington intend this sprawling poem to serve as a libretto? Given the absence of set pieces (arias) and choruses, the poem initially seems more appropriate as a text for an oratorio. But the reality of the impending concert date may have forced his hand. Ellington adjusted his plans, and his poem was finally expressed in music by his orchestra of marvelous jazz artists alone. How did Ellington musicalize his text?

First movement: Black, *section one, "Work Song."*

The opening lines of the poem read:

> A message is shot through the jungle by drums.
> Boom! Boom! Boom! Boom!
> Like a tom-tom in steady precision.
> Like the slapping of bare feet across the desert
>   wastes.
> Like hunger pains . . . [21]

The opening section does indeed begin with kettledrums "in steady precision." The poem goes on to describe Boola's catastrophic experiences with the torture and displacement of slavery for six pages before actually mentioning the work song:

> Out of this deep dream of freedom
> Evolved the only possible escape
> Freedom of expression in song.
> Out of this great need for freedom
> The work song was born.
> Not a song of triumph. Not a song
> Of burden. A song punctuated
> By the grunt of a heaving pick
> Or axe. A song punctuated by the swish
> And thud of a sledgehammer.

The "Work Song," a pounding seven-note theme stated by the trumpets and saxophones in unison, is distinguished by a quickly falling fifth and rising third that outlines the tonic triad of E-flat. It serves as a leitmotif that appears throughout *Black, Brown and Beige*. Whether the music depicts slaves at Emancipation Day fearful of leaving the plantation, folks in their Sunday best singing a spiritual, the discovery of the blues, or sophisticated Harlemites going off to war, the "Work Song" theme is woven in, a reminder of the roots shared by all African Americans, black, brown, or beige—to which Stanley Crouch, writer, critic, and Ellingtonian, adds *bone*.[22]

In the development of the "Work Song" section, Ellington has the baritone saxophone explore the leitmotif at length. In skilled hands, like those of Harry Carney, for whom Ellington was writing, the solo sounds improvised even though Ellington wrote every note in his manuscript score. The leitmotif is further transformed into a tightly harmonized jazz fanfare for a quartet of trumpets, and it shows up in another solo "improvisation" for the string bass. For his final "Work Song" formulation, Ellington recasts the sledge-hammer rhythm of the leitmotif, selecting perhaps the most extraordinary of hues from his orchestral spectrum, an evocative "plunger" trombone, which sounds like the cries of a human voice.

The plunger technique was first developed in Ellington's band by "Tricky Sam" Nanton. Nanton placed a *trumpet* straight mute deep into his trombone bell. He then compressed and released the mostly high-pitched sounds (sometimes raucous gut-bucket growls) by manipulating a rubber crown—a plumber's toilet plunger—across the opening of the bell. It sounds easy, but trombonists have been trying to emulate Nanton's "plunger" style for decades with little or no success.[23]

The "Work Song" section closes with a softly held incomplete cadence. An alto saxophone reaches out, introducing itself with a fragmentary tune marked *Religioso* in anticipation of the second section of *Black*, "Come Sunday."

"Come Sunday" was made famous in a vocal rendition (text by Ellington) by the great spiritual and gospel singer Mahalia Jackson, who recorded it with the Ellington orchestra—the only time she agreed to appear with a jazz ensemble—in 1958. But it was first conceived as a purely instrumental work, albeit one inspired by Ellington's poetry:

> Came Sunday, Boola was irresistibly drawn
> To that pretty white house with the steeple
> So tall, shining there in the sun. Everyone
> Who entered there was scrubbed and polished
> And all dressed up. How happy they seemed!
>
> When the white voices inside rang out
> In triumph . . . the blacks outside would grunt
> Subdued approval. When the white voices inside
> Were raised in joyous song, the blacks outside
> Hummed along, adding their own touches.
> Weaving Gorgeous melodic, harmonic, rhythmic patterns.
> Thus the spiritual was born.
> Highly emotional Worshipping of God in song.

Short, lyrical statements by solo trombone and trumpet introduce the "song," rendered not by voices, but as a collection of *Religioso* instrumental testimonies. "Come Sunday" follows the traditional thirty-two-measure AABA pattern, but there the similarity ends. The A section begins unusually on the dominant seventh chord with an added thirteenth in the melody, the first in a series of abstract harmonies. The music slowly rises, "Weaving Gorgeous melodic, harmonic, rhythmic patterns," resting on nonchordal tones: a flatted fifth and a ninth. A closing phrase swoops down an octave and a half: "white voices inside rang out / In triumph." The music holds still, catching its breath: "the blacks outside . . . grunt / Subdued approval." Muted trombones slide a spiritual "amen" church cadence into place, establishing home, the tonic chord.

When I recorded "Come Sunday" with the Louie Bellson band, I honored Duke's admonition not to allow anyone to imitate Johnny Hodges. And keeping in mind how Ellington realized the text of his poem with gentle instrumental colors—veritable sermons by Ray Nance's warm and sweet violin and Hodges's poignant alto sax—I asked Clark Terry, a treasured jazz creator who was with Ellington for almost a decade, to interpret what had been the Hodges alto sax solo on his flugelhorn. Terry played the slow phrases tenderly and without an apparent breath, using circular breathing. One listens in awe to this "Highly emotional / Worshipping of God in song." I suspect Ellington would have approved.

The music of *Black* closes with a joyous release, a hard-swinging section titled "Light" after the poem:

> Oh, well, here's something new . . . Let's sing About this. Our work
>   lightens . . . our song lifts . . .
> But the spiritual slips in and out as we see
> And learn new things. Boola worked
> And dwelt in song . . .
>
> The slave song broadened, covering all things
> Sometimes soft . . . sometimes loud. A rainbow
> Of color, complete with pot of gold. Paradise
> To come. On their way to heaven in tempo.
> The pulse, the beat was ever present.
> Boom! Boom! Boom! Boom!

Second movement: Brown, *section one, "West Indian Dance."*

The poem "Brown" describes the historic battles fought by African Americans on behalf of America. In each case, "Boola was there":[24] the Indian rebellion of 1652 on the side of the colonials; on the Boston Commons alongside Crispus Attucks, who "shed his black blood in the birth struggle / Of this great republic!"; in the War of 1812, his "heart was filled" when "came the seven hundred free Haitians / Of the Fontages Legion to descend / Upon the British at the Siege of Savannah"; with Nat Turner and the Abolitionists, on the Underground Railway and the Civil War battlefield, in the long struggle that led to emancipation; and finally, at San Juan Hill in the Spanish-American War, soon after which "Boola got the blues!"

The poem "West Indian Dance" depicts Boola's reaction to Haitian drums:

> the echo of Africa
> Was loud here
> Tropical jungles. Savage drums . . .
> Religious drums . . . Sexual drums . . .

This is reflected in the music of "West Indian Dance," breaking away from the more serious "tonalizations" of *Black* as Ellington unleashes the drum-driven island rhythms of the *corrida* (dash or sprint), exposing another facet of the jazz diadem, the "Latin tinge."

The music of "Emancipation Proclamation," the second section of *Brown*, slows down the pace a bit in order to celebrate the ultimate victory for African American soldiers, "His God-given rights [*sic*] to be free!" In the poem Ellington tempers this elation, reminding the reader that while "it was sweet to be one's own! / A sad note was sounded in the hearts of old folk." Instead of enjoying their retirement, they would be thrown off the farms and plantations where they had spent their lives.

Ellington musicalizes these conflicting emotions by juxtaposing a swinging celebrational music, "Boola jumped for joy!"—originally depicted with elegant humor by cornetist Rex Stewart—with a string of worrisome duets for two of the older folks. Their raspy voices are represented by a "plunger" trumpet and "plunger" trombone; they blend, they bicker, and finally totter off, shaking with age and resignation.

The poem "Brown" also describes a new kind of music: the blues, a result of the love triangles that surfaced when black soldiers returned from the Spanish-American War to find their ladies with other men:

> A medal hung proudly from his chest,
> But where were her arms for his head to rest?
> And soon he learned someone had to lose
> That's how Boola got the blues.
> The Blues . . .
> The Blues ain't . . .

For "The Blues," the third and final musical section of *Brown*, Ellington turned to his vocalist, Bette Roche. Only the first two lines of the song come from the poem. Ellington expands upon them, creating an entirely new text. Could this be a model of how an operatic libretto would have evolved from his poem? Note that the opening three lines are mirrored at the end of the song:

> The Blues
> The Blues ain't—
> The Blues ain't nothin'
> The Blues ain't nothin' but a cold grey day
> And all nite long it stays that way.
> Ain't somethin' that leaves you alone
> Ain't nothin' you should want to call your own
> Ain't somethin' with sense enough to get up and go
> Ain't nothin'
> Like nothin' I know
> The Blues don't
> The Blues don't know nobody as a friend
> Ain't been back nowhere where they're welcome back again
> The low ugly mean Blues.
> The Blues ain't somethin' that you
> Sing in rhyme
> The Blues ain't nothin' but a dark cloud markin' time
> The Blues is a one way ticket
> From your Love to nowhere
> The Blues ain't nothin' but a black crepe veil ready to wear
> Sighin'
> Cryin'
> Feels most like Dyin'!
> The Blues ain't nothin'
> The Blues ain't—
> The Blues

Most of Ellington's musical gems are formulations of the twelve-bar blues, a matrix he never tired of and one for which he would never run out of ideas. "The Mooch," "Creole Love Call," "Transblucency," and "Things Ain't What They Used to Be" are all twelve-bar blues. Even what he called his "extended concert pieces"—*Grand Slam Jam* and *Harlem*—contain long sections of twelve-bar blues. Yet, for the "Blues" section from *Black, Brown and Beige*, he follows his mentor "Dad" (Will Marion) Cook's proscription: "First you find the logical way, and when you find it, avoid it, and let your inner self break through and guide you."[25]

Starting with its abstract, almost atonal introduction, the harmony, bar structure, and melodic contour of "The Blues" section are a jazz world away from the standard blues. Well into the piece, after the singer finishes the first chorus of the song and steps back to listen, Ellington calls upon his trombones to wail a demonstration chorus of the twelve-bar blues—later recycled and developed into a separate instrumental work called the "Carnegie Hall Blues." A tenor sax interlude leads us back to the song, its final lick being a quote of the "Work Song" leitmotif. Ellington's song "The Blues" is a masterpiece *about* the blues.

Beige

Beige is the longest and the most enigmatic of the three movements and the one that departs almost entirely from the poetry. The poem "Beige" reveals Ellington's most heartfelt philosophic testimony about the African American experience. The focus shifts from the metaphoric world of Boola to Harlem, from the mythical to the autobiographical.[26] Boola becomes Ellington:

> Harlem! Black Metropolis!
> Land of mirth!
> Your music has flung
> The story of "Hot Harlem"
> To the four corners
> Of the earth!

"Hot Harlem" is aptly expressed by the opening jungle-style music of *Beige*, a tom-tom-driven music we associate with Ellington's Cotton Club days. The distinguished critic and author Albert Murray argues that the jungle style was satire, wordplay—the asphalt jungle, not the Congo;[27] an urbane notion that is not supported by Duke's descriptive words and phrases in the opening stanza of "Beige" the poem: "primeval beat of the jungle . . . scorching . . . primitive jungle calls . . . wild . . . joyous . . . exciting as Stravinsky!" [*sic*].

The poem's mood turns bitter, but Ellington's music does not follow. The poem asks:

> But did it [Harlem's music] ever speak to them
> Of what you really are?
> Did it say to them . . .
> "The joy I'm giving,
> Is the foil I use to lose my blues
> And make myself an honest living!"
> Did it speak to them
> That all your striving

To make your rightful place with men
Was more than jazz and jiving!
How could they fail to hear
The hurt and pain and anguish
Of those who travel dark, lone ways
The soul in them to languish . . .

Later in the poem Ellington welcomes the end of black minstrelsy and
Harlem's newfound community pride and self-esteem:

Yes, Harlem!
Land of valiant youth,
You've wiped the make-up from your face,
And shed your borrowed spangles.
You've donned the uniform of truth,
And hid the hurt that dangles
In heart and mind. And one by one
You've set your shoulders straight
To meet each challenge and to wait
Till justice unto you is done!

If the music of *Beige* cannot be reconciled with the mix of anger and
pride found in the poem, what, then, is its story?

We know that Ellington originally intended that somewhere toward the
end of *Beige*, the very last lines of his poem were to be sung:

Once more, you've heard your country call,
Patient, willing to give your all.
Once more, the word is sent to you
[sung from here on]
And the black, the brown, the beige
Is ready for the chance to wage
The fight for right 'neath the red, white and blue!

Why not remind the gala audience assembled in Carnegie Hall — in support
of Russian War Relief! — that African Americans were again fighting for their
country while awaiting true emancipation?

The sung section was tried out at a preview performance held in Rye
High School in Rye, New York, the night before the Carnegie Hall performance, which is where, according to one of Ellington's admirers, critic
Barry Ulanov, "the 'flagwaving' finale featuring vocalist Jimmy Britton was
cut."[28] Nevertheless, Ellington made sure his message was heard. He spoke
to the Carnegie Hall audience before each of the movements, and his ver-

bal introduction to *Beige*, preserved on the archival "location" recording, ends with a paraphrase of the text: "The Black, the Brown, the Beige is ready for the chance to fight for the Red, White and Blue!" This serves as one of several clues to *Beige's* musical narrative.

I believe that the music of *Beige* tells a story about a group of Negro soldiers in World War II. They are on a weekend leave, attending a "Sugar Hill Penthouse" party in Harlem. Following the excitement of the opening jungle music, a stride piano belts out a tune that Ellington composed in his teens, "Bitch's Ball," gaily announcing an all-night social affair. But the mood turns sad as we hear a dirge based upon the four notes of the jungle theme. Ellington then introduces a series of party dances, each again derived from the jungle theme, beginning with a slow seductive waltz.[29] Ellington's titles, written into the score, suggest a scenario as well. After the "Waltz," a medium fox-trot, "Cy-Runs," is interrupted, by a fire siren or a vixen or both. These are followed by a swinging "Rok [sic] Waltz"; a ballad, "Last of Penthouse"; and "Sugar Hill Penthouse Reprise,"[30] a slow version of "Waltz."

As the last slow dance, "Sugar Hill Penthouse Reprise," is being whispered by closely harmonized saxes, a fanfare interrupts. It is time to go. Gospel piano chords introduce a reprise of "Come Sunday"; its final "amen" cadence aches with nostalgia. A morning church bell is sounded. The "amen" is slowly expanded by the piano, becoming a powerful cadenza that explodes into a patriotic, flag-waving, orchestral finale; a stirring anthem is sounded in the trumpets above, while below the baritone sax and trombones strut through themes from the entire score. Ellington's piano returns in a "medium stride" to introduce the final shout-chorus.[31] We hear bits and pieces of "Come Sunday" and "Work Song." I envision the young soldiers and their ladies brimming with the emotions of love, of God and country; and as they part, a final trumpet scream blots out all fears and doubts.

This rich mix of jungle music, party dances, Sunday church atmosphere, and patriotic bombast reflects the complexity of the Harlem community described in Ellington's poem. Ellington is telling us that the American Negro, black, brown, and beige, arrived here out of great suffering, built this land, fought its enemies, gained freedom, and gave it spirituals, the blues, and jazz, which reached out to the "four corners of the globe." Nevertheless, while they march off again to fight, true equality is still withheld. The music of *Beige*, like the poem, is, after all, a political work—Ellington's musical expression of words later to be eloquently spoken by Dr. Martin Luther King Jr.: "How long, O Lord?"

Ellington the Composer

The autograph and copyright scores of *Black, Brown and Beige* reveal some fascinating information about Ellington's composing practices. For example, on the opening pages of the *Beige* autograph there are asterisks indicating six different high-pitched vertical chords—clusters (seven or eight interlocking notes) identified by the numbers 1 through 6. These clusters, led by a clarinet in its highest register, function as "hits"—short, sharp chords that punctuate the wild jungle theme being grunted out by low trombones and baritone sax. The numbers are a shorthand for the clusters when next they appear, relieving Ellington from having to write out the seven or eight interlocking notes every time. On the bottom margin of the first page of the autograph, Ellington identifies the asterisks as "Piano Theme." Why are the clusters called "Piano Theme"? The first five clarinet notes at the top of the clusters spell out (in minor) a variant of the theme from "Work Song," with its characteristic falling fifth and rising third.[32]

Thus, at the very moment Duke is introducing us to "Hot Harlem" and its new jungle-music leitmotif, a reflection of Boola, of the past, shines down from above.

Furthermore, the clusters are an example of "secret voicings," the "Ellington sound," which has often been explained away as the result of individual musicians adding their own dissonant, accidental harmonies. Duke himself encouraged this quaint notion of collaborative composition through his constant use of the first-person plural: "Our impressions of the Far East." Typical of the musician's stories that perpetuate this myth is one about trumpeter and composer Thad Jones from the time he first joined the band. A tune was called, but the part was missing from Jones's band book. Looking over at a nearby player's part, he began blowing along, making up harmonies as he went, only to hear Cootie Williams growl, "Get offa my note!"

The most remarkable discovery, one already noted, was that nearly all the improvised-sounding solos in *Black, Brown and Beige* were written by Ellington himself, the most striking example being a long solo cadenza by Ben Webster in *Beige*.[33]

Eleven chords are struck and held by the orchestra. Above each of these "stop chords," the tenor sax plays a short solo. In the archival location recording we hear Ben Webster adding his own after-licks and impeccable phrasing, but the critical notes are Duke's. And what notes! Above the first and third chord, the tenor sax quotes "Work Song." Above the second chord we hear the tune from "Sugar Hill Penthouse." Above the final chord the tenor sax begins with the jungle theme and unwinds with a preview of the melody that is about to follow, "Last of Penthouse."[34]

Here Ellington does for his solo-filled works what Beethoven did for his piano concertos: composing cadenzas rather than leaving them, as tradition had it, to the improvising skills and good taste of soloists. I doubt that Duke would approve of my bringing attention to this parallel. In stark contrast to his contemporary Gershwin, who sought acceptance by the musical establishment as a "legitimate" composer, Ellington rejected the notion entirely. Whenever we talked about his music, he spoke of feelings or images — about people standing outside a church they could not enter and harmonizing with the beautiful music they heard from within, knowing they all shared the same God. How then can I justify analyzing his compositional secrets?

The answer lies in the realization that I do this for myself, to legitimize my own passion for this music and that of others like me who, despite brainwashing by the academy of our youth, have been drawn to and nourished by Ellington's music. Not withstanding my sense that Duke would not approve, I find myself compelled to demonstrate how complex is the compositional process that creates his seemingly happy-go-lucky music, how even the defining idea of jazz-inspired music — a tenor saxophonist "taking off" on an improvised flight — was controlled, bent, premeditated by Ellington in the service of his muse, and how he crafted his music from his own poetry.

Afterword

My own story continues. I make all sorts of joyful noises whenever possible. Thanks to Duke Ellington, I have learned that what I believed to be separate worlds of music—the European world of Dvořák, Ellington's African American macrocosm, and Bernstein's conflation of the two—are really one. All the stories in my book are about the transfer of the center of creative power from Europe to America, Dvořák being the prophet and Ellington its fulfillment.

Dvořák's Neighborhood

I have re-created Dvořák's America, in part, by reading crumbling old newspapers and playing his "American" works and those of his pupils. I also "walked in his moccasins," so to speak, here and abroad.

In the Czech Republic I found everything lovingly preserved and maintained. Besides his country house, Vysoka, there is a charming Dvořák Museum in Prague not far from his last apartment. His archives are splendidly preserved, and his birthplace, Nelahozeves, is now a state-supported tourist attraction.

In America, only a few vestiges of Dvořák's Old World remain, and they are fast disappearing. The Midway Plaisance, near the University of Chicago, site of the exotic villages over which Ferris's wheels once loomed, is now a grassy field, good for strolling, sunning, and sports by day and an unsafe expanse by night. In New York City the Church of Our Lady of Perpetual Help, built in 1887 for Bohemian-speaking Catholics, where Dvořák sought the comfort of his mother tongue as he offered a Mass for the Dead for his beloved *Tatinku* (Little Father), was torn down less than a year after I "discovered" it and told an excited priest about its Dvořák connection.[1] Lüchow's German restaurant, the place where H. L. Mencken reports that his drinking buddy, music critic and novelist James Gibbons Huneker, took Dvořák for his first Manhattan cocktail and got him sloshed, is but a fond memory.[2] Still, there is enough left of his old neighborhood—the Washington Irving House, St. George's Episcopal Church, and Stuyvesant Square Park—to afford the stroller authentic flashes of the turn-of-the-century ambience.

In the spring of 1990 I walked Dvořák's daily path along Seventeenth Street, from the north wing of Washington Irving High School, where the conservatory once stood, to his house a few blocks east—a path that would lead me smack dab into the middle of a landmarking battle, trying to save the Dvořák House from the wrecker's ball.

In the middle of the first block, I passed the side entrance to what was Scheffel's Beer Hall, built in 1894. I can imagine Dvořák, who was a lover of beer and had a daily pail delivered to his house, stepping in for a quick mug. Scheffel's was, at the time of my walk, home to a jazz club named Fat Tuesday's. Its strikingly massive Renaissance revival facade, around the corner on Third Avenue, featured a hologram of Dizzy Gillespie. Over ballooned cheeks and bent horn, Dizzy's eyes followed me no matter where I stood—an amusing reminder of my furiously eclectic musical *olam*.

I crossed Third Avenue and took in a lovely block lined almost completely with nineteenth-century brownstones. The block opened onto the uptown side of Stuyvesant Square Park, and I became aware of St. George's,[3] the church where Harry T. Burleigh reigned for over forty years as baritone soloist and where many of his art songs and arrangements of spirituals were first heard. I soon passed the statue of Peter Stuyvesant, dubbed by Dvořák "the one-legged pirate." Before me, breaching the park, was Second Avenue, a street the Maestro feared crossing alone.[4]

On the far side of Second Avenue, my Dvořák reverie was shattered. Historical Seventeenth Street was abruptly taken over by massive modern hospital buildings, two even connected by an overpass. I had almost forgotten what I was searching for when, halfway to First Avenue, the hospital's tasteless architectural jumble gave way to a brave row of nineteenth-century houses. To my pleasant surprise, at 327 East Seventeenth Street, I came upon

FIGURE 18-1
The Dvořák House. Photograph by the author, 1990.

the modest brownstone in which the Dvořák family kept a five-room flat during their two and a half years in America.

The Dvořák House

Mounted upon the facade of the house was a handsome bronze plaque. In the center was a large bas-relief portrait of Dvořák, identified in large letters:

FIGURE 18-2
Dvořák House Memorial Plaque. Created by Agon Agopoff
for the Czechoslovak Cultural Circle, mounted on
December 7, 1941.

THE FAMOUS CZECH COMPOSER ANTONIN DVOŘÁK
(1841–1904) LIVED IN THIS HOUSE FROM 1892 UNTIL 1895.

This was surmounted by the following text in smaller letters, also cast as part
of the plaque:

IN MEMORY OF HIS 100TH BIRTHDAY AND FOR FUTURE GENERATIONS OF
FREE CZECHOSLOVAKIA, THE GRATEFUL GOVERNMENT IN EXILE CAUSED
THIS INSCRIPTION TO BE ERECTED ON DECEMBER 13TH 1941. LONGING
FOR HIS CZECH HOME, YET HAPPILY INSPIRED BY THE FREEDOM OF
AMERICAN LIFE, HE WROTE HERE AMONG OTHER WORKS THE NEW
WORLD SYMPHONY, BIBLICAL SONGS, THE CELLO CONCERTO.

A dedication ceremony had been held in the house on the afternoon of
December 13, 1941, only a few days after the sneak attack on Pearl Harbor.
The musicians, old friends, and dignitaries assembled in Dvořák's former living room had much to think about. Mayor Fiorello LaGuardia, who, along
with Governor Herbert H. Lehman and Franklin Delano Roosevelt, made
up the heroic triumvirate of my youth, gave the opening remarks:

The war will be long and difficult but a new world will come into existence, free from the attacks of fanatical dictators. . . . Dvořák produced much that will live forever, and his music will be played and his name will be honored when the names of Hitler, Mussolini, and the Mikado [*sic*] will be found only by referring to the criminal[s] . . . of history.[5]

Jan Masaryk, foreign minister of the Czech government-in-exile, then spoke. It was Masaryk's father who, with the help of President Woodrow Wilson, finally succeeded in establishing Czechoslovakia as an independent nation after World War I. Dvořák, and his American house, were for the Czech American community and the Czech government-in-exile a precious symbol of that legacy:

> We Czechoslovakians and Americans of Czechoslovakian descent swear by the memory of Dvořák that we will do everything in our power to help the new world, because by so doing we will help to compose the real "new world symphony" of free people.

Three representatives from the New York Philharmonic were in attendance: Bruno Walter, its music director and conductor; Arthur Judson,[6] who represented the board; and a member of the orchestra's viola section, Joseph Kovařik, Dvořák's former assistant, who had lived in the house with the Dvořák family forty-nine years earlier.

Violinist Fritz Kreisler came to pay his respects. It was Kreisler who renamed Dvořák's Sonatine for Violin and Piano the *Indian Lament*. The sonatine, one of Dvořák's "American" works, holds the significant opus number 100, set aside by the composer for a new work to honor and entertain his two eldest children—Antonin, age ten, and Otilie, age fifteen. Their first rendition, in that very room was, in Dvořák's own words, "[my] favorite premiere."[7]

Dvořák's old pupils Edward B. Kinney[8] and Harry T. Burleigh also attended. Burleigh had just celebrated his seventy-fifth birthday, a time for reflection, and being back in the house must have rekindled poignant feelings.

Two youthful Czech-born artists—pianist Rudolf Firkusny and Metropolitan Opera star Jarmilla Novatna—performed several of the *Biblical Songs*, also composed in the House. Little did they know that fifty years later they would become active in the, alas, unsuccessful campaign to rescue the Dvořák House from the territorial ambitions of nearby Beth Israel Hospital.

When I first came upon the Dvořák House in 1990, it was apparent that the building had been emptied.[9] It had all the earmarks of a major restoration—or a demolition—about to happen. I quickly wangled an appointment to gain entry, "in the interest of musicological research," and made sure to bring my camera.

Not surprisingly, in the hundred years since Dvořák lived there, the building had undergone some modernization, the most radical change being an interior circular staircase between the street level and the first (parlor) floor. But the principal rooms, which overlooked the rear garden and the street, retained their original marble mantelpieces, and much of the woodwork survived as well. The window shutters were still folded into their paneled boxes, and the massive doors and window frames were intact.

I imagined where Dvořák set the grand piano that William Steinway sent over from his Fourteenth Street showroom—in the back room near the garden window, with the north light coming over his right shoulder. I envisioned the Kneisel (String) Quartet during one of their visits, set up in the corner next to the fireplace. I fancied the quartet's cellist, Alwin Schroeder, sitting across from the piano, reading through the cello concerto, the "first hearing in history," in February 1895, and Dvořák's children playing the sonatine. I wondered: in which room did Burleigh sing to Dvořák?

I joined the battle to save the Dvořák House. We gave concerts, formed a committee of distinguished "friends," and lobbied local and national politicians. But within fourteen months of my first visit, the house was no more.

For one brief period our efforts seemed to have been rewarded. On February 26, 1991, the City Landmarks Commission officially designated the Dvořák House a "Historic Landmark," but four months later the designation was overturned by the city council—the first reversal of its kind. In the interim we enlisted William Warfield to sing "Goin' Home" at a city council meeting. I helped arrange a "Save the Dvořák House" concert at St. George's to raise public awareness. The hospital countered, calling upon its deepest political connections, and convinced Isaac Stern, savior of Carnegie Hall, to declare on television, "We have the music, Dvořák was there for only a short time, why keep a building that has changed beyond recognition?" To my naive surprise, the *New York Times* came down against us. On March 7, 1991, an article appeared on their editorial page under the headline, "Dvořák Doesn't Live Here Anymore." It was an embittering experience, my first real encounter with city politics and raw, arrogant power.[10]

I was heartsick over the destruction of the central icon of Dvořák's American period and mortified before my Czech friends who—coming from a country where historic churches, synagogues, and houses both modest and grand are cherished and lovingly maintained—could not understand why the United States would allow such a desecration.

I was also particularly saddened for Jarmilla Novatna. Having sung at the dedication of the house fifty years earlier, she was more than just another concerned artist. Novatna was, in the greater sense, a trustee. And knowing that she had been there with Burleigh, Kovařik, Kreisler, and others who had worked with the master made the hundred years between myself and Dvořák almost fathomable.

We did not give up. One of the most devoted Save the Dvořák House proponents, the architect Jan Pokorny, made arrangements to have the bas-relief plaque and the parlor floor fireplace mantels removed and placed in storage at the Bohemian National Hall on Manhattan's East Seventy-third Street. The hall was erected in 1896 by the Czech community with the help of Dvořák, who raised money for it when he first arrived in New York. These elements will become part of a new Dvořák Museum that will occupy one floor of the building.[11]

One of our enemies was ignorance. Had the battle to save the Dvořák House taken place a year later, when the one hundredth anniversary of Dvořák's American adventure got underway and a cascade of Dvořák articles and celebrations descended upon us, I firmly believe the house would still be standing. Maybe a Dvořák Museum on Stuyvesant Square Park would have had a chance.

Within two years of the house's demolition, his music began enjoying a remarkable revival. New York's leading classical music station placed ads in the *New York Times*: "Dvořák Is Dynamite." *Rusalka*, Dvořák's most celebrated opera, was mounted for the first time at the Metropolitan Opera on November 11, 1993. In 1997, Seventeenth Street along Stuyvesant Square Park was renamed Dvořák Place, and a statue of Dvořák was erected in the park not far from the lost house.

The general public has become far more aware of Dvořák, his music, and his American story. Part of that story is the heightened awareness he brought to the bountiful riches of African American music.

The Composer-Collector Generation

Dvořák's "Negro music idea" came at the time of, and no doubt influenced, a rising generation of Negro writers and composer-collectors who independently realized that their effusive culture of story, song, and movement had to be documented and put down on paper.

The elegant author James Weldon Johnson described New York's early Negro musical community in great detail in his *Black Manhattan* (1930). He also edited and wrote the introduction for *The Book of American Negro Spirituals*, with musical arrangements by his brother, the composer James Rosamond Johnson.[12] The vaudevillian and musical entertainer Tom Fletcher documented everything he could recall in his *100 Years of the Negro in Show Business*, from his youth as an actor in the 1880s—a field hand in a dramatization of *Uncle Tom's Cabin*—through his days in vaudeville and as a jazz musician in the 1930s.

These writers were joined by a group of Negro "composers" who were as much, or more, collectors and notators of black musical memories. In this I include Ernest Hogan's far from unusual aural hijacking and reworking of "All Coons Look Alike to Me," described earlier. I also include Harry T. Burleigh. Well over half of Burleigh's 215 published works are settings of traditional spirituals and Negro songs. He also published two "collections," comprising over 207 Afro-American Folk Songs.[13]

The most compelling example of the composer-collector is W. C. Handy, the peripatetic cornetist, bandleader, composer, arranger, black music historian, and music publisher. Handy's true contribution was in "uncovering," no less "fathering," the blues, a style of playing he learned and practiced well before it became a form he could write down. Handy caught the public's attention with his celebrated "first," the "Memphis Blues," composed in 1909 and published in 1912. He went on to become a New York–based sheet music publisher who branched out into art songs, solo piano pieces, and choral works by other composers. He published a significant collection of well over a hundred spirituals, supplying his own harmonizations and arrangements. In the elaborate introduction to his lovingly assembled 1926 anthology *The Blues*,[14] Handy carefully transcribes and notates the old foot and hand "pats" that propelled and underpinned shouts and play songs, along with work songs and jubas from his youth. I recently visited the offices of the Handy Brothers publishing house, a family-owned business since 1915, and was greeted by a smiling and rightfully proud grandniece, Edwinna Handy, who guided me into a set of rooms that appear to be unchanged from the first half of the last century. Long lines of shelves overflow with yellowing sheet music. There are brick-shaped packets of octavo choral music and stock arrangements by the yard. Period photos cover the walls: Handy with the Duke, with Victor Herbert, Dizzy Gillespie, Louis Armstrong, Sarah Vaughan; Handy fronting ancient bands and salon orchestras; greetings from eager vaudeville acts and minstrel stars; a tribute from Gershwin. The office is a veritable salon, museum, archive, and retail sheet music outlet. Once a hangout for song pluggers, arrangers, and bandleaders on the prowl for gigs, stocks, and publishing deals, it was the place to talk about the good old days with W. C., a grand old man of African American music, who was there.

A keen historical memory is also evident in the work of finished composers such as Will Marion Cook and, of course, his protégé, Duke Ellington. The sum total of this American master's prolific impressions, portraits, narrated stories such as *A Drum Is a Woman*, and the larger works, *Black, Brown and Beige* and *Harlem*, comprise an African American *Gesamtausgabe*, a complete black history artwork.

During my research and writing I was often struck by the conscious search for, and development of, an African American instrumental voice. The European symphony orchestra Dvořák taught his students to write for was too inflexible, too interconnected with court dances, Protestant hymns, and the Italian aria for African American–inspired music. It did not include the dance-driven oscillating sounds of strummed instruments — banjos, mandolines, and guitars — nor the bones, tambourine, and trap drums favored at the time by Negro musicians and entertainers. All of these instruments not only made for good steady rhythm, they also allowed the players to sing while they fiddled, struck, or strummed, often in three- and four-part harmony. If there was to be an African American orchestra, voices would have to be included — as they were in the Clef Club Orchestra — or else they would have to be replaced by instruments that could replicate Negro singing.

A New African American Orchestra

> We must strike out for ourselves, we must develop our own ideas and conceive an orchestration adapted to our own abilities and instincts. . . .
> Neither should a black symphony orchestra be organized to sound like a white one. —James Reese Europe

The search for an African American instrumental voice, that collection of saxes, trumpets, trombones, traps, brass, and string basses, and guitars that we now call a big band or a jazz band — the predecessors of today's electrified rock bands — was taken up in earnest by Will Marion Cook, Ford Dabney, and James Reese Europe, three composers and bandleaders who moved to New York City from Washington, D.C., to make their fortune.[15]

First came Cook's and Ernest Hogan's "playing, singing, dancing" Memphis Students Band (1905), also known as the Nashville Students, a twenty-member ensemble that featured the juggling "trick trap-drummer" Buddy Gilmore. For Jim Europe, who played in the band, it became a model for the society string orchestras that he would put together for the dancers Irene and Vernon Castle starting in 1913, and for his crowning achievement, the Clef Club Orchestra of 1912–15.

According to James Weldon Johnson, Ford Dabney "organized and directed a jazz orchestra which for a number of years was a feature of Florenz

Ziegfeld's roof-garden shows." Johnson sees Dabney and Europe as "the grand daddies of the unnumbered jazz orchestras that have followed."[16]

Jim Europe was getting ever closer to his dream of "an orchestration adapted to our own abilities and instincts," with his 369th Army band, "the Hellfighters" (1917–19), which featured hot drumming and "jazz breaks" for clarinet, solo cornet, and trombone. It was around the same time that Will Marion Cook's urbane Southern Syncopators orchestra appeared in London with its star soloist, Sidney Bechet, playing New Orleans–style jazz on clarinet and his newfound soprano sax.

A photograph of the Southern Syncopators taken for a poster advertising their monthlong engagement in Paris in 1921 shows thirty-seven musicians surrounding Maestro Cook. The instrumentation is not unlike that of the hybrid band Whiteman would lead at Aeolian Hall three years later: there are seven strings, eight brass, five saxes, flute, clarinet, two pianists, four banjos, two drummers (including "juggling" Buddy Gilmore), and seven singers.[17]

Mark Tucker points out that Cook, Europe, and Dabney brought their groups to Washington in the 1910s and 1920s, the formative years of another bandleader and composer from the nation's capital, Duke Ellington.[18]

Ellington's Washingtonians of 1927 still contained the makings of the earlier string bands; a hot drummer, a violinist, a string bass, and a banjo player. But the Washingtonians also featured a harmonic core rendered by three saxophones—the missing human voices?—and the unique trombone and trumpet work of "Tricky Sam" Nanton and Bubber Miley. They were inventing and refining the "black and tan fantasy" sounds that would soon distinguish Ellington's celebrated New York Cotton Club orchestra.

Ellington had lots of company. By the late 1920s a blaze of bandleaders, both black and white, were leading hot jazz orchestras of up to a dozen or so players and employing skilled arrangers, the unsung heroes of American music, to create their own unique repertoire. Whiteman's thirteen-piece Palais Royal Orchestra, often augmented for grand events such as the Aeolian Hall concert, had Grofé and later Bill Challis as the lead arrangers, and the Fletcher Henderson nine-piece Roseland Ballroom orchestra played "charts" by Don Redman and Henderson, to name the most prominent. But none of the above, neither bandleader nor arranger, was a world-class composer. With Duke Ellington, Dvořák's imperative was realized in ways that no one, including Duke's erstwhile teacher, Will Marion Cook, could have imagined.

Duke Ellington stands alone as the foremost American genius who remained loyal to the improvisational, tonal, and rhythmic endowments of African American music. His universe was an orchestra of brilliant jazz artists, one he never found wanting. With a light but firm tether, he drew and followed them along a trail of discovery, leaving glorious artifacts in his path.

Notes

Chapter 1

1. Eric Blom, ed., *Grove's Dictionary of Music and Musicians*, 5th ed. (New York: St. Martin's Press, 1954), 1:872.

2. Tchaikovsky made a better deal than Dvořák, earning $100 a day for his twenty-five-day stay in America, mostly to conduct at the 1891 opening of Andrew Carnegie's new Hall of Music. He also directed parts of four concerts with a small touring orchestra put together by Victor Herbert; they appeared in Boston, Baltimore, Washington, and Philadelphia. Tchaikovsky lived lavishly and went home with a thousand rubles ($600). See Elkhonon Yoffe, *Tchaikovsky in America* (New York: Oxford University Press, 1986), 160, 178.

3. Dvořák also appeared in Leeds, Edinburgh, Cambridge, and Manchester. He conducted in Russia and Germany during this period as well.

4. Jitka Slavikova, "A Brief Observation about the Dvořák Cello Concerto," *Report of the International Musicological Congress, Dobris, 17th–20th, September 1991* (Praha: Ustav pro hudebni vedu Akadamie ved Ceske republiky, 1994).

5. Emma Lazarus, "The New Colossus," inscribed on the pedestal of Frederic Auguste Bartholdi's mammoth Statue of Liberty.

6. Other "American" works of Dvořák include a Te Deum, the *Biblical Songs*, Sonatine (for violin and piano), the String Quintet (opus 97), the *American Suite*, and the cantata *The American Flag*.

CHAPTER 2

1. To quote from his self-published instruction manual: "To assist amateur players in giving the Joplin Rags that weird and intoxicating effect intended by the composer is the object of this work." Scott Joplin, *School of Ragtime* (New York: The author, 1907).

2. Curt Sachs, *World History of the Dance*, trans. Bessie Schönberg (New York: W. W. Norton, 1937), 367–373, 444.

3. Eileen Southern, *The Music of Black Americans*, 1st ed. (New York: W. W. Norton, 1971), 135.

4. John Fanning Watson's 2nd revised edition, *Annals of Philadelphia and Pennsylvania, in the Olden Time* (1850); quoted in Southern, *The Music of Black Americans*, 54.

5. Southern, *The Music of Black Americans*, 95–98.

6. The Thirty-first Regiment bivouacked on Port Royal Island south of Charleston from the winter of 1862 to the summer of 1864. The regiment then moved to Folly Island. George Gershwin spent four weeks on Folly Island in the summer of 1936 soaking up the music of the Gullah community in preparation for composing his *Porgy and Bess*.

7. [Sir Walter Scott, coll.,] *Minstrelsy of the Scottish Border*, 1802–3.

8. Thomas Wentworth Higginson, "My Life in a Black Regiment," *Atlantic Monthly*, June 1867, 685–94.

9. The symphony manager tried to calm me down. The minstrels were within their rights. We believed in free speech, etc., etc. For decades, a traveling director and producer, who also played the role of the interlocutor, had been setting up shop in small towns through Texas and Louisiana to direct the locals in their popular entertainment. In 1964 President Lyndon Baines Johnson, a good ol' Texas boy himself, forced the passing of the Civil Rights Act, and the Corpus Christi Lions Club Minstrels disappeared soon after.

10. Mel Watkins, *On The Real Side: Laughing, Lying, and Signifying* (New York: Simon and Schuster, 1994).

11. Duke Ellington, *Black, Brown and Beige*, typescript c. 1943, Ruth Ellington Archive, copy in author's files.

12. The Georgia Minstrels (1865–87) and the Hyer Sisters Minstrels were lodestones for the most advanced and highly schooled musicians as well as the most natural talents around. Their success tells us that they delivered enough of what was expected by white showgoers while displaying and developing their artistry. Black minstrel troupes even succeeded, once in a while, in integrating the seating of their mixed audiences.

13. Symphonic music written "under the influence of ragtime" included Debussy's "Golliwog's Cake-walk," Virgil Thomson's *Symphony on a Hymn Tune*, and part of Stravinsky's *L'histoire du soldat*.

14. On camera, Blake told us about the "first time I ever heard the word ragtime." He was around ten (more likely fourteen) years old when his mother surprised him as he was noodling around the keyboard. "Get that ragtime out of this house!" she scolded.

15. Clef Club photograph. On the right front—melody—side sit six mandolins, three "first" banjos, a violin, and a flute; on the left are one violin, nine tenor banjos, and one five-stringed folk banjo. Behind them, divided left and right, sit ten guitars

in all, including four harp guitars, one bass guitar and a bass banjo. Grouped together in the middle are seven cellos. Behind them sits a trap drummer with timpani. Three double basses are nearby. Bringing up the rear on both sides are ten men without instruments standing on their chairs. They would be the pianists, some of whom played "four hands." William Tyers leads the minstrel band in the rear. Like Jim Europe, he holds a baton and wears white tie and tails.

16. The minstrel band, as far as I can make out, has three cornets, a trombone and a tuba, a drummer, (one saxophone?), and six other men who are probably woodwind players or violinists. The front-liners have six banjos and seven tambourines.

17. In the photo, Tyres holds a baton and wears white tie and tails, as did Europe. The names of the minstrel band members appeared in an advance notice for the Monster Melange published in the *New York Age*, May 18, 1911.

18. In 1871 the music director at newly established Fisk University in Nashville, George L. White, selected nine singers and a pianist from among his student choir of former slaves; Ella Sheppard, pianist, Maggie L. Porter, Jennie Jackson, Minnie Tate, Eliza Walker, Phoebe J. Anderson, Thomas Rutling, Benjamin M. Holmes, Greene Evans, Isaac P. Dickerson and George Wells. It was his idea to raise funds for the school by presenting students in formal concerts of Negro songs and spirituals. By the time they completed their first successful tour up and down the eastern seaboard, under the sponsorship of abolitionist minister Ward Beecher of Brooklyn, White had chosen a name for his ensemble: The [Fisk] Jubilee Singers.

19. Leviticus 25: 8–17, and Exodus 21: 2–11.

20. Southern, *The Music of Black Americans*, 272.

21. J. B. T. Marsh, *The Story of the Jubilee Singers*, rev. ed. (Cleveland, 1892), 40–42. White never quite forgave himself that he did not answer the thunderous encore that followed with "John Brown" in the original version!

22. Marsh, *The Story of the Jubilee Singers*, 42.

CHAPTER 3

1. *New York Times*, October 10, 11, and 13, 1892.

2. Dvořák's style for October 14, 1892.

3. Antonin Dvořák, *Korespondence a Dokumenty* (Praha: Supraphon, 1985), 155–56.

4. That Dvořák seemed reluctant to complete the orchestration, even though most of the "American Flag" had been composed by the time he arrived, comes as no surprise. Dvořák must have realized the work was inferior and arranged it so that "American Flag" did not become his first American work. The piece, in my view, is as uninspired and awkward as the poem. It would have gotten him off to a bad start.

When Freedom from her mountain-height
Unfurled her standard to the air,
. . . And gave into his mighty hand
The symbol of her chosen land.

"American Flag" was eventually given its premiere on May 4, 1895, one month after Dvořák sailed forth from America for the last time. Gustav Schirmer arranged to have it presented by the New York Musical Society in Madison Square Garden with F. G. Dossert conducting. A review in the *New York Daily Tribune*, May 6, 1895, reeked with disappointment: "A composition in which it is impossible to find spontaneity of thought or treatment, which is barren of originality."

5. The Metropolitan Orchestra was most certainly from the Metropolitan Opera where the concert was to have taken place. In addition to Anton Seidl, conductor of the Met's German repertoire, who led them in Liszt's *Tasso*, Dvořák conducted his own works, and R. Henry Warren, the chorus master, led the "National Hymn, America."

6. *New York Herald*, October 22, 1892. Higginson's Carnegie Hall address, "Two New Worlds: The New World of Columbus and the New World of Music," is not included in the voluminous books, articles, and diaries with which Higginson documented his life.

7. Carnegie Hall Program, October 21, 1992.

8. Not that Dvořák's liberal humanist sympathies had to be coaxed. He had a daily calendar for 1893, which he must have gotten at the World's Columbian Exhibition, since it featured pictures and homilies by prominent Czechs from Chicago. Among the mundane entries of income and expenses, one finds "Very kind man," written next to the name of a prominent Czech freethinker whom Dvořák had met in Chicago, F. B. Zdrubek. Author's file copy from the Dvořák Archive in Prague.

9. *New York Herald*, May 28, 1893.

10. *Reaching Out: An Epic of the People of St. Philip's Church* (New York: Custombook, 1986). Trinity Episcopal Church was chartered by the King of England in 1697 as the "sole and only" parish of the Church of England in the city of New York. In 1704, under the aegis of the Society for the Propagation of the Gospel in Foreign Parts, Trinity Episcopal reluctantly allowed enslaved Africans to begin the study of catechism under the direction of an enterprising businessman, Elias Neau, who had himself formerly been a slave and a Huguenot.

11. The critic and author James Gibbons Huneker, who acted as the press representative for the National Conservatory and taught there as well, "gave special attention to an all Negro piano class. . . . Paul Bolin and Henry Guy were especially talented." Other clues suggest there was also a separate choir for the African American students. But Dvořák's composition class and his orchestra included women as well as African Americans. "Harry" P. Guy, among the earliest ragtime song composers, was active in early Detroit bands. According to Rudi Blesh, "Guy once sang for the Fisk Jubilee Singers [and] unionized the Detroit musicians." Rudi Blesh and Harriet Janis, *They All Played Ragtime* (New York: Alfred A. Knopf, 1950), 104–5.

12. Edward B. Kinney's name surfaced at a reception following the dedication of the new Dvořák statue on Seventeenth Street (October 1997) at which I spoke about Dvořák's life on Stuyvesant Square. A woman who introduced herself to me as Kinney's daughter-in-law asked, "Did I know anything about him?" She was very white, very blonde. I related the few details that I could recall about him and my understanding that he was African American. She was quite surprised. She told me that Kinney him-

self wrote a short memoir in which he said that he descended from a Scottish family that arrived in America in the eighteenth century. A few days later Mrs. Kinney called to say that her family was intrigued by my news. They wanted to know everything I might have learned about Edward B. Kinney. She sent me a copy of his memoir, which only added to the mystery. In reviewing all of my Kinney references, I now realize that his identity could be interpreted either way. Kinney's memoir describes two other black churches, besides St. Philip's, that he worked for. In 1896, Kinney went to Egypt for a year—"Ill health took me abroad"—at the same time he joined the Bahai faith, which, he notes in his memoir, professes "unity between all races."

Kinney lived at several addresses in the West Fifties in midtown Manhattan, not far from St. Philip's and the Marshall Hotel on West Fifty-third, a gathering place for the leading black entertainers, yet, according to his family, he was a member of the New York Athletic Club, not exactly Negro stomping grounds in the 1890s.

Perhaps in my eagerness to add to my list of Dvořák's black students, I leaped to a convenient conclusion. But my gut feeling is that, like Maurice Arnold, one of his African American colleagues at the conservatory, Kinney decided to "pass" and spent the last part of his life as a white man.

13. Dvořák, *Korespondence a Dokumenty* (Editio Supraphon, Praha, Vol. 3, 1989), November 19, 1894, letter 319.

14. Anne Key Simpson, *Hard Trials: The Life and Music of Harry T. Burleigh* (Metuchen, N.J.: Scarecrow Press, 1990), 12.

15. "Naturally I knew a great deal about the symphony, as I saw the Dr. two or three times a week and knew he was at work on it." Victor Herbert, principal cellist at the premiere of the *New World* Symphony. See Edward N. Waters, *Victor Herbert* (New York: Macmillan, 1955), 87.

16. When Waters left the Maryland plantation in 1832, he was described as being "five feet eight inches in height and of a bright mulatto complexion, partially blind, orderly and intelligent, about thirty-two years of age." Despite his difficult beginnings, Waters put his daughter Elizabeth, the mother of Harry T. Burleigh, through college. She tutored Greek and Latin while doing janitorial work for the Erie Public Schools. Simpson, *Hard Trials*, 3, 4.

17. Harry T. Burleigh, interview by Louis Biancolli, *New York Herald Tribune*, April 15, 1935.

18. From a program note for the New York Philharmonic, March 1918.

19. Charlotte Murray, *The Story of Harry T. Burleigh*, quoted in *Hymn* 17, no. 4 (October 1966): 104.

20. Camille W. Zeckwer, " Dvořák as I Knew Him," *Étude* 37, no. 2 (1919): 694–702.

21. *Musical America*, April 12, 1914, 21–27.

22. *New York Herald*, Sunday, May 21, 1893. The *Herald* gave generous space to Dvořák's news. The article "Real Value of Negro Melodies" announced that the conservatory "is to be thrown open free of charge to the Negro race." A letter from Jeanette Thurber elaborates, "The Conservatory proposes to enlarge its sphere of usefulness by adding to its departments a branch . . . for colored students of talent. . . . Two young but efficient colored pupils have already been engaged as teachers . . . for their own race, in addition to the rest of the faculty—Harry Burleigh of Erie, New York [*sic*]

and Paul Bolin, of Poughkeepsie." Thurber had no intention of taking this radical step alone. She adds, "It is believed that the decision of the Conservatory to move in this new direction will meet with general approval. . . . Several of the trustees have shown special interest in the matter. Prominent among these is Mrs. Colin P. Huntington." Thurber's political skill matched her vision, and she clinched the argument by invoking Dvořák, who "expresses great pleasure at the decision of the trustees and will assist its fruition by sympathetic and active cooperation."

23. Dvořák 's sophisticated use of English—"They are pathetic, tender, passionate, melancholy, solemn, religious, bold, merry, gay or what you will . . . suits itself to any mood or purpose . . . nothing in the whole range of composition that cannot be supplied with themes from this source . . . moves sentiment in [the American musician]"—came as a surprise to many and encouraged naysayers to question its provenance. Dvořák had in fact spent some effort learning English for his nine concert tours in Great Britain. The music critic Henry Edward Krehbiel reported, "He speaks English fluently." *New York Tribune*, Oct. 16, 1892.

24. The full run of Dvořák articles in New York (*NYH*) and Paris (*PH*), the span of May 21–28, 1893:

> Sunday, May 21, *NYH*: Dvořák interview, "In the Negro melodies of America I discover all that is needed for a great and noble school of music."
>
> Monday, May 22, *PH*: Dvořák interview summary.
>
> Friday, May 26, *PH*: Joachim and Rubinstein interviewed about Dvořák's theory.
>
> Saturday, May 27, *PH*: Bruckner interviewed, "A Cold Water Douche."
>
> Sunday, May 28, *PH*: Hans Richter interviewed.
>
> Sunday, May 28, *NYH*: Summary of *Paris Herald* interviews.
>
> Sunday, May 28, *NYH*: Dvořák announces his new symphony and says that it "reflects Negro melodies."
>
> Sunday, May 28, *NYH*: Editorial page comment on Dvořák's "welcome utterance."

25. Sylvester Russell, "The Great Dvořák Dead," *Indianapolis Freeman*, June 4, 1904.

26. Quoted in Gilbert Chase, *America's Music, from the Pilgrims to the Present*, 1st ed. (New York: McGraw-Hill, 1955), 355; from Edward MacDowell, *Critical and Historical Essays* (Boston: Arthur P. Schmidt, 1904.) MacDowell also asked rhetorically, "Why cover a beautiful thought with Negro clothes cut in Bohemia [with] the badge of whilom slavery rather than with the stern but at least manly and free rudeness of the North American Indian?" For John Knowles Paine's reaction, see the *New York Herald*, Sunday, June 4, 1893.

27. Chase, *America's Music*, 394.

28. *Indianapolis Freeman*, June 4, 1904.

29. Arthur Bird also described a concert in Dresden at which a Negro melody was played, to the delight of Rubinstein. He felt that "the Germans are at a standstill. . . . The French are far ahead. . . . My ideal is for an American School—a mixture of French and German." *Paris Herald*, May 26, 1892, 1. According to *Baker's Biographical Dictionary of Music and Musicians*, 4th ed. (New York: G. Schirmer, 1940), 109,

Arthur Bird was permanently settled in Berlin by 1886. A four-movement Suite no. 3, op. 32, by Bird was premiered by Theodore Thomas at the World's Columbian Exposition on June 12, 1893, and played again on July 7, this time at an all–American music concert along with works by Dvořák's pupils Henry Schoenfeld and Harry Rowe Shelley.

30. The Vienna report began, "I have been fortunate enough to obtain the opinion of several . . . distinguished musicians with regard . . . to Dr. Anton Dvořák's theory that the future music of the *Western world* [author's italics] must be based upon its Negro melodies." *Paris Herald*, May 27, 1892.

31. The Vienna reporter elicited more anthropological notions from "a compatriot of Dr. Dvořák," Eusebius Mandyczewski: "The airs or melodies of a race . . . especially among the Slavonic nations, could never be considered as forming the basis of its future music." This was an obvious slap at the "Slavonic Dances" of his so-called compatriot. *Paris Herald*, May 28, 1892.

32. We have yet to identify the anonymous newspaperman at the *New York Herald* who touted these stories. Possibilities include the music critics Gustav Kobbé, A. Steinberg, and T. P. White, all of whom are listed as *New York Herald* critics in the "1899 Music Directory and Musicians Register." Musicologist Michael Beckerman has also gotten interested in sleuthing out our éminence grise. But his primary candidate, the engaging charlatan Horace Creeley, is, in my view, a far stretch.

33. Burghauser, "Commentary, IXth Symphony in E Minor," *Pressfoto* [Prague] (1972): 26.

34. Dvořák, letter to Karal Baštař, in Dvořák, *Korespondence*, 155–56.

CHAPTER 4

1. According to Kovařik, Dvořák was accompanied by his wife and his daughters, Otilie and Anna. Dvořák visited the fair June 4–5, August 8–18, and September 18–19, 1893.

2. Lionel Davis, translation of a contemporary diary entry in "Dvořák and American Music," in *Student Musicologists at Minnesota* 5 (Minneapolis: University of Minnesota, College of Liberal Arts, Dept. of Music, 1971–72).

3. Dvořák Archives, letter 665.

4. Eugene Levy, *James Weldon Johnson* (Chicago: University of Chicago Press, 1973), 41.

5. *Daily Columbian*, August 24, 1893. Chicago's *Daily Columbian* was assembled from articles that appeared in other Chicago newspapers: the *Daily InterOcean*, the *Daily Tribune*, and the *Chicago Record*. To these were added a weekly schedule of events and official announcements. When "The Committee on Ceremonies" announced the schedule of "Special World's Fair Days" (from May 9 through October 13) in the May 5 issue of the *Daily Columbian*, "Colored people" was listed for August 25. "Liberia" was assigned July 26 and "Hayti," August 16. "Bohemian Day" was not listed. Its date, August 12, was originally assigned to the "I.O. Foresters."

6. *Daily Columbian*, August 26, 1893.

7. The southern exhibitors at the fair predicated their participation upon the barring of blacks, with one exception: a display and demonstration of the agricultural and industrial skills being taught at Booker T. Washington's Hampton Institute. This offended Douglass and the Haitian Pavilion circle, who were quite familiar with, and diametrically opposed to, Washington's philosophy. Washington had declared, "The agitation of questions of social equality is extremist folly. . . . The opportunity to earn a dollar in a factory just now is worth infinitely more than the opportunity to spend a dollar in an opera house." Cotton States' Exposition, Atlanta 1895; quoted in Langston Hughes and Milton Melzer, *A Pictorial History of the Negro in America* (New York: Crown, 1956), 244.

8. *Daily Columbian*, August 26, 1893; and Virginia Cunningham, *Paul Laurence Dunbar and His Song* (New York: Biblo and Tannen, 1969). The after-concert article in the *Daily Columbian* made no further mention of the Jubilee Singers. In addition to those scheduled to appear, J. Arthur Freeman sang "The Shadows Deepen" by Dudley Buck; Isabelle Beecher Howard, sister of the author of *Uncle Tom's Cabin*, was introduced; and Madame Desiree Plato also sang Giacomo Meyerbeer's "Lieti Signor." "The best performer," Sydney Woodward, born a slave on a Georgia plantation in 1860, sang an aria from Giuseppe Verdi's *I due Foscari* and an unlisted encore. John Douglass played a violin fantasy from *Il Trovatore*. Strothotte was the accompanist for all.

9. *Daily Columbian*, May 4, 1893.

10. The Ferris wheel was the most popular attraction of the fair and quickly became its symbol. Designed by George Washington Gale Ferris, a bridge builder from Pittsburgh, it was actually two wheels, with thirty-six cars suspended between them that could accommodate as many as fourteen hundred people. The wheels "rotated on an axle forty-five feet long and nearly a yard in diameter—the largest single piece of steel ever forged." Each car of the Ferris wheel had a tiny lunch counter, and people spent entire days on it. Sol Bloom, *The Autobiography of Sol Bloom* (New York: G. P. Putnam's Sons, 1948).

11. Henry Edward Krehbiel, *Afro-American Folksongs: A Study in Racial and National Music* (1913; reprint, New York: Frederick Ungar, 1962), 64–65.

12. Mary White Ovington, *Half a Man: The Status of the Negro in New York* (1911; reprint, New York: Negro Universities Press, 1969), 72. According to Reid Badger in a conversation we had, Ovington mistakenly cites the 1893 Chicago World's Fair, rather than the San Francisco fair, for the Williams and Walker Dahomeyan masquerade.

13. *In Dahomey* toured for seven months in 1902–3 before a booking in a major Broadway theater, the New York—a first for a full-length black musical comedy—where it opened on February 18, 1903, and had a respectable run of fifty-three performances. Next came the London run of well over two hundred performances (starting in May of 1903) after which the company toured England and Scotland (winter–spring 1904) before returning to the States for a forty-week coast-to-coast tour that ended in June 1905. A second troupe opened in London in the fall of 1904.

14. *In Dahomey*, script and vocal score at London Theatre Museum. The words of the song are by Cecil Mack and Will Marion Cook.

15. Virginia Cunningham, *Paul Laurence Dunbar*, 106–7.

16. Al Rose and Eubie Blake, *Eubie Blake* (New York: Schirmer Books, 1979), 17, 151.

17. Blesh and Janis, *They All Played Ragtime*, 191. "The Dream" is described as an unpublished slow-drag rag with a tango (habanera) bass by Pickett, but possibly composed as well by Jack the Bear, who is immortalized in Ellington's composition of the same name. Since Pickett told Blake he *learned* it at the fair, another author is implied.

18. Tom Fletcher, *100 Years of the Negro in Show Business: The Tom Fletcher Story* (1954; reprint, New York: Da Capo Press, 1984), 137.

19. *Chicago Defender*, May 1, 1915.

20. Will Marion Cook, *Illinois Record*, May 14, 1898; reprinted from *The Prospect*, an African American monthly that apparently came and went with its one issue, that of April 1898. Lawrence Gushee, "The Nineteenth-Century Origins of Jazz," *Black Music Research Journal* 14, no. 1 (Spring 1994): 1–24.

21. The *Oxford English Dictionary* offers several examples of usage for the word *rag*, "a program of satirical revues," and the notion of *rag* as gossip. The latter appeared, not unexpectedly, in *Punch*, December 5, 1885: "We had a good rag when he was away."

22. Fletcher, *100 Years of the Negro in Show Business*, 138–41.

23. Joseph J. Kovařik, *Reminiscenses of Dvořák*, a series of letters between Kovařik and Dvořák biographer Otakar Šourek between 1927 and 1945 now at the Dvořák Museum in Prague.

24. Markéta Hallová and Jitka Slavikova, both musicologists, were members of the editorial team that organized and published the letters of Dvořák in Prague's Dvořák Archives. Dr. Hallová became the director of the Dvořák Museum in Prague. She now heads all the national music museums in the Czech Republic. Dr. Slavikova is an author and journalist and co-edits the principal music journal of the Czech Republic, *Houdebni Rozhledy*.

25. Otakar Dvořák, *Antonin Dvořák, My Father* (Spillville, Ia.: Czech Historical Research Center, 1993), 23–24. This is a translation from the Czech by Miroslav Nemëc of an unpublished manuscript written in 1961. John Clapham reported that Otakar "told me that the family came into contact with the Indians daily, and that at his father's request the whole group assembled at the inn on two or three occasions of native singing and dancing." Clapham also reported that the managers of the "Kickapoo Indian Medicine Show" hired Indians from various tribes but called them Iroquois. Big Moon, the oldest Indian in the Spillville troupe, was possibly a Hunkpapa. John Clapham, "Dvořák and American Indians," *Musical Times* 107 (1966): 863.

26. It would be another twenty years before Grand Central Station was completed.

CHAPTER 5

1. John Clapham, *Dvořák* (New York: W. W. Norton, 1979), 201.

2. "Dvořák on His New Work," *New York Herald*, December 15, 1893.

3. I have been able to identify the following composition students of Dvořák:

The composition class at the National Conservatory:
    Maurice Arnold* [Strathotte] (1865–1937)
    Michael J. Banner (1868–1941)
    Laura Sedgwick Collins (1857–1941)
    Will Marion Cook* (1869–1944)
    Rubin Goldmark (1872–1936)
    William Arms Fisher (1861–1948)
    Edward B. Kinney* (1863–1950)
    Harvey Worthington Loomis (1865–1930)
    Henry [Harry] Rowe Shelley (1858–1947)
    Henry Waller
    Camille W. Zeckwer (1875–1956)
Unofficial composition students at the conservatory:
    Harry T. Burleigh* (1866–1949)
    Edwin Franko Goldman (1878–1956)
    Clara Anna Korn (1866–?)
American composition students who worked with Dvořák in Europe:
    John Spencer Camp (1858–1946) (Camp also in New York, 1893)
    Harry Patterson Hopkins (1873–?)
    Bedrick Vaska Alois Reiser
    Zamernik (first name unknown)
Students whose affiliation is unclear:
    Alfred S. Baker
    Jenny Leighton
    Arthur Reginald Little
        *African American

4. According to Copland, "Other talented musicians, George Gershwin, Leopold Godowsky II and Frederick Jacobi, studied with Goldmark during my time with him." Aaron Copland and Vivian Perlis, *Copland, 1900 through 1942* (New York: Saint Martins/Marek, 1984), 28.

5. There is a most curious musical coincidence in Goldmark's trio. The theme of the middle movement is built upon a six-note sequence: a triadic figure and a downward swoop to a "wrong note" landing. The second appearance of the sequence exactly outlines the notes of Billy Strayhorn's tune "Take the A Train"—but in slow motion.

6. May 31, 1992. It was the centennial celebration for Dvořák's American residency. I had organized another Dvořák Legacy concert a month earlier at the Graduate School of the City University of New York (CUNY), Thursday April 15, 1992:

Dvořák's American Legacy
    Rubin Goldmark: Romanze and Scherzo from Trio, op. 1 (1893)
        Joel Lester, violin; André Emelianoff, cello; Agustin Anievas, piano
    Will Marion Cook: Swing Along (1903)
        Vanessa Ayers, mezzo-soprano, and Stephen Mahr, piano
    George Gershwin: Lullaby for String Quartet

The Meridian Quartet: Sebu Serinian, Lisa Tipton, violins; Eric DeGioia, viola; Deborah Assael, cello

Aaron Copland: Sonnet III for Piano (unpublished, 1920–21)
Agustin Anievas

Duke Ellington: Three Vocalises:
The Mooch(1927)
Creole Love Call (1927)
Transblucency(1946)
Melodee Savage, soprano
The Aaron Copland School of Music Jazz Ensemble: Dennis Joseph, clarinet; Steven Henry, trumpet; William Cepeda, trombone; Stephen Mahr, piano; Daniel Burwasser, drums; David Chevan, bass

Antonin Dvořák: Finale from the String Quartet in F, "The American" (1893)
The Meridian Quartet

7. Zeckwer, Camille W. "Dvořák as I Knew Him," *Étude* 37, no. 2 (1919): 694–702.

8. Jablonski passes on the Gershwin family legend about Gershwin bringing Goldmark his *Lullabye* for string quartet, something he had composed three or four years earlier. After studying the piece for a moment, Goldmark is supposed to have said, "It's good, very good. . . . It's plainly to be seen that you have already learned a great deal of harmony from me." Edward Jablonski, *Gershwin* (New York: Doubleday, 1987), 42–43. The story first appears in David Ewen's biography, *A Journey to Greatness: The Life and Music of George Gershwin* (New York: Henry Holt, 1956), 85.

9. *Juilliard Review* 3 (fall 1956): 15–16. From an address given on March 18, 1956, for the dedication of the Goldmark Wing at City College, his alma mater.

10. "Edwin F. Goldman Remembers Antonin Dvořák," unpublished manuscript, c. 1940, copy in the Dvořák Museum, Prague. Goldman joined the Metropolitan Opera Orchestra in 1898, founded his first Goldman Band in 1918, and was a composer of light music, such as "On the Mall," a favorite singalong march with which he often ended his summer concerts in Central Park.

11. Rupert Hughes, *Famous American Composers* (Boston: L. C. Page, 1900), 135–39. After a tour of Bulgaria, Turkey, and Hungary, Arnold studied at the Cologne Conservatory and finally with Max Bruch in Breslau. He returned to St. Louis, where he taught violin and served as a conductor for opera companies.

12. H. Wiley Hitchcock. *Music in the United States* (Englewood Cliffs, N.J.: Prentice-Hall, 1969), 133.

13. *New York Herald*, May 21, 1893.

14. *New York Herald*, January 24, 1894.

15. *New York Herald*, January 21, 1994, and January 24, 1894. The exception was a "child pianist," Bertha Vysanska, who played the piano solo in Liszt's *Hungarian Fantasy*. According to Lonnie Goodkind, the longtime friend and manager of William Warfield, his aunt Bertha and her brother Daniel, who was concertmaster of the conservatory orchestra, made a surprise middle-of-the-night visit to Dvořák's house in Prague. They rang the bell at the garden gate and soon "an old man with a lantern came to the gate and shouted, 'Vysanski!'"

16. Sissieretta Jones's *nom de guerre* was borrowed from the internationally celebrated diva Adelina Patti. Madame Jones had distinguished herself at the White House of Benjamin Harrison, on the concert stage, and with her own vaudeville company, Black Patti's Troubadors. According to John Graziano, she did finally appear at the fair on September 25, 1893, at the Women's Pavilion.

17. *New York Herald*, May 21, 1893.

18. Maurice Arnold, *American Plantation Dances* (P.L. Jung–International, 1894).

19. Copland's "Music for a Great City" (1964) is the only symphonic work that requires sandpaper blocks, according to James Blades, *Percussion Instruments and Their History* (London: Faber and Faber, 1970), 397, 458.

20. *New York Herald*, January 24, 1894.

21. Clapham, 133.

22. The address is listed under Maurice Arnold in the archives of the 1930 National Census. Is there any significance to the fact that Maurice Arnold used "Strathotte" at the fair and the conservatory, when he was black, and "Arnold" for the rest of his professional life? His *New York Times* obituary explains that Arnold was his professional name. His death certificate is filed under Strathotte.

23. Langston Hughes, *The Weary Blues* (New York: Knopf, 1926).

24. Arnold's career was aptly summed up by Goldman: "Arnold wrote much music . . . but he never achieved the success and recognition he deserved. He was entirely too modest for his own good, and never seemed able to bring himself to the fore. The work which Dvořák admired the most, was Arnold's 'American Plantation Dances,' [which] Dvořák frequently conducted . . . as did Seidl and other conductors. [Arnold] died in New York in 1937, practically unknown." Goldman, "Edwin F. Goldman Remembers Antonin Dvořák."

25. A review of a National Conservatory concert that Dvořák directed only a month earlier noted, "Prominent among the violins and tympani [Burleigh] were several colored men." *New York Herald*, December 5, 1893.

26. *Theatre Arts*, September 1947, 61–65. John White (1855–1902) was in Cook's time the organist at the Church of the Ascension. White was a student of Rheinberger in Munich and went back there in 1896, never to return to the United States. The author played trumpet and conducted in the Church of the Ascension in the late 1950s for the organist Vernon de Tar and recorded Rheinberger Organ Concertos with E. Power Biggs for Columbia Records in St. George's—Burleigh's Church.

27. Fletcher also traveled with Cook and his "Syncopated Orchestra" in 1919–20 (Fletcher, *100 Years of the Negro in Show Business*), 129, 258. Cook coached the Memphis Students band and "gave a hand in whipping them into shape" when they were first formed in 1905, according to James Weldon Johnson, *Black Manhattan* (1930; reprint, New York: Atheneum, 1968), 120–21.

28. Edward Kennedy [Duke] Ellington, *Music Is My Mistress* (New York: Doubleday, 1973), 96. The Czech author Josef Skvorecky wrote in a letter to me on June 29, 1995, that he had seen and misplaced a photocopy of the "insulting" review, possibly in the *Metropolitan Magazine* or *New York Magazine*. The review characterized Cook as a "Black Rémeny" and Skvorecky surmised that Cook was doubly insulted, first by

being assigned a borrowed identity—a common humiliation for talented blacks of the time (Black Patti, Black Melba)—and compounded by being compared to the violinist Edouard Rémeny, known more for his gypsy flash than his classical musicianship.

29. *London Tattler*, May 20, 1903.

30. In its dramatized form, *Uncle Tom's Cabin* was a perennial favorite of African American audiences. See Fletcher, *100 Years of the Negro in Show Business*, 8. According to the *Encyclopedia Britannica*, Harriet Beecher Stowe's novel (1852) was a "disguised pamphlet against the Fugitive Slave Laws." "Slavery," *Encyclopedia Britannica* (Chicago: William Benton, 1965), Vol. 20, p. 783.

31. I am indebted to John Graziano, who found, among Dunbar's papers at the Schomburg Library, a publishing contract for *Clorindy* between Dunbar, Cook, and W. Witmark and Sons, dated 1895. This could have been based upon Cook's idea for the show and could help explain the falling-out between Cook and Witmark four years later, after *Clorindy* actually opened and proved to be a hit.

32. *New York Herald*, January 23, 1894.

33. W. E. B. Du Bois, "The Negro in Literature and Art," in *W. E. B. Du Bois: A Reader*, ed. Meyer Weinberg (New York: Harper and Row, 1970). Sometimes called "Swanee River," the song was often sung by the Fisk Jubilee Singers and by Noble Sissle when he served as drum major and solo singer with James Reese Europe's Hellfighter's Band in France.

34. *Minstrel Songs Old and New* (Boston: Oliver Ditson, 1892), 3–5. Kovařík brought the pages to Dvořák. His handwritten note in the margin identifies these pages as the actual ones Dvořák used (Dvořák Museum Archives, Prague).

35. These days we are careful about the distinction between arranger and orchestrator. An arranger dresses up the music, even going so far as to recompose it. The orchestrator assigns the composer's exact notes to the various instruments. The roles—composer, arranger, orchestrator—are often so intermingled they can hardly be sorted out. But, with very few exceptions, only the composer gets royalties. Arrangers and orchestrators are, in the parlance of the trade, "guns for hire." Dvořák was in this instance primarily an orchestrator.

36. *New York Herald*, January 24, 1894.

37. Most appropriately, the manuscript has found its way to the (Stephen) Foster Hall Collection at the University of Pittsburgh, a prize of the collection. The collection also holds the original hand-copied orchestral parts from the 1893 concert. One of each of the string quartet parts is in Dvořák's hand.

38. Goldman, "Edwin F. Goldman Remembers Antonin Dvořák."

39. "The Great Dvořák Dead," *Indianapolis Freeman*, June 4, 1904.

CHAPTER 6

"The Talented Tenth" was the rubric assigned to African American intellectuals at the end of the nineteenth century who, like Paul Laurence Dunbar and W. E. B. Du Bois, were dedicated to the "elevation of the race."

1. Andrew G. Paschal, ed., *A W. E. B. Du Bois Reader* (New York: Macmillan, 1971), 19–26.

2. Alfred A. Moss Jr., *The American Negro Academy: Voice of the Talented Tenth* (Baton Rouge: Louisiana State University Press, 1981), 25–26.

3. Moss, *The American Negro Academy*, 50, offers an explanation for Dunbar's discomfort with the name "African Institute." He found that before the Civil War, when returning to Africa was the only acceptable goal for many free people of color, "African" was their identity of choice. "Colored" came into vogue after emancipation, to distinguish themselves from the "great masses of newly freedmen." The younger Dunbar, unhappy with the class distinction, saw "Negro" as all-inclusive. Dunbar argued further that thanks to the Civil War, in which his own father had served, emancipation was the law of the land and they were now truly, and firstly, Americans. Paul Dunbar's father, Joshua Dunbar, a former slave who escaped to Canada from Kentucky via the underground railroad, was forty years old when he enlisted in the Fifty-fifth Regiment of the Massachusetts Volunteer Infantry. He was enrolled in Company F, which boasted the best chorus in the regiment, and maintained the seventeen-piece Regimental Band and a "drum corps of twenty, mostly lads from twelve to fifteen years of age." The regiment was sent to the Sea Islands of Georgia by ship in late July 1863. Dunbar senior took sick and was given a disability discharge on October 28, 1893. Charles B. Fox, *Record of the Service of the Fifty-Fifth Regiment of Massachusetts Volunteer Infantry* (Cambridge: John Wilson and Son, 1868).

4. David Levering Lewis, *W. E. B. Du Bois* (New York: Henry Holt, 1993), 172–73.

5. Dunbar missed hearing Du Bois's paper. He was in England on a recital tour and was brought up to date when he stayed at Crummell's London residence later that spring. This may have been when Crummell asked Dunbar to start a "monthly magazine . . . for purely Negro literature." But fate had other plans.

6. One member "felt that the ablest blacks had to be recognized on terms that went beyond race." Another argued, "If you put a Negro under the refining influence of the 19th century, he is no longer a Negro." See Lewis, *W. E. B. Du Bois*, and Moss, *The American Negro Academy*.

7. The bibliophile Arthur A. Schomburg was invited to join the academy in 1914; the author and poet James Weldon Johnson, in 1915.

8. *Theatre Arts*, September 1947, 61–65.

9. M. Christine Boyer, *Manhattan Manners* (New York: Rizzoli, 1985), 75.

10. In the words of Dunbar's first biographer, Lida Keck Wiggins, "[Dunbar] woke at dawn on his 24th birthday to find himself famous." Wiggins was referring to the June 27, 1897, issue of *Harper's Weekly*, which came out with William Dean Howells's full-page review in praise of Dunbar's second book of poems, *Majors and Minors*. In fact Dunbar woke up in London that morning quite aware of his shrinking cash, not of his growing fame. Wiggins, *The Life and Works of Paul Laurence Dunbar* (1907, Naperville, Ill.; reprint, Grand Rapids, Mich.: Cadace Press, 1996).

11. Virginia Cunningham, *Paul Laurence Dunbar and His Song* (New York: Biblo and Tannen, 1969), 155. She writes that Cook and Burleigh "introduced [Dunbar] to James Weldon Johnson, and his brother J. Rosamond Johnson" but apparently did not

know that Dunbar had already met James Weldon at the fair. See Eugene Levy, *James Weldon Johnson* (Chicago: University of Chicago Press, 1973), 41.

12. Mercer Cook papers, Moreland-Spingarn Research Center, Howard University.

13. Both meetings ended with Williams and Walker giving Cook train fare back to Washington. *Theatre Arts*, September 1947, 61–65.

14. In either September–October of 1897 or January–February of 1898. I have established these windows of opportunity by comparing corresponding dates of their known calendars and that of their contemporaries such as James Weldon Johnson.

15. Wiggins, *The Life and Works of Paul Laurence Dunbar*, 108.

16. Published posthumously by his son in *Theatre Arts*, September 1947, 61–65.

17. Mercer Cook, interview by Joseph Skvorecky, tape recording, (month and date not recorded) 1980. A copy of this interview is in the author's files.

18. *Theatre Arts*, September 1947, 61–65.

19. Braham descended from a fascinating musical family dating back to eighteenth-century England. Americans include Harry Braham, a theater producer and the husband of Lillian Russell, and John, conductor of the first American production of *H.M.S. Pinafore* and Cook's defender.

20. There was an earlier, and decidedly different racial confrontation involving Rice and a conductor. When Herman Perlet refused to direct the orchestra for a Negro dancer whom Rice had engaged to do a dancing specialty in his successful vaudeville revue *1492*, Rice took over the baton and completed the rehearsal "after a fashion." *New York Sun*, July 22, 1894.

21. Johnson, *Black Manhattan*, 103. Johnson does not acknowledge another early "all-black" show, *A Trip to Coontown*, which opened off Broadway in Jacobs Third Avenue Theater four months earlier than *Clorindy*. There are some important differences; above all, *A Trip to Coontown* did not have an original score but was built around established popular songs.

CHAPTER 7

1. Carl Bamberger (1902–1987) graduated from the University of Vienna and conducted in German opera houses. He immigrated to the United States via Russia in 1936 and was both conductor and teacher at Mannes from 1937 to 1975. Among his students are Julius Rudel, George Cleve, and the author. The Mannes School became a college in 1953.

2. David Mannes, *Music Is My Faith* (New York: W.W. Norton, 1938), 213. John Thomas Douglas who is not to be confused with the Washington-based Negro violinist Joseph Douglass, Frederick Douglass's grandson and Jim Europe's teacher.

3. Fletcher, *100 Years of the Negro in Show Business*.

4. Mannes's prediction that Negro musicians would enter American symphony orchestras in thirty or forty years was far too optimistic. At the beginning of the twenty-first century, the conspicuous absence of African Americans in the ranks of our orchestras, major or minor, is an embarrassment, enigma, scandal . . . take your pick.

5. *Grove's Dictionary of Music and Musicians*, 3d ed., vol. 6, American suppl., rev. 1928 (New York: Macmillan, 1946), 301.

6. The faculty included the organist Melvin Charlton, a graduate of the National Conservatory, and the violinist Joseph Douglass.

7. Mannes observed Europe's rehearsals and became anxious when he found out that Europe was forced to rehearse the orchestra in small sections and would first be bringing the entire ensemble together for the concert itself. Mannes's fears were for naught.

8. *New York Evening Journal*, editorial, May 1, 1912.

9. The fourth and final concert was directed by the school's director, J. Rosamond Johnson.

10. *New York Times*, March 12, 1914.

11. *Musical America*, March 21, 1914.

12. *New York Post*, March 13, 1914.

13. "A Negro Explains Jazz," *Literary Digest*, April 26, 1919, 28.

14. Gunther Schuller, *The Swing Era* (New York: Oxford University Press, 1989), 46.

15. Gilbert Seldes, *The Seven Lively Arts* (New York: Harper Brothers, 1924), 158.

16. Paul Whiteman and Mary Margaret McBride, *Jazz* (New York: J. H. Sears, 1926), 16.

17. Copland and Perlis, *Copland, 1900 through 1942*, 25.

CHAPTER 8

1. George Gershwin and Ira Gershwin, *The Gershwin Songbook* (New York: Simon and Schuster, 1960), vi.

2. David A. Jasen and Trebor Jay Tichenor, *Rags and Ragtime* (1978; reprint, Mineola, N.Y.: Dover, 1989), 7.

3. Quoted in Riccardo Scivales, *Keyboard Classics* 14 (July–August 1994): 25.

4. Eubie Blake, interview by John Wilson; quoted in Joan Peyser, *The Memory of All That* (New York: Simon and Schuster, 1993), 41–42.

5. Edward Jablonski, *Gershwin* (New York: Doubleday, 1987), 230; *George Gershwin's Song Book* (New York: Random House limited edition, 1932).

6. The string quartet was published posthumously in 1968 by Ira Gershwin as *Lullaby*.

7. Vodery's papers also contain Gershwin's piano-vocal holograph for *Blue Monday Blues*, the very material that Vodery worked from. With the permission of the Gershwin Estate, I obtained copies of both.

8. There are a few early-twentieth-century exceptions to the mixing taboo on Broadway: *The Gold Bug* (1896), previously mentioned; *The Southerners: A Study in Black and White* (1904); the headlining of Bert Williams in several editions of the *Ziegfeld Follies*; and Edna Ferber and Jerome Kern's *Show Boat* (1927).

9. Ellington's *Beggar's Holiday* was based on John Gay's *Beggar's Opera*. Ellington did finally conquer the Great White Way. In February 1981, six years after his passing,

Sophisticated Ladies, a plotless, almost-all-black musical featuring Ellington's best-known songs, began a two-year run on Broadway.

10. Whiteman returned to *Blue Monday Blues* in 1925 with a new orchestration by Ferde Grofé and a new title, *135th Street*. The occasion was his second "experiment in modern music."

11. At some point in the early history of *Porgy and Bess*, the "black cast only" condition was attached to the licensing rights for all future productions of *Porgy and Bess*. Although no one seems ever to have seen the proscription in writing, it was confirmed in conversations I had in 1996 with executives at Tams Witmark and with legal representatives in charge of licensing productions of *Porgy and Bess*.

12. *New York Times*, November 28, 1995.

13. *Stage Magazine*, October 1935, 25–28.

14. "Profanation," the second movement of the *Jeremiah Symphony*, derives from the traditional blessing of the Haftorah, sung at every bar and bat mitzvah. In 1963 Bernstein wrote his Symphony no. 3 (*Kaddish*) in memory of the death of the first Catholic president. A year later *Fiddler on the Roof*—book by Joseph Stein, music by Jerry Bock, lyrics by Sheldon Harnick, based on stories by Sholem Aleichem—triumphed on Broadway.

15. In 1943 Weill composed a ninety-minute oratorio, *We Will Never Die*, to a text by Ben Hecht, "A Memorial to the Two Million Jewish Dead in Europe." The number is not a misprint—the final figure of six million was yet to come.

16. This Met production of *Porgy and Bess* was presented without cuts. Quite a bit of music had been struck between the 1935 Boston tryout and the New York opening when the director, Rouben Mamoulian, made Gershwin shrink his work to Broadway-musical size. Nevertheless the complete vocal score was published with an insert that contained an extraordinary caveat: "*Note* / This is the Original Unabridged Version of *PORGY and BESS* / Due to time limitations in the theatre, the actual playing version has several deletions. / The Publisher."

17. In 1992 the musicologist Charles Hamm consulted with me on an article he was writing about cuts made in *Porgy and Bess* for its 1935 Broadway premiere. Hamm felt that the newfound interest in performing the complete opera score without cuts was misguided. I had already been on a similar search in hopes of recording a "Broadway Porgy" that re-created the original forces with the 1935 cuts, perhaps in the original Alvin Theater (now the Neil Simon Theater). I led him to the heirs of Alexander Smallens, the first music director and conductor of *Porgy and Bess*, who kept the score that Smallens used in the pit. Like Steinert's, it was a heavily marked vocal score with penciled orchestral cues and, to Hamm's delight, all the cuts. By the time Steinert died, his papers and scores were scattered, and, saddest of all, the film he made of scenes from the original show had disappeared. See Hamm, "The Theatre Guild Production of *Porgy and Bess*," *Journal of the American Musicological Society* 40, no. 3 (1987): 495–512.

18. Two Gershwin contemporaries I have known, Virgil Thomson and Milton Rettenberg—a childhood friend of the Gershwins—believed that Gershwin had a ghost orchestrator in his friend Bill Daly. This was an old story that Daly denied. I asked

Morton Gould, a master orchestrator who played for Gershwin and "knew all the guys" in the music scoring world back then, what he thought. His answer was typically cryptic. Gould played piano at a pre-production "tryout" session of orchestrations for *Porgy and Bess* led by Gershwin. Gould would never say what he thought—that Gershwin, who needed to test his work out, was an amateur scorer when compared to himself—but he did not accept the ghost orchestrator idea.

19. We do not know whether Gershwin had mastered enough of the art and craft of orchestration or had enough lead time to attempt the scoring of his jazz-band accompaniment himself. But he was already composing with instruments in mind. The string scoring of his *Lullaby* is quite refined, with a skillful use of harmonics and double stops—was this perhaps done with Goldmark's help? There are also definite instrumental notations sketched into the holographs (original manuscripts) for both *Blue Monday Blues* and the two-piano score of the *Rhapsody In Blue*.

20. *Modern Music*, November–December 1935, 16–17.

21. Milton Rettenberg, interview by author, tape recording c. 1983.

22. Reducing an orchestration is not to be confused with reorchestrating; five brass instead of seven still sounds like brass.

23. When I conducted *Porgy* in 1968, there was still no printed score, only a photocopy of Gershwin's autograph.

24. Denecke went on to become timpanist in the Cleveland Orchestra under Artur Rodzinsky, the Pittsburgh Symphony Orchestra under Fritz Reiner, and the Minneapolis Symphony Orchestra under Dimitri Mitropoulus.

25. I passed on Mueller's name to Joan Peyser. He became an important source for her book *The Memory of All That* and sold her a self-portrait George had given him.

26. In the vocal score of *Strike Up the Band*, only the overture has very specific instrumental indications and countermelodies. Gershwin was documenting his scoring.

27. Berlin, although unable to read or write down his own music, was not intimidated by his arrangers. According to Jay Blackton, who conducted many of Berlin's shows, "When Irving wrote a song and dictated it (playing it on the piano) to Helmy Kresa, the piano part was sacred, that was the way Irving wanted the orchestra to play it, with his little answers between phrases and nothing else." Mary Ellin Barrett, *Irving Berlin: A Daughter's Memoir* (New York: Simon and Schuster, 1994), 238.

28. Ellington quotes Will Vodery, who advised him that when "you write a [theater] score, don't ever arrange it," adding that when you do so, "you are confined by your own personal prejudices." *Music Is My Mistress*, 186.

29. There are signs of exuberance in *An American in Paris* that I would chalk up to inexperience, such as the clever little countermelodies Gershwin weaves around his Paris "walking themes," superfluous fillers that, for a time, I tried unsuccessfully to bring into the open. He also fusses too much with the violin parts: passages that would be most effective in octaves or unison are passed between the first and second violins in a sort of faux counterpoint. The closing lick, a dramatic reiteration of the slow theme by a single saxophone, needs, and gets, reinforcement from most conductors. Scoring aside, both the Concerto in F and *An American in Paris* are distinguished by

their memorable flapper-age tunes, soaring themes, and gorgeous blues harmonies. And, given a good orchestra, neither the listener nor the average musician is aware of any problems.

30. William Paley, the chairman of the board at CBS, provided the studio orchestra that read through the orchestrations.

31. The Concerto in F reading took place in the Globe Theater, in mid-November 1925. Bill Daly conducted as George played. It was not recorded. Gershwin must have taken pride in this, his first major orchestration effort. Gershwin's case as an orchestrator wasn't made any stronger when, three seasons later, Whiteman, who felt he was "entitled," had Grofé rescore the Concerto in F for his orchestra, again a jazz hybrid, and presented and recorded it in this form with Roy Bargy as soloist in fall 1928. In a conversation, Ed Jablonski quoted Al Simon, a close friend of the Gershwins: "George was not happy about the rescoring of the concerto." But Gershwin could well have stopped Whiteman's arrogation, especially for a premiere recording, which requires the publisher's, and therefore the composer's, permission. Yet he did not intercede.

32. *Porgy and Bess*, RCA Victor C25-1-8. Recorded in early October 1935 on a four-record set of 78s just as *Porgy and Bess* was getting ready to open in New York. The Eva Jessye (African American) choir sang. Alexander Smallens shared the conducting duties with Nathaniel Shilkret. So much for Gershwin's resolve about all-black casts. Then again, perhaps it was after Tibbets and Jepson were heard that the all-black cast proscription was introduced. The closest thing we have to an original cast recording was made when *Porgy and Bess* was first revived in 1942. On this recording of excerpts, Ann Brown sings the role of Bess as well as Clara's "Summertime."

33. Phyllis Bash sang Serena, James Randolph sang Crown, and Michael Montel directed.

34. Several cameo parts, the Strawberry Woman and Crab Man, were assigned to members of the Texas Southern University choir, which continued to sing with the Corpus Christi Symphony in performances of *Candide*, Mahler's Symphony no. 2, and Mozart's Requiem.

CHAPTER 9

1. Conductors included Georg Solti, Leopold Stokowski, Josef Krips, and Nadia Boulanger (I was her offical escort), and among the sixty-three soloists were violinists John Corigliano, Isaac Stern, and Zino Francescatti; and pianists Rudolf Serkin, Van Cliburn, Malcolm Frager, and André Previn.

CHAPTER 10

1. Reid Badger, *A Life in Ragtime: A Biography of James Reese Europe* (New York: Oxford University Press, 1995), 84.

2. Kurt Dieterle, interview by author; film, February 14, 1984. Dieterle remained a

member of the Whiteman band after the Aeolian Hall Concert and was concertmaster for the next eleven years. Information about the Whiteman *Rhapsody in Blue* rehearsals, premiere, and subsequent tour are from the author's many interviews with pianist Milton Rettenberg in 1983–85. Rettenberg played in many Whiteman orchestras in the 1920s as well as the band that toured the Aeolian Hall concert in the spring of 1924.

3. Thomas A. DeLong, *Pops: Paul Whiteman, King of Jazz* (Piscataway, N.J.: New Century, 1983), 36–88. I am indebted to DeLong for facts and figures, and for the personalities involved in the Aeolian Hall concert, and for introducing me to many Whiteman devotees, in particular Carl Johnson, curator of the Whiteman Collection at Williams College, and members of the Whiteman family.

4. DeLong, *Pops*, 101.

5. Ellington, *Music Is My Mistress*, 71.

6. Gunther Schuller, *Early Jazz* (New York: Oxford University Press, 1968), 258.

7. Whiteman and McBride, *Jazz*, 3, 20.

8. *New York Times*, February 13, 1924.

9. Tape of Canadian Broadcast interview in Whiteman Archive, Williams College.

10. The complete Aeolian Hall program:

True Form of Jazz:
Ten Years Ago: La Rocca, "Livery Stable Blues"
With Modern Embellishment: Baer, "Mamma Loves Papa"
Comedy Selections:
Silver, "Yes, We Have No Bananas"
Thomas, "So This Is Venice"
Legitimate Scoring vs. Jazzing:
Schonberger, "Whispering"
Recent Compositions with Modern Score:
Braham, "Limehouse Blues"
Rose, "Linger Awhile"
Kern, "Raggedy Ann"
Zez Confrey, Piano:
Confrey, Medley of Popular Airs—"Kitten on the Keys," "Ice Cream and Art," "Nickel in the Slot"
Flavoring a Selection with Borrowed Themes:
Grofé, "Russian Rose"
Semi-Symphonic Arrangement of Popular Melodies:
Berlin, "Alexander's Ragtime Band," "A Pretty Girl Is Like a Melody," "Orange Blossoms in California"
Part II:
Herbert, *A Suite of Serenades: Spanish, Chinese, Cuban, Oriental.*
Adaptation of Standard Selections to Dance Rhythm:
Logan, "Pale Moon"
MacDowell, "To a Wild Rose"
Friml, "Chansonette"

George Gershwin, Piano:
Gershwin, *A Rhapsody in Blue*
In the Field of Classics:
Elgar, *Pomp and Circumstance*

11. In addition to Virgil Thomson, Frankie Gershwin, George's sister, and the society band leader Lester Lanin attended the 1924 original and my 1984 re-creation (March 1984).

12. Herbert, born in 1851, studied cello with Bernhardt Cossmann, principal cellist of the Leipzig Gewandhaus Orchestra under Felix Mendelssohn. In Vienna, at age twenty, Herbert played principal cello in the Johann Strauss Orchestra, then directed by Eduard Strauss. A year later he performed with Franz Liszt and Camille Saint-Saëns at a summer festival in Zurich. In 1886 Frank Damrosch, musicologist, choral conductor, and the brother of Walter, brought Herbert and his wife, Therese Forster, a Wagnerian soprano, to America to join the Metropolitan Opera Company for its fourth season.

As a solo cellist, Herbert performed most notably in the American premieres of the Brahms Double Concerto under Theodore Thomas, and Dvořák's *Dumka* Piano Trio, with the composer at the keyboard. He was principal cellist for the New York Philharmonic and for Tchaikovsky's first American orchestra tour. Herbert became music director of the Twenty-second Regimental Band, replacing Sousa's rival, Patrick Gilmore, in 1893. He served as music director of the Pittsburgh Symphony from 1898 to 1904. In 1909 Edison hired Herbert to be one of the first artists recorded on cylinder (he conducted his own orchestra). Among his compositions are over fifty operettas, including *Babes in Toyland*, *Naughty Marietta*, and *The Red Mill*. Edward N. Waters, *Victor Herbert: A Life in Music* (New York: Macmillan, 1955).

13. The concert manager Maxime Gershunoff was my partner for this "attraction," which was titled "The Birth of the *Rhapsody in Blue*."

14. Whiteman turned his library over to Williams College, but Grofé had smuggled out his original score of the *Rhapsody in Blue* after the two men had a dispute. Legally, the score belonged to Whiteman, who had paid for it. The following storm of angry emotions was finally calmed when Grofé donated the score to the Library of Congress and a photocopy was given to Whiteman and hence to Williams College.

15. Gershwin was a perennial student. After his studies with Goldmark, Gershwin sought out Nadia Boulanger in Paris, but she turned him down, not wanting to disturb his muse. There are Gershwin family anecdotes about George asking Ravel to give him orchestration lessons. He did work with Wallingford Riegger, Henry Cowell, Arnold Schoenberg, and especially Joseph Schillinger. Typical Schillinger formulas for harmonic progressions abound in *Porgy and Bess*. Schillinger's mathematically based system is not a substitute for musical inspiration, as aptly demonstrated by his own mundane compositions, but it did challenge Gershwin to find fresh ways to compose.

16. Victor 35822, A and B.

17. The *Suite of Serenades* turned out to be a new and quite brilliant orchestration of a recent work tailored to fit Whiteman's augmented dance band, rather than the entirely new *American Suite* that had been announced.

18. Leonard Bernstein, "A Nice Gershwin Tune," *Atlantic Monthly*, April 1955, 40–41. Despite his carping reservations, Bernstein also said: "I vividly remember causing a sensation as a Harvard undergraduate by announcing that I loved the music of Tchaikovsky. It was considered an outrageous heresy: Tchaikovsky was located one pigeonhole beneath contempt at the time, as was Verdi. One of the most egregious victims of [this] musical *haute-couture* in our century has been George Gershwin. The 'higher criticism' does not permit that name to enter the category of significant composers." Charles Schwartz, "An Appreciation," introduction to *Gershwin: His Life and Music* (1973; reprint, New York: Da Capo Press, 1979), unpaginated.

19. Schwartz, *Gershwin: His Life and Music*, 91.

20. Ibid., 88.

21. Schwartz, Appendix I, "Remarks About Gershwin's Music," in *Gershwin: His Life and Music*, 326–28.

22. Constant Lambert, *Music Ho!* (London and Plymouth: Latimer Trend, 1937), 210–11.

23. Debussy quote: André Fontainas, "Mes souvenirs du Symbolisme"; quoted in Oscar Thompson, *Debussy: Man and Artist* (New York: Tudor Publication, 1940), 102–3.

24. In Whiteman's time, the heckelphone had been around for only twenty years. It was developed at Wagner's behest—he was always searching for the ideal alphorn—and finally perfected in 1904 by Heckel and Sons, the German instrument makers best known for their bassoons. They gave it their family name.

During our searches for a heckelphone, we were offered several bass oboes. But they have a markedly less robust sound. One of the few heckelphones in New York turned up at the Metropolitan Opera. They must have purchased their heckelphone, no. 25, for the prominent part it plays in Richard Strauss's *Salomé* (composed the same year the instrument was perfected, 1904), which the Met first performed in 1907. We were able to borrow it for the occasion.

25. Dean belonged to an ensemble that performed Renaissance and baroque music on sackbuts (an early form of the trombone) and cornets (a cross between a recorder and a natural [valveless] trumpet), rather than the type of horn Bix Beiderbecke had favored.

26. Dieterle went out to Los Angeles with the Whiteman band for the movie *The King of Jazz*. An avid golfer, he roomed with Bing Crosby, who sang with the band at the time.

27. To finance my first reconstruction, I "went liquid" and for the most part used my own funds along with some from the Gershwin family, ASCAP, BMI, Vincent Sardi Jr., and others. I am happy to report that the concert earned back every dime and a little over.

CHAPTER 11

1. See Badger, *A Life in Ragtime*.

2. Fletcher, *100 Years of the Negro in Show Business*, 263.

3. Seldes, *The Seven Lively Arts*, 158.

4. The concerts took place on Monday, Wednesday, and Friday, July 10, 12, and 14. From Queens College, where I teach, came my musical assistants, Adam Zeichner and Ellie Hisama. They kept track of all our contracts and communications with solo artists, and with the contractors for three distinctly different orchestras. They helped me with the library—with the collection and distribution of music for the other conductors, the choirs, and the orchestras. And they oversaw the complex rehearsal schedule and making sure everyone got paid. Peter Pretsfelder was my logistics and publicity contact with Carnegie Hall. It sounds quite difficult on paper, but the excitement of realizing these unusual programs carried us along.

5. In 1911, at the very same time the Clef Club was beginning to appear in public, Joplin was trying to launch his ragtime opera *Treemonisha*. He may have wanted it to receive an important hearing on its own and steered clear of the Clef Club. James Europe was not unaware of Joplin. In 1915, at the Palm Gardens on East Fifty-eighth Street, the Orchestra of the Settlement House for Colored Children, for whom the Clef Club was giving benefit concerts at Carnegie Hall, did perform an excerpt from *Treemonisha*: the opening of act 2, "The Frolic of the Bears." The conductor was E. E. Thomson, later an assistant director of the 369th Band under James Reese Europe. Joplin did not live to see a complete performance of *Treemonisha*.

6. In 1911, one year before the choir appeared at the Clef Club concert, St. Philip's consecrated its new church on West 134th Street. With the nearby apartment houses built and managed by the church, St. Philip's was joining the new Harlem development opening up to African Americans. St. Philip's continues to serve as the spiritual home for prominent people in the arts and public affairs, such as the late Supreme Court justice Thurgood Marshall. George Walker, of Williams and Walker, and Ada Overton, the choreographer and actress, were married in the old St. Philip's on June 29, 1899. A few years later, on December 27, 1916, the composer and founder of the National Association of Negro Musicians, Robert Nathaniel Dett, was married in the new St. Philip's.

7. Coleridge-Taylor's father was a native of Sierra Leone. His mother was English. The third of his cycle of choral settings from Wordsworth's *Hiawatha* enjoyed a triumphal premiere at Albert Hall in 1900.

8. Badger, *A Life in Ragtime*, 22.

9. Frank Wess also recorded with Nat "King" Cole, Ella Fitzgerald, Sarah Vaughan, Frank Sinatra, Tony Bennett, Dinah Washington, Lou Rawls, and Sammy Davis Jr.

10. Jester Hairston was a graduate of Tufts and also studied at Juilliard. He left New York for Hollywood in 1936 with the Hall Johnson Choir, when the choir was engaged to sing for the film score of *Green Pastures*, and never looked back. Hairston directed the choir for Dimitri Tiomkin's score for *Lost Horizons*; William Grant Still was the film's orchestral arranger. Soon Hairston began working as a film actor. At the time of our Clef Club concert, Hairston lived in Los Angeles, where he was a regular on *Amen*, a TV sitcom. He also composed its theme song.

11. Words and music by Will Marion Cook.

12. For Conrad's first selection we followed the historical precedent of 1912, substi-

tuting Saint-Saëns's "Mon coeur s'ouvre à ta voix" (from *Samson et Dalila*) for Foster's "Suwanee River." Clearly, Europe's soprano, Elizabeth Payne, had insisted on singing a work that would show off her voice and artistry.

13. Mannes, *Music Is My Faith*, 18. On a harp guitar, the bass strings float freely along a separate neck and are plucked individually by the thumb of the right (strumming) hand in oom-pah fashion. This neck juts out above, and at a slight upward angle to, the regular fingerboard of an oversize six-string guitar. The photograph of the Clef Club orchestra shows several players using normal six-string guitars, but the majority are harp guitarists.

14. "The Negro's Place in Music," *New York Evening Post*, March 13, 1914.

15. Natalie Curtis-Burlin, "Black Singers and Players," *Musical Quarterly* 5 (1919): 502–4; quoted in Badger, *A Life in Ragtime*, 65.

16. Marion Cumbo, interview by author, tape recording, March 31, 1989 at a nursing home in Riverdale, New York. Cumbo was ninety-one years old at the time.

17. Europe was not the only trained violinist who took up another string instrument. The black violinist John Thomas Douglas, David Mannes's teacher, was an excellent guitarist. And, from the high percentage of mandolin players in the Clef Club, I suspect many others found this practice expedient as well.

18. Fletcher, *100 Years of the Negro in Show Business*, 263. Bill Tyers was a respected New York composer, orchestrator, and conductor from the turn of the century until his death in 1924. Tyers's "Trocha" was singled out by Europe as the first tango composed in the United States.

19. Harry T. Burleigh, *From the Southland* (New York: William Maxwell, 1910).

20. James Weldon Johnson describes the "biting attack and infectious rhythm" of Europe's "Clef Club March," "and on the finale [the trio], bursting into singing. The effect can be imagined, the applause became a tumult." (Johnson, *Black Manhattan*, 124.)

21. Not even the copyright files were able to yield three of Europe's pieces, and I had to find substitutes for other works of his. "Hula," "Lorraine Waltzes," and "Strength of the Nation March" were replaced by "Hi-Lo, Hawaiian Waltz," "Castle's Lame Duck Waltz," and "Hi! There! March," respectively. I also decided against trying to re-create the Royal Poinciana Quartet's singing—or was it singing and playing?—of two vestigial minstrel pieces, "Old Black Joe" and "Take Me Back to Dixie." It was more important, I argued with myself, to bring back Bill Warfield, Barbara Conrad, and the already-researched sound of the Versatile Entertainers on the second half of the program. So I had them join forces for a song that the Clef Club featured at one of their early concerts, "Play That Barber Shop Chord."

Mea culpa: In the final days preceding the concert, the ragtime historian Ed Berlin came up with one of the songs that was originally performed by the Versatile Entertainers Quintet, J. Rosamond Johnson's "You're Sweet to Your Mammy Just the Same." It was a typical coon song containing the unfortunate lyric, "Even though your hair is nappy, you're sweet to your Mammy just the same." My musicological virtue was on the line. I called Betty Allen, one of the finest singers of her generation and a musical friend—we had performed J. S. Bach's *St. Matthew Passion*, Richard Wagner's *Tristan und Isolde*, Gustav Mahler's *Das Lied von der Erde*, and Beethoven's

Ninth Symphony together—who, as a member of the Carnegie Hall board, was a strong advocate for the series. Betty, who is African American, told me what I wanted to hear: "don't do it."

22. Berresford, Rye, and Walker, "The Versatile Four: Ambassadors of Syncopation," *VJM* [*Vintage Jazz Mart* magazine] (1995): 9–12.

23. The term "trap drummer" originated in the vaudeville pits, where the drummer was responsible for any and all "traps"—nonpitch sounds such as whips, whistles, trains, horns, and tin pans. The name was passed on to the early jazz drummers, who carried their traps or trap set. See Blades, *Percussion Instruments and Their History*.

24. Berresford, Rye, and Walker, "The Versatile Four," 9.

25. There were separate rehearsals with the singers and strummers alone, and two with the entire ensemble.

26. Certain key players who had perfected the ragtime style led the way: our drummer, Chuck Spies; our lead banjoist, Eddy Davis; the tuba player, Vince Giordano; and Allen Dean and Dave Bargeron on cornet and gutbucket trombone.

27. Although the phrase "eight to the bar" to describe the ragtime rhythmic impulse first appears in the title of "Beat Me Daddy, Eight to the Bar!"—a tune written in 1940 by Don Raye, Hughie Prince, and Eleanor Sheehy during what Vince Giordano calls "the boogie-woogie zoot-suit" age—I suspect it dates from an earlier time and have taken the liberty of using it to explain some of the challenges one faces when trying to recreate an earlier vernacular style.

28. H. H. Stuckenschmidt, *Twentieth Century Music*, trans. Richard Deveson (New York: World University Library, McGraw-Hill, 1969), 86–87. Other rag-inspired works by Stravinsky from this period include "Piano Rag-Music" and *Ragtime for Eleven Instruments*.

29. Other swinging accompanists behind Rainey include pianist Georgia Tom Dorsey; guitarist Tampa Red; cornetists Joe Smith and Thomas Ladnier; and trombonist Kid Ory.

30. It has often been noted that an identical practice of tripletizing, or double-dotting what appear to be even notes, was in vogue during the baroque period. This is aptly known as *notes inégales*. The rub is, where and when was it applied? We fortunately have recordings of ragtimers and swing players as guides.

How *inégale* are the notes that produce the swing effect? The line of demarcation is far more subtle and not neatly drawn. I once visited the Institut de Recherche et de Coordination Acoustique-Musique (IRCAM), the experimental music laboratory created by the French Arts Council for Pierre Boulez. An experiment was in progress to investigate, by use of a computer, the proportions of long-short that produce swing. The triplet gives us a simple two-to-one. The fellow running the experiment told me he was finding out that at certain tempos you could go as high as seven-to-one and still get a swing effect.

31. The concert also had music by Ethelbert Nevins, Charles Ives, and William Wallace Gilchrist.

32. I thank Richard B. Woodward for assembling this cluster in his "Jazz Wars," *Village Voice*, August 9, 1994, 27.

33. According to Tom Riis, the preeminent authority on early all-black Broadway shows, "Swing Along" was probably composed as early as 1898.

34. Jon Pareles, *New York Times*, July 17, 1989. "Re-creating a Night When History Was Made."

CHAPTER 12

1. "The Hot Bach," interview by Richard O. Boyer, *New Yorker*, 1944; reprinted in Tucker, *The Duke Ellington Reader*, 241.

2. Josef Skvorecky, *Dvořák in Love* (New York: Alfred A. Knopf, 1986).

3. For example, S. Frederick Starr, "Oberlin's Ragtimer: Will Marion Cook," *Oberlin Alumni Journal* (fall 1989): 13–15. Starr is an educator and jazz clarinetist. The National Public Radio show *Fresh Air* did an hour-long broadcast on Cook in the winter of 1999.

4. *Bandanna Land* was the first black musical to play at the Majestic Theatre on Columbus Circle and Fifty-ninth Street as well at the Belasco in Washington, D.C.

5. Abbie Mitchell (c. 1884–1960) was a student of Jean de Reszke in Paris. In addition to her work in black musicals, she sang major operatic roles and was a well-known vocal recitalist of new music, lieder, and spirituals. She also appeared in the original production of Lillian Hellman's *Little Foxes* (1939) as one of a quartet of Negro house servants who functioned as a Greek chorus. Toward the end of her career, Mitchell taught. See Georgia A. Ryder's article in *Notable American Women—The Modern Period: A Biographical Dictionary*, ed. Barbara Sicherman and Carol Hurd Green (Cambridge: Belknap Press of Harvard University Press, 1980).

6. Mercer Cook papers, Moreland-Spingarn Research Center, Howard University.

7. The song was sung to Mitchell's stage character.

8. Mercer Cook, interview by Joseph Skvorecky, tape recording, 1980. A copy of this interview is in the author's files.

9. *New York Times*, May 23, 1905; quoted in Gerald Bordman, *American Musical Theatre* (New York: Oxford University Press, 1978), 201.

10. Southern, *The Music of Black Americans*, 369.

11. Carl Van Vechten, *Nigger Heaven* (New York: Grosset and Dunlap/Alfred A. Knopf, 1926).

12. Mercer Cook Papers, Moreland-Spingarn Research Center, Howard University.

13. Kurt Schindler, Schindler File, New York Public Library. The Schindler file is an in-house memo written for his firm, G. Schirmer, describing the music of Cook for a new publication. Schindler (1882–1935) trained under Richard Strauss and Felix Mottl in Berlin before coming to America in 1905 to join the conducting staff of the Metropolitan Opera. He founded New York's MacDowell Chorus (later known as the Schola Cantorum) and prepared them for appearances with Mahler and the New York Philharmonic (1911). Schindler was music director for New York's most exclusive synagogue, Temple Emanu-El, where Harry T. Burleigh was the baritone soloist and

Melvin Charlton was the organist. For a time, Charlton was also chairman of the music department at Bennington College.

CHAPTER 13

1. Deems Taylor, *Of Men And Music* (New York: Simon and Schuster, 1937), 83; Chase, *America's Music*, 571; Richard Franko Goldman, "American Music: 1919–1960," in *The Modern Age, 1890–1960*, ed. Martin Cooper, vol. 10 of *The New Oxford History of Music* (London and New York: Oxford University Press, 1974), 596.

2. "Mischa, Yascha, Toscha, Sascha," Ira and George Gershwin's humorous takeoff on four Russian-Jewish violinists, was composed in 1921 but first published in 1932.

3. New York: Alfred A. Knopf, 1948, 50–61.

4. The original 1926 score, now at the Music Division of the New York Public Library, was used only four times. It has huge penciled or crayoned cues, with arrows and pictures of propellers, drawn in by Goossens (and/or Vladimir Golschmann, who had conducted it in Paris). These are reminders to give an early warning to and then bring in the "mechanical effects" persons. This leads me to suspect that they did not have orchestral parts with bars of rest and exact entrances and exits marked in musical notation, or that they could not be counted on to keep their place even if they could read music.

5. Eugene Goossens, *Overtures and Beginners* (London: Methuen, 1951), 244–45.

6. Compact Disc. Music Masters Classics 67094 and Musical Heritage Society 513891L: *Ballet Mécanique*, George Antheil's Carnegie Hall Concert of 1927, recreated and conducted by Maurice Peress, The Mendelssohn String Quartet, Charles Castleman, violin; Randall Hodgkinson, Ivan Davis, piano; the New Palais Royal Orchestra and Percussion Ensemble.

7. Francis Picabia was born in Paris in 1879 and died in New York in 1953. He was impressed by Alfred Steiglitz's "Photo-Secession" exhibit during his visit to New York for the Armory Show in 1913. Steiglitz took his Gallery 291 name from its address, 291 Fifth Avenue. In 1916 Picabia returned to Barcelona, opened his own Gallery 391, and began publishing the magazine.

8. *Zukunst* [Vienna] 2, no. 3 (1923); quoted in Linda Whitesitt, *The Life and Music of George Antheil, 1900–1959* (Ann Arbor: UMI Research Press, 1983), 9.

9. After Charles Amirkhanian, program booklet (New York: Carnegie Hall, July 2, 1989).

10. Pianola, a registered brand name, has been accepted in England and elsewhere as the generic term for player piano.

11. See Igor Stravinsky, *Pianola Works*, played on Pianola by Rex Lawson, Music Masters CD 67138-2.

12. There have been several attempts to present the film and the music together. The first was a performance at New York's Museum of Modern Art on October 18, 1935, which wisely used the Pianola rolls alone. Nevertheless, the enormous time disparity

between the twelve-to-fourteen-minute film and the twenty-seven minutes of music on the rolls leaves a great deal of choice for anyone trying to meld the two. Besides the Pianola music alone, there are two other versions to consider: the 1925–27 Paris–New York version—the Pianola rolls with percussion ensemble—and the 1952–53 revision.

The Swedish Film Institute made a video c. 1993 joining the 1952–53 revised version to a color tinted print, ostensibly by Léger. While its timing (sixteen minutes) works better, it is in my view a gloss on the original and thereby a new work. At this point in time any "synchronisme musical" will be a chance—ergo appropriately Dadaist—affair.

13. *Der Tag* [Vienna], September 25, 1924. See program brochure for an evening dedicated to Frederick Keisler: "A Tribute to Anthology Films Archives," presented at the Museum of Modern Art on October 19, 1977, and the Kennedy Center on November 10, 1977.

Fernand Léger, who is most often associated with the film, came on board after most of the film was shot and edited. See William Moritz, "Americans in Paris," in *Lovers of Cinema*, ed. Jan-Christopher Horak (Madison: University of Wisconsin Press, 1995).

14. *New York Times*, February 22, 1954.

15. Before I met Lawson, I had naively assumed that once found, the rolls could simply be played on a good automatic (electrified) player piano while I conducted the rest of the musicians.

16. I later learned that it is actually better for the preservation of the rolls to play them once in a while, but the Curtis rolls sit in pristine silence to this day.

17. Randy Kerr restores and repairs player pianos and collects 1920s American memorabilia. At his home in Queens, New York, Randy showed me a Gershwin letter and an original Oscar.

18. Virgil Thomson, *Virgil Thomson* (New York: Alfred A. Knopf, 1966), 82.

19. Copland and Perlis, *Copland, 1900 through 1942*, 127.

20. I was able to perform *A Jazz Symphony* thanks to a photocopy I found while rummaging about the bottom of the Antheil drawer at the office of his New York publisher, Eugene Weintraub. After some deciphering (Antheil had scribbled changes in pencil over the ink original), parts were prepared, and it was presented at Dick Hyman's Summer Jazzfest, held at New York's Ninety-second Street YMHA, with Ivan Davis as solo pianist, in July 1987.

21. The original *Americana/A Jazz Symphony* was scored for four saxophones doubling on clarinets and oboes, three trumpets, three trombones, banjo, tuba, traps, xylophone, and a small string section. After its Carnegie Hall debut, *A Jazz Symphony* was not performed in this original scoring until July of 1987. As with his *Ballet Mécanique*, Antheil reworked *A Jazz Symphony* in 1957 (a far more successful reworking than that of the *Ballet Mécanique*), replacing its solo piano and expanded jazz-band instrumentation with a band of brass and woodwinds alone.

22. *Louis Armstrong, in His Own Words*, ed. and introd. Thomas Brothers (New York: Oxford University Press, 1999), 106.

23. From a handwritten notation on the face page of the holograph score of the revised *Jazz Symphony*, copy in the author's files.

24. *New York World*, April 11 or 12, 1927.

25. Copland and Perlis, *Copland, 1900–1942*, 75.

26. Charles Amirkhanian, program booklet (New York: Carnegie Hall, July 2, 1989). Amirkhanian goes on to say: "The 'Second Sonata for Violin, Piano and Drum,' is rife with quotations from salon and popular music of the day, with the violin often representing the music of the past and the piano the music of Antheil's envisioned 'future.' The furious piano cadenza, with its brutal repetitions of a single obsessive phrase of chord clusters, points the way to the compulsive repetition in *Ballet Mécanique*, and by implication, to the minimalist aesthetic of Terry Riley, Steven Reich and Philip Glass which arose forty years later."

27. The 1927 concert opened with the String Quartet no. 1, which was then followed by the sonata. In 1989 I reversed this order.

28. At the 1927 Carnegie Hall concert, Antheil's String Quartet no. 1 was played by the Musical Arts quartet: Sascha Jacobson, first violin; Bernard Ocko, second violin; Louis Kaufman, viola; and Marie Roemat-Rosanoff, cello. For the 1989 Carnegie Hall re-creation it was performed by the Mendelssohn Quartet: Ida Levin and Nicholas Mann, violinists; Katherine Murdock, violist; and Marcy Rosen, cellist.

29. Whitesitt, *The Life and Music of George Antheil*, 103.

30. Her accompanist was Daniele Amfitteatrov. Il Duce serenaded them in turn on his own violin, and their meeting was reported in the press: "Mussolini complimented Miss Rudge on her technique and musical feeling. . . . It was rare to find such depth and precision of tone 'especially in a woman.'" *New York Herald*, "wire from Rome," March 16, 1927.

31. Whitesitt, *The Life and Music of George Antheil*, 105–6.

32. Ibid., 105.

33. The computerized player pianos that are commercially available at this writing can sound up to twenty-four notes at one time, whereas Antheil's rolls call for over thirty notes. And predictably, in November 2000, a performance purported to be "the original Ballet Mécanique" was organized with the help of the Yamaha piano company utilizing sixteen digital-playback spinet pianos linked together.

34. Antheil's autobiography was titled *Bad Boy of Music* (Garden City, N.Y.: Doubleday, Doran, 1945).

35. I have worked with two remarkable, if very different, students of Antheil: Benjamin Lees, who composes powerful and exquisitely crafted symphonies and concertos, and Earl Robinson, a unique composer who refined and redirected his superb skills to support socially conscious causes with works like the *Ballad for Americans*, "Joe Hill," *The Lonesome Train*, and a stirring banjo concerto, *How Can I Keep from Singing*.

36. Zakariasen, *New York Daily News*, July 14, 1989; Page, *Newsday*, July 15, 1989; Kozinn, *New York Times*, July 15, 1989; Elliot, *New York Post*, July 14, 1989.

CHAPTER 14

1. Lewisohn Stadium was built with the gift of Adolph Lewisohn in 1915. Located between Amsterdam and Convent Avenues and between 136th and 138th Streets, its concrete oval of twenty-four tiers seated 6,000, and there was room below for 1,500 standees. It was demolished in 1973 "in favor of academic expansion."

2. "Pulp and Circumstances," in Gerald Early, *Tuxedo Junction: Essays on American Culture* (New York: Ecco, 1989), 201.

3. The world premiere of the *Kaddish* Symphony had been in Israel in December 1963. The American premiere, promised to the Boston Orchestra, was in February 1964. Only afterward (April 12–17, 1964) could Bernstein perform and record the work with the New York Philharmonic.

4. The song on the piano rack became "Thank You," the final part of the Gloria section of *Mass*.

5. Richard Boone played Lincoln, and Martin Gable and Nancy Kelly were Senator and Mrs. Douglas. The score was by David Amram.

6. Although Davidson and I thought we had successfully put *Candide* back on its feet in 1966—an opinion we still share—within a few years Bernstein teamed me up with a brilliant Chicago-based writer and director, Sheldon Patinkin, who was preparing his own concert version for Grant Park. We eventually presented this version at Lincoln Center for Bernstein's fiftieth birthday in 1968.

7. The short list of Gordon Davidson's productions that reached Broadway includes *Angels in America, The Trial of the Catonsville Nine, The Shadow Box, Zoot Suit, Children of a Lesser God,* and *In the Matter of J. Robert Oppenheimer.* Carroll O'Connor became the writer and star of Norman Lear's groundbreaking television sitcom *All in the Family.* Peter Wexler went on to design major productions for Broadway and Hector Berlioz's *Les Troyens* for the Met, and created special concert settings for the New York Philharmonic's Promenade Concerts at Lincoln Center and their summer concerts in Central Park.

8. The *Candide*-to-end-all-*Candide*s tour closed after a run at the new Kennedy Center with me back in the pit. The long-awaited Broadway revival came in 1973, when Hal Prince got into the act with his frothy, fey *Candide* confections, with a new libretto by Hugh Wheeler.

9. A paraphrase on the title of Arthur W. Little's book *Harlem to the Rhine: The Story of New York's Colored Volunteers* (New York: Covici, Friede, 1936), which documents the musical and battle exploits of James Reese Europe's regiment in World War I.

10. The unusual liturgical form of Bernstein's *Mass* (condensed):

Kyrie
Kyrie eleison	"Lord, Have Mercy"
Christus eleison	"Christ, Have Mercy"

A Simple Song/Alleluia
Kyrie eleison	"Lord, Have Mercy" / Kyrie March
In Nomine Patris	"Almighty Father"

Epiphany	
Confiteor*	
Trope	"I Don't Know"
	"Easy"
Meditation I	
Gloria	
Gloria tibi	"Glory to You"
Laudamus te	"We Praise You"
Gratias agimus tibi	"We Give Thanks"
Dominus Deus	"Lord God"
Qui tollis	"Who takest away"
Qui sedes ad	"Who sittest"
Quoniam tu solus	"You Are Holy"
Cum Sancto Spiritu	"With the Holy Spirit"
Trope	"Half of the People"
	"Thank You"
Meditation II	
Epistle	"The Word of the Lord"
Gospel-Sermon	"God Said"
Credo	
Credo in unum deum	
[*normal position of Confiteor in Roman Catholic Mass]	
Trope: Non Credo	"And Was Made Man"
	"Hurry"
	"World without End"
	"I Believe in God"
Meditation III (De Profundis I)	
Offertory (De Profundis II)	
The Lord's Prayer	"Our Father"
Trope	"I Go On"
Sanctus	"Holy, Holy"
	"Hosanna"
Benedictus	"Blessed Is He Who Comes"
Kadosh	
Agnus Dei	
Agnus Dei	"Lamb of God"
Dona nobis pacem	"Grant Us Peace"
Fraction	"Things Get Broken"
Pax: Communion	"Secret Songs"

11. Carol Neblett went topless in *Thaïs* in the late 1960s, and others soon followed. I conducted a production of *Manon Lescaut* for the Washington Opera in 1969, directed by Richard Pearlman, in which Teresa Stratas and Harry Theyard were to appear in the altogether on film making love while the orchestra played the third act entr'acte. The film was made, but we lost our soprano, and the shocker was scrapped.

12. I had known Webster since his Harvard days, when he caught the attention of the symphony world by taking the Harvard-Radcliffe orchestra on a successful South American tour.

13. The members of the Street Chorus for the premiere performance of *Mass* were John D. Anthony, Margaret Cowie, David Cryer, Ed Dixon, Eugene Edwards, Tom Ellis, Joy Franz, Judy Gibson, Carl Hall, Lee Hooper, Larry Marshall, Gina Penn, Mary Bracken Phillips, Carole Prandis, Benjamin Rayson, Marion Ramsey, Neva Small, Louis St. Louis, Barbara Williams, Walter Williams, Walter Willison, and Ronald Young.

14. Bernstein reserved for himself the scoring of the most important, and delicate, portions of *Mass*: "Simple Song," "Meditations," "Thank You," "Epistle," and all the choral writing. Once he completed composing, he returned to orchestrating and scored everything from the Offertory through to the end — more than three-quarters of the work.

15. Alan Titus, who now has a sizable bass-baritone voice and sings in major European houses, was a high baritone in 1971 with a bright and beautiful sound. In my view, the recording of Alan Titus singing the role of the Celebrant, as coached by Bernstein, sets the very highest standard for twentieth-century American diction and musicianship. Compact Disc CBS M2 31008.

16. The call came from Diana Shumlin, the show's production coordinator. In retrospect the decision was probably inevitable, but it came as a complete surprise. "Don't tell anybody," she began, "but Lenny wants you to conduct the opening performance." My heart leaped, but my hand never left the phone. "Don't tell anybody" — indeed, I called my manager and asked her to engage the best publicist she knew.

17. "Quadraphonic speakers," new at the time, disappeared after a short spurt of interest. The idea returned in full force in the 1990s as "surround sound," when home video theaters came into vogue.

18. On the Columbia recording, the voice we hear is that of the Celebrant.

19. Jack Anderson, *The Anderson Papers* (New York: Random House, 1973), 171–72.

CHAPTER 15

1. Transcription of White House archival recording, June 14, 1965, Lyndon Baines Johnson Library, Austin, Texas.

2. *The Golden Broom and the Green Apple* was orchestrated by Joe Benjamin, Ellington's bassist and copyist at the time.

3. Louie Bellson, interview by author in New York City, 1993, and in Palo Alto, California, July 1996.

4. I am able to pinpoint the exact date and place of my meeting with Ellington (February 19, 1970 at the Staten Island Auditorium) thanks to "The Duke Ellington Chronicle," compiled by Joe Igo and edited by Gordon Ewing (1988), which is kept at the Duke Ellington Collection, Archives Center, National Museum of American History, Smithsonian Institution, Washington, D.C.

5. The archival "location recording" is actually a compilation of the Boston follow-up performance (Symphony Hall, January 28, 1943), and the Carnegie Hall premiere. The scores for *Black, Brown and Beige* were "distributed in England by Campbell Connelly."

6. Ellington was in Washington, D.C., at the time preparing for the *Second Sacred Service*, which, according to Igo and Ewing's "Chronicle," was performed at the National Presbyterian Church on March 14 and 15, 1970.

7. The *Symphonic Suite from Black, Brown and Beige* has become one of my signature pieces. I conducted it for the inauguration of the Lyndon Baines Johnson Library with the Austin Symphony. With the old Kansas City Philharmonic I did it at both Leavenworth Penitentiary and Carnegie Hall, where the suite formed the centerpiece of an entire evening devoted to Ellington. In 1988 I returned to Carnegie Hall for an all-Ellington concert with the American Composers Orchestra. Along with the *Symphonic Suite* we did my transcription/orchestration of Ellington's piano concerto *New World A-Comin'* (1944) with Sir Roland Hanna as soloist, the magnificent concerto grosso *Harlem*, and the ballet suite *Three Black Kings*, featuring the saxophonist Jimmy Heath. The latter two works were scored by Luther Henderson Jr. The American Composers Orchestra recorded this concert for Music Masters: *Four Symphonic Works by Duke Ellington*, MM7011-2-c. The author edited all four works for publication, and they are now available through G. Schirmer.

8. *The River* was commissioned by the American Ballet Theatre. Alvin Ailey was the choreographer. Ellington provided ABT with a "rehearsal tape" for which he himself played the score on piano. But they needed the music written out so that their own pianist could play for rehearsals, stopping and starting as needed. Ellington then scored the work for his band, had it copied and recorded at his own expense, and sent the tape to ABT, thinking the instrumental sounds and rhythms would be even more inspirational for the company to rehearse with. ABT insisted they still needed a written-out piano part. So I was called upon to transcribe Ellington's piano tape, as was the jazz organist Wild Bill Davis, who was then playing with the band. Davis ended up doing the bulk of the work.

CHAPTER 16

1. January 14–24, 1971. Igo and Ewing, "Chronicle."

2. At the time Ellington's regular orchestra of fifteen or sixteen players included four trumpets, three trombones, and sometimes a guitar.

3. In the January 2001 issue of the New York Duke Ellington Society *Bulletin*, Thomas Harris recalled being at the Rainbow Grill that night and how he feared the actor was about to embarrass himself when, with "his eyes somewhat glazed . . . he began to speak, slowly, resonantly, like an incantation: 'I see about me faces of grey and black.'" Harris realized that Burton, the son of a coal miner, was reciting an old Welsh miner's ballad about men covered with coal dust.

4. *Queenie Pie*, typed manuscript at Ellington Archive, Smithsonian Institution.

5. Barry Ulanov, *Duke Ellington* (New York: Da Capo Press, 1975), 241–42. *Jump for Joy* includes a skit about an elegantly dressed African king and queen about to be visited by an expedition from an American searching for the original source of jazz. "Oh, damn," says the queen. "Yes, my dear, we shall have to get out our leopard skins again." A. H. Lawrence, *Duke Ellington and His World: A Biography* (New York: Routledge, 2001), 304.

6. Ellington could fit three systems of score on a single sheet of standard twelve-staff music paper. Two or three sheets would suffice for a fully fleshed out three- or four-minute gem.

7. According to the Canadian orchestrator Ron Collier, Ellington wrote out this full score in response to Collier's complaint that he was overworked and running out of time, trying to finish scoring *Celebration*, a piece Ellington wrote in honor of the 150th anniversary of the city of Jacksonville, Florida, in 1972.

8. The Ellington transcriber, scholar, and conductor Andrew Homzy provided me with these "translations." Others—ADDI, SOUL FLOT, FIFE, and SOSO—were used "as is," the last being from the *African Asian Suite*.

CHAPTER 17

1. Quoted in Ulanov, *Duke Ellington*, 258.

2. A solo trombone would have been redundant of the movement's introduction; the solo lies too high for the French horn; and the English horn would evoke pastoral settings such as those in Rossini's *William Tell* Overture and Berlioz's *Symphonie fantastique*.

3. Albert Murray, "Storiella Americana as she swyung [*sic*]: Duke Ellington, the Culture of Washington, D.C., and the Blues as Representative Anecdote," *Conjunctions* 16 (1991): 217–18.

4. *Newsweek*, February 1, 1943, 50.

5. According to Hoefsmit and Homzy, in 1965, when Ellington began performing a truncated version of *Black* ["Montage"] on a regular basis, he recorded most of *Beige* (SAJA 7 91234-2), but he never performed it in public. See Hoefsmit and Homzy, "Chronology of Ellington's *Black, Brown and Beige*," *Black Music Research Journal* 13, no. 2 (fall 1993): 161.

6. Author's *Black, Brown and Beige* chronology:

   1965: Heard *Black* with Ellington's Orchestra at White House
   1970: Premiered own orchestration of an orchestral *Suite from Black, Brown and Beige* with the Chicago Symphony,
   1977: Performed suite with Kansas City Philharmonic in Leavenworth Penitentiary, and in Carnegie Hall, the latter being a concert dedicated to Ellington that also featured the Modern Jazz Quartet
   1988: Performed jazz band original with American Jazz Orchestra, Cooper Union

1989: Performed jazz band original as part of Ellington's entire 1943 Carnegie Concert in a re-creation at Carnegie Hall (Landmark Series)

1993: Recorded jazz band original suite on compact disc featuring the Louie Bellson Band with Clark Terry and Joe Williams (Music Masters 65096-2) *Duke Ellington, Black, Brown and Beige.*

1997: Performed jazz band original at Stanford University and in San Francisco, featuring Louie Bellson Band with Joe Williams

1999: Performed jazz band original with Carnegie Hall Jazz Band (John Faddis, director), the author conducting

7. Mark Rosenzweig, archivist and Labor and Communist Party historian, in an e-mail to the author, July 7, 2001.

8. "Goings On," January 23, 1943, 5.

9. Commissioned by Paul Whiteman for his Carnegie Hall concert on December 25, 1938.

10. "Koko" opened the second half, replacing "Flaming Sword" and the three Strayhorn pieces. Mercer Ellington's "Blue Serge" and "Jumpin' Punkins" were dropped, but his "Moon Mist," originally composed for Ray Nance on jazz violin, was played just before *Black, Brown and Beige.* Our re-creation followed suit.

11. Whiteman and McBride, *Jazz,* 200.

12. I myself transcribed one of Ellington's "lost" pieces for Mercer, *New World A-Comin',* a piano concerto composed as the big new concert piece for Ellington's second Carnegie Hall appearance on December 11, 1943. The title comes from Roy Ottley's *New World A-Coming* (Boston: Houghton Mifflin, 1943). Ottley was a reporter for New York's *Amsterdam Star News.* His "test tube" study of Harlem "held up to full glare to reflect Black America," and his impassioned predictions inspired Ellington to go beyond the historical "tonal portrait" he explored in *Black, Brown and Beige* and into the future.

Of course, Ellington never committed his solo piano part to paper—so I obliged. I then made an orchestral version of *New World A-Comin'* that was recorded under my direction by the American Composers Orchestra with Sir Roland Hanna as soloist; *Four Symphonic Works by Duke Ellington,* Music Masters 7011-2-C.

13. Other players in the re-creation of Ellington's Carnegie Hall debut concert were saxophonists Jerry Dodgion, Walt Weiskopf, Mark Lopeman, Bill Easley, and Scott Robinson; trumpeters Rande Sandke, Glenn Drews, and Spanky Davis; trombonists Dave Bargeron, Art Baron, and Joel Helleny; violinist John Blake; bassist Jay Leonhart; and drummer Grady Tate.

14. *Black, Brown and Beige,* Music Masters 65096-2. We assembled to record on October 20–22, 1992. The Louie Bellson band included saxophonists Frank Wess, Phil Bodner, Bill Easley, Ted Nash, Scott Robinson, and Joseph Temperly; trumpeters Clark Terry, Marvin Stamm, Robert Millikan, Barrie Lee Hall, and Anthony Kadleck; trombonists Britt Woodman, Art Baron, and Alan Raph; bassist John Beal; pianist Harold Danko; guitarist Gene Bertocini; and violinist Lesa Terry.

15. I found myself adding even more details to Cohen's transcription-edition gleaned

from the same recording, as had pianist-conductor Dick Hyman before me. This turned out to be an a makeshift cut-and-paste-affair, but thanks to my caring musicians, it worked. Until Ellington's autograph scores for *Black, Brown and Beige* surfaced in the Smithsonian's archive collection, this chain of sources served as the means by which Ellington's music could be re-created.

16. Thanks to the Stamford Jazz Festival, Jim Nadel, director; the Chicago Jazz Orchestra, Bill Russo, director; the Carnegie Hall Jazz Band, John Faddis, director; and computer-autographer Omar Castanos, with the knowledgeable assistance of musicologist-autographer John Howland.

My four editorial sources were: Ellington's holograph manuscript; a photocopy of the "copyright" score (a copyist's condensation of Ellington's manuscript for registration at the U.S. Copyright Office) loaned to me by Ruth Ellington; the Tempo Music/Campbell Connelly edition; and, where necessary, my transcriptions of the bass and drum parts and piano solos from the location recording.

17. In order of appearance: Peter Watrous, *New York Times*, January 25, 1999; Gary Giddins, *Village Voice*, February 16, 1999; Gene Seymour, *Newsday*, January 25, 1999; Robert L. Daniels, *Variety*, January 28, 1999; Will Friedwald, *JAZZIZ*, April 1999.

18. *Black, Brown and Beige* received standing ovations in subsequent performances: by the Chicago Jazz Orchestra under Bill Russo, composer and veteran trombonist and arranger for Stan Kenton's "thundering herd," and by the Carnegie Hall Jazz Band under John Faddis.

19. Mark Tucker also believes that the final version of the poem was written close to, perhaps in preparation for, the composition of the music (c. 1943), a plausible notion. See Tucker, "The Genesis of *Black, Brown and Beige*," *Black Music Research Journal* 13, no. 2 (fall 1993): 73–74.

20. Howard Taubman, "The 'Duke' Invades Carnegie Hall," *New York Times Magazine*, January 17, 1943, 30.

21. Duke Ellington, "Black, Brown and Beige," typescript, c. 1940. Copy in author's files; original held in the Duke Ellington Collection, Smithsonian Institution, Washington, D.C. Portions of the poem have appeared in the author's liner notes for *Four Symphonic Works by Duke Ellington* (1989); Peress, "My Life with *Black, Brown and Beige*," *Black Music Research Journal* 13, no. 2 (fall 1993): 155–57; and Tucker, "The Genesis of *Black, Brown and Beige*," 77.

22. Stanley Crouch, interview by author, 1999.

23. It is quite possible that Nanton actually sang through his trombone as well. This was in fact how Jack Fulton, trombonist for the Whiteman band, played the haunting solo in Ferde Grofé's "On the Trail"—the "call for Philip Morris" theme—from the *Grand Canyon Suite* when the work was first recorded by the Whiteman orchestra in 1932.

24. Irving Kolodin in the Carnegie Hall program for January 23, 1943, describes "Boola" as "The term Negros use to symbolize the perpetual spirit of the race through time. . . . When a discussion of some important phase of American history is under way . . . one of the group is sure to say: 'Yes, Boola was there all right.'"

25. Ellington, *Music Is My Mistress*, 97.

26. Ellington returns to the subject of Harlem, his home turf from the 1920s on, in what I consider his masterwork for jazz band and orchestra, *Harlem*, written in 1950.

27. Albert Murray, 1990, conversation with the author, New York City.

28. Ulanov, *Duke Ellington*, 250–51.

29. The "Jungle" and "Sugar Hill Penthouse" themes appear below:

30. Mark Tucker pointed out to me in 1993 that while this title appears in the Campbell-Connelly score, it does not appear in the manuscript.

31. "Medium" refers to tempo, a moderate speed. "Stride" is a style of piano playing in which the left hand alone sets the rhythm, leaping ("striding") between low bass notes and off-beat chords in the middle register. A "shout-chorus" is the last and most intense in a series of choruses.

32. The "Jungle Theme" tonal clusters are shown here in the left example; a variation of the "Work Song" theme appears on the right.

33. See Wolfram Knauer, "'Simulated Improvisation' in Duke Ellington's *Black, Brown and Beige*," *Black Perspective in Music* 18 (1990): 20–38.

34. The *Beige* quotations in Webster's solo appear below:

AFTERWORD

1. Dvořák learned of the death of his father, Frantisek Dvořák, in early April 1894. He normally attended mass every morning, probably at St. Mary Magdalen, a

German-speaking congregation a few blocks due east from his house on Seventeenth Street. (Mary Magdalen, located between Avenues A and B, was taken down when Stuyvesant Town was built.) But for this occasion Kovařik reports that Dvořák went up-town to the Church of Our Lady of Perpetual Help (on Sixty-first Street between First and Second Avenues), built not long before, in 1887, by the Redemptorist Fathers as a national church for Bohemian-speaking Catholics.

In the spring of 1998 the New York Times ran an article announcing the demolition of Our Lady of Perpetual Hope. I wrote a letter, which was published, telling about Dvořák's trip uptown to say a mass for his father in Czech.

2. Mencken, "My Life as Author and Editor," unpublished ms., Baltimore, Md., Enoch Pratt Free Library, Appendix X, 118–20.

3. On the Sixteenth Street side of St. George's rises a bell tower with curiously elongated flying turrets, a miniature version of Tyn Church, which dominates the old town square of Prague and served as an inspiration to the prominent Czech Jewish architect Leopold Eidlitz.

4. Kovařik, Memoirs, Dvořák Museum Archives, Prague.

5. Bill King, music critic from the New York Sun, was present at the dedication of the Dvořák House. His article (December 15, 1941) is one source for this information. Olin Downes of the New York Times also attended but did not write an article.

6. Arthur Judson was among the most powerful figures in American concert life. In 1941 he was both a board member of the New York Philharmonic and the founder and president of Columbia Artists Management.

7. Paul Stefan, Anton Dvořák (New York: Greystone Press, 1941), 225.

8. The New York Herald, January 21, 1894, misidentified Kinney as "Edward H. Kinney (pupil of Dr. Dvořák)." His full name is Edward Beadle Kinney Jr.

9. The Gramercy Park Association confirmed my fears: "Yes, the Dvořák House was in contention. The new owners, Beth Israel Hospital, want to replace it with a new, albeit-to-scale, building with four stories instead of three." To seal its fate, the hospital announced that they were slated to receive a $1 million grant from the Robert Mapplethorpe Foundation to set up an AIDS outpatient clinic on that very site, even though they owned several identical houses close by.

10. Musicians the likes of Yo-Yo Ma, Kurt Masur, and Wynton Marsalis joined ranks with Rudolf Firkusny and Jarmilla Novatna and wrote letters on behalf of the house. The Czech Artists Academy sent a petition signed by all of its members from Prague to Mayor David Dinkins. Václav Havel, president of Czechoslovakia, tried to help through diplomatic channels. But we were no match for the hospital's high-powered public relations firm. They lobbied city council members, emboldened the anti-landmark editorial writers at the New York Times, and arranged for negative TV coverage.

11. The author is a member of the new Dvořák Museum Planning Committee.

12. James Rosamond Johnson, The Book of American Negro Spirituals, introd. James Weldon Johnson (New York: Viking Press, 1925). A subsequent volume, The Second Book of American Negro Spirituals, was published in 1926.

13. Afro-American Folk Songs (Henry Edward Krehbeil) New York: G. Schirmer,

1914, thirteen songs; and *Old Songs Hymnal*, New York: The Century Company, 1929, 194 works. Also see Simpson, "Catalogue," 363-401.

14. W. C. Handy, *The Blues* (New York: Albert and Charles Boni, 1926).

15. The epigraph above is from James Reese Europe, *New York Evening Post*, March 13, 1914, reprinted in Robert Kimball and William Bolcom, *Reminiscing with Sissle and Blake* (New York: Viking, 1973), 60–61.

16. Johnson, *Black Manhattan*, 120.

17. Author's copy, from the collection of James Reese Europe Jr.

18. Mark Tucker, *Ellington: The Early Years* (Urbana and Chicago: University of Illinois Press, 1991), 14.

Selected Discography

Bernstein, Leonard. *Candide* (original Broadway cast recording). Legacy Records 86859.

———. *Mass* (original cast recording conducted by the composer). Sony Classical SM2K 63089.

Copland, Aaron. Piano Concerto. Aaron Copland, piano; Leonard Bernstein, conductor. Sony Classical S2K 47232.

Dvořák, Anton. Symphony no. 9 (*From the New World*). Karel Ancerl, conductor; Czech Philharmonic. Supraphon MD 3662.

Gershwin, George. *Porgy and Bess* (1935 tryouts). Ann Brown, Todd Duncan, Abbie Mitchell; conducted by the composer. Musical Heritage Society 5129239. Available from www.musicalheritage.com.

"Ellington's *Black, Brown and Beige*." Compilation, conducted by Maurice Peress. Musical Heritage Society 513633L. Available from www.musicalheritage.com.

"Four Symphonic Works by Duke Ellington." *Harlem; Suite from Black, Brown and Beige; New World a'Comin'; Three Black Kings*. Compilation, conducted by Maurice Peress. Musical Heritage Society 5168303. Available from www.musical heritage.com.

"Digital George: A Collection of Gershwin Classics." Conducted by Maurice Peress. Musical Heritage Society 513380W. Available from www.musicalheritage.com.

"Whiteman's Aeolian Hall Concert of 1924; The Birth of the *Rhapsody in Blue*." Conducted by Maurice Peress. Musical Heritage Society 5266573. Available from www.musicalheritage.com.

In addition, *Dvořák and America*, a documentary film by Lucille Carra, Brian Cotoir, and Maurice Peress (PBS Home Video, 2000), is available from www.pbs.org; and a specially prepared CD of privately recorded works (Will Marion Cook, "Overture to *In Dahomey*" and *Swing Along*; Maurice Arnold Strathotte, *Plantation Dances*; James Reese Europe, *Clef Club March*; and George Antheil, *Jazz Symphony* and an excerpt from *Ballet Mécanique*) is available from httyger@aol.com.

Selected Bibliography

Antheil, George. *Bad Boy of Music*. Garden City, N.Y.: Doubleday, 1945.

Badger, Reid. *A Life in Ragtime: A Biography of James Reese Europe*. New York: Oxford University Press, 1995.

Beckerman, Michael B. *New Worlds of Dvořák: Searching in America for the Composer's Inner Life*. New York: W. W. Norton, 2003.

Burton, Humphrey. *Leonard Bernstein*. New York: Doubleday, 1994.

DeLong, Thomas A. *Pops: Paul Whiteman, King of Jazz*. Piscataway, N.J.: New Century, 1983.

Ellington, Duke. *Music Is My Mistress*. New York: Doubleday, 1973.

Emerson, Ken. *Doo-Dah!: Stephen Foster and the Rise of American Popular Culture*. New York: Simon and Schuster, 1997.

Ewen, David. *A Journey to Greatness: The Life and Music of George Gershwin*. New York: Henry Holt, 1956.

Fletcher, Tom. *100 Years of the Negro in Show Business: The Tom Fletcher Story*. 1954. Reprint, New York: Da Capo Press, 1984.

Ford, Hugh. *Four Lives in Paris* [includes a chapter on Antheil]. San Francisco: Northpoint Press, 1987.

Pollack, Howard. *Aaron Copland: The Life and Work of an Uncommon Man*. New York: Henry Holt, 1999.

Simpson, Ann Key. *Hard Trials: The Life and Music of Harry T. Burleigh*. Metuchen, N.J.: Scarecrow Press, 1990.

Skvorecky, Josef. *Dvořák in Love: A Light-Hearted Dream*. New York: Knopf, 1987.

Southern, Eileen. *The Music of Black Americans*. New York: W. W. Norton, 1971.

Starr, S. Frederick. *Bamboula: The Life and Times of Gottschalk*. New York: Oxford University Press, 1994.

Tibbetts, John, ed. *Dvořák in America*. Portland: Amadeus Press, 1993.

Tucker, Mark. *The Duke Ellington Reader*. New York: Oxford University Press, 1993.

———. *Ellington: The Early Years*. Urbana: University of Illinois Press, 1991.

Watkins, Mel. *On the Real Side: Laughing, Lying, and Signifying*. New York: Simon and Schuster, 1994.

Index